WHERE THE RIGHT WENT WRONG

Also by Patrick J. Buchanan

The New Majority

Conservative Votes, Liberal Victories

Right from the Beginning

The Great Betrayal

A Republic, Not an Empire

The Death of the West

· PATRICK J. BUCHANAN ·

WHERE THE RIGHT WENT WRONG

HOW NEOCONSERVATIVES SUBVERTED
THE REAGAN REVOLUTION AND
HIJACKED THE BUSH PRESIDENCY

Thomas Dunne Books

ST. MARTIN'S GRIFFIN ❧ NEW YORK

THOMAS DUNNE BOOKS.
An imprint of St. Martin's Press.

www.stmartins.com

Library of Congress Cataloging-in-Publication Data

Buchanan, Patrick J. (Patrick Joseph), 1938–
    Where the right went wrong : how neoconservatives subverted the Reagan revo-
lution and hijacked the Bush presidency / Patrick J. Buchanan.
        p. cm.
    ISBN 0-312-34115-6 (hc)
    ISBN 0-312-34116-4 (pbk)
    EAN 978-0312-34116-9
    Includes index (p. 269).
    1. United States—Politics and government—2001– 2. War on terrorism, 2001–
3. Conservatism—United States. 4. United States—Foreign relations—Islamic
countries 5. Islamic countries—Foreign relations—United States. 6. United
States—Economic policy—2001–

JK275 .B83 2004

2004558171

First St. Martin's Griffin Edition: May 2005

10 9 8 7 6 5 4 3 2 1

CONTENTS

AMERICAN EMPIRE AT APOGEE

Not even the British Empire at its zenith dominated the world in the way the United States does today. U.S. forces are deployed in lands the soldiers of Victoria never saw. Our warships make port calls on all continents. Our military technology is generations ahead of any other nation's. Our GDP is 30 percent of the global economy.

Brand names like Coca-Cola, McDonald's, and Levi's are household words from Kathmandu to Kurdistan. The music the young listen to around the world is American or an imitation thereof. Americans annually claim the lion's share of the Nobel prizes in science, medicine, and economics. Hollywood films are the world's most watched. The dollar is the world's reserve currency. The International Monetary Fund that keeps scores of nations from bankruptcy is headquartered in Washington and responsive to the U.S. Treasury. The American language, English, is the lingua franca of the Internet and the International Elite.

When crises erupt—in the Balkans, the Caucasus, Kashmir, or the Mideast—U.S. diplomats are the brokers of truce. By almost any measure—military and economic power, technology, standard of living, cultural dominance, social and political freedom— America is the gold standard, the "hyperpower" of the Quai d'Orsay's resentment.

Yet one recalls the story Lincoln is said to have told friends gathered to see him off as he departed Springfield to take up the leadership of his sundered nation. An Eastern monarch, said Lincoln, asked his wise men to come up with words that would everywhere and always be true. The wise men went away and reflected, and when they returned they gave the king these words: "This, too, shall pass."

Let us hope that is not true of America, said Lincoln.

Yet, it is true. All republics, all empires, all civilizations pass away. The Roman republic began to die the day that Caesar's legions crossed the Rubicon to make him dictator of Rome. Cicero knew it. The crowds did not, or did not care. Four hundred years later, Alaric the Goth led his army over the Alps to ring down the curtain on the world's greatest empire.

What brought Rome down? A loss of faith in the old gods and old virtues? Degeneration of the aristocracy? The corruption of the people with bread and circuses? The follies of dissolute emperors? The wealth dissipated in war? The collapsing birth rate? The immigrant invasion of barbarians who had no love for Roman culture or history? Displacement of Rome's soldiers with foreign conscripts?

These were the symptoms of impending death. What was the cause?

The emperor Julien the Apostate, Gibbon's hero in *The Decline and Fall of the Roman Empire,* believed Rome could not survive Constantine's embrace of a Christianity that forswore the martial virtues for "Love thy neighbor." The empire could not survive the loss of the old pagan faith. When a religion dies, the culture and the civilization that grew out of it die with it. And indeed, as Rome was invaded by barbarians, popes would stand at the city gates to plead for mercy from the likes of Attila the Hun.

In our time, empires collapse more suddenly. The twentieth century was a graveyard of empires. The Austro-Hungarian, German, Russian, and Ottoman perished in the Great War. The Empire of the Sun was reduced to ashes in 1945. The British Empire, which encompassed a fourth of the world's surface and a fifth of its people, vanished within a quarter century of its "finest hour" in 1940.

A Soviet empire that spanned a dozen time zones from the Bering Sea to the Elbe, with outposts in Southeast Asia, the Mideast, Africa, and even the Caribbean and Central America, succumbed to a collapse of faith and will in 1989. All the empires of the twentieth century are gone. Only the American empire endures.

But the invasion of Iraq and the war to impose democracy upon that Arab and Islamic nation that has never known democracy may yet prove a textbook example of the imperial overstretch that brought down so many empires of the past. Fallujah, where U.S. Marines were withdrawn before completing their mission to eradicate the guerrillas and terrorists who had murdered four Americans and desecrated their bodies, may prove the high tide of an American empire that has begun its long retreat.

IN THE TRAIN carrying him to Fulton for his Iron Curtain speech in 1946, a rueful Churchill confessed to his American companion, "If I were to be born again, I would wish to be born in the United States. Your country is the future of the world. . . . Great Britain has passed its zenith."

A startling admission from the personification of British patriotism. Yet, the great man's melancholy was understandable. For Churchill had been first lord of the Admiralty at the apex of empire and had watched from the wheelhouse as the great ship went down. Historians search the nineteenth century for the causes of Britain's collapse. Some say the embrace of free trade led to her fall from industrial primacy. The British paid a hellish price in two world wars for their dependence upon imports for the necessities of national life.

In the late nineteenth century, Great Britain seemed to accept the idea that money is wealth, and financial primacy more important than manufacturing power. To sustain a world-trading system of her own creation, Britain sacrificed national interests, even as we Americans now sacrifice national interests on the altar of that Moloch of modernity, the global economy.

Yet, if we were to name one cause of the fall of Britain, it would be war. The Boer War was Britain's Vietnam. With it came a loss of faith in the superiority of British civilization and spread of the heretical idea that a British Empire that denied self-determination to peoples of color was no longer morally defensible.

Then, for ten years between 1914–1918 and 1939–1945, Britain was locked in mortal battle with the mightiest land power in Europe. Britain alone fought both world wars from the first day to the last. By 1945, she was bleeding, bankrupt, exhausted, finished. She would relinquish her empire, sink into socialism, become a Marshall Plan mendicant, and cede the great decisions on the destiny of Europe and of the world to the Americans. By the end of Winston Churchill's last premiership, Britain was a shadow of the world power whose inner cabinet he had entered in 1911.

A year later, came the ultimate affront. General Eisenhower had chafed under Churchill's wartime command. Now President Eisenhower ordered Churchill's successor, Anthony Eden, to abandon Suez with a threat to sink the British pound. America then rudely shouldered Britain aside to assume her imperial role. By Churchill's death in 1965, nothing remained of the empire upon which the sun had never set. Indeed, the poet Shelley's couplet comes to mind: "Nothing beside remains. Round the decay / Of that colossal Wreck, boundless and bare / The lone and level sands stretch far away." Writes Labor Party statesman Sir Roy Denman:

> At the beginning [of the twentieth century], Britain, as the centre of the biggest empire in the world, was at the zenith of her power and glory. Britain approaches the end as a minor power, bereft of her empire. . . . Britain will end the century little more important than Switzerland. It will have been the biggest secular decline in power and influence since seventeenth-century Spain.

"Though the object of being a Great Power is to be able to fight a Great War," wrote British historian A. J. P. Taylor, "the only way of remaining a Great Power is not to fight one." Britain fought two. In World War I, she lost 720,000 dead. In World War II, another 400,000. In ten years of war, Britain had sunk the blood of the best and bravest of her young, and the accumulated treasure of her empire.

America, however, stayed out of the world wars longer than any other power and thus suffered fewer losses. Not until four years after British, French, Germans, and Russians had started slaughtering one another at a rate of six thousand a day did the doughboys arrive to turn the tide on the Western Front, only six months before the armistice.

Not until four years after Hitler overran France did the Higgins boats appear off Normandy, just eleven months before V-E Day. In both world wars, we played Fortinbras in *Hamlet,* coming upon the carnage in the final scene in the bloodstained throne room to take charge of affairs.

During the Cold War, America avoided a war with a Soviet Union that could have wreaked far greater havoc and destruction on us than was visited on Britain in two world wars. We are the last superpower because we stayed out of the great wars of the twentieth century longer than any of the other powers, and we suffered and lost less than any of them.

SINCE THE COLD War's end, however, all the blunders of Britain's ruling class in its march to folly have been replicated by our elites, from the arrogance of power to the alienation of allies to the waging of imperial wars where no vital U.S. interests were at risk. Spurning the counsel of John Quincy Adams, America now goes abroad in search of monsters to destroy.

For a century and a half, America held to Washington's dictum of no "permanent alliances." Now we have treaty guarantees out to fifty nations on five continents and troops in a hundred countries. Some 150,000 U.S. soldiers are tied down in seemingly endless wars in Afghanistan and Iraq. Should the United States confront another crisis anywhere on earth, the bankruptcy of our foreign policy would be transparent to the world.

President Bush has declared it to be U.S. policy to launch preemptive war on any rogue regime that seeks weapons of mass destruction, a policy today being defied by North Korea and Iran, both of which have programs to produce nuclear weapons. The president has also declared it to be U.S. policy to go to war to prevent any other nation from acquiring the power to challenge U.S. hegemony in any region of the earth. It is called "the Bush Doctrine." It is a prescription for permanent war for permanent peace, though wars are the death of republics. "No nation," warned Madison, can "preserve its freedom in the midst of continual warfare."

In 2003, the United States invaded a country that did not threaten us, did not attack us, and did not want war with us, to disarm it of weapons we have since discovered it did not have. His war cabinet assured President Bush that weapons of mass destruction would be found, that U.S. forces would be welcomed with garlands of flowers, that democracy would flourish in Iraq and spread across the Middle East, that our triumph would convince Israelis and Palestinians to sit down and make peace.

None of this happened. Those of us who were called unpatriotic for opposing an invasion of Iraq and who warned we would inherit our own Lebanon of 25 million Iraqis were proven right. Now our nation is tied down and our army is being daily bled in a war to create a democracy in a country where it has never before existed.

With the guerrilla war, U.S. prestige has plummeted. The hatred of President Bush is pandemic from Marrakech to Mosul. Volunteers to fight the Americans have been trickling into Iraq from Syria, Saudi Arabia, and Iran. In spring 2004, revelations of the sadistic abuse of Iraqi prisoners at Abu Ghraib prison sent U.S. prestige sinking to its lowest levels ever in the Arab world. We may have ignited the war of civilizations it was in our vital interest to avoid. Never has America been more resented and reviled in an Islamic world of a billion people.

At home, the budget surpluses of the 1990s have vanished as the cost of the Afghan and Iraq wars has soared beyond the projections of the most pessimistic of the president's economic advisers. The U.S. budget deficit is above 4 percent of GDP. With a trade deficit in goods nearing 6 percent of GDP, the dollar has lost a third of its value against the euro in three years. One in six manufacturing jobs has disappeared since President Bush took the oath. By mid-2004, the president had failed to abolish a single significant agency, program, or department of a Leviathan government that consumes a fifth of our economy. Nor had he vetoed a single bill.

America's native-born population has ceased to grow. Its birth rate has fallen below replacement levels. U.S. population growth now comes from immigrants, legal and illegal, from Asia, Africa, and Latin America. The religious, ethnic, and racial composition of the country, a child of Europe, is changing more rapidly than that of any other great nation in history in an era when race, religion, and ethnicity are tearing countries apart. The melting pot no longer works its magic. Newcomers are not assimilating. We are becoming what Theodore Roosevelt warned against our ever becoming—"a polyglot boardinghouse for the world."

The American people have demanded in every survey that illegal immigration be halted and legal immigration reduced. But the president and Congress refuse to do their constitutional duty to defend the states of the Union from what has become a foreign invasion.

U.S. primary and secondary education is a disaster area. Test scores have been falling for decades and are below those of almost every other developed nation. In our universities, ignorance of American history has reached scandalous proportions and rising percentages of students in the hard sciences come from foreign lands.

The Republican Party, which had presided over America's rise to manufacturing preeminence, has acquiesced in the deindustrialization of the nation to gratify transnational corporations whose oligarchs are the party financiers. U.S. corporations are shutting factories here, opening them in China, "outsourcing" back-office work to India, importing Asians to take white-collar jobs from Americans, and hiring illegal aliens for their service jobs. The Republican Party has signed off on economic treason.

And though seven of the nine sitting justices were nominated by Republican presidents, Republicans have failed to rein in a Supreme Court that is imposing a social, moral, and cultural revolution upon our country.

Then there are the ominous analogies to the Rome we read about in school: the decline of religion and morality, corruption of the commercial class, a debased and decadent culture. Many of America's oldest churches are emptying out. The Catholic Church, the nation's largest, is riven with heresy, scandal, dissent, and disbelief.

Yet, measured by the yardstick that counts in this capital city—power—the compassionate conservatism of George Bush is a triumph. Republicans in 2004 control both houses and have dominated Congress for a decade.

Since the Goldwater defeat in 1964, Republicans have won seven of the ten presidential contests to become "America's Party." The nation has seemed as much in tune with the GOP of today as it was with the party of Harding and Coolidge in the Roaring Twenties. But victory has come at a high price: the abandonment of principle.

Historically, Republicans have been the party of the conservative virtues—of balanced budgets, of a healthy skepticism toward foreign wars, of a commitment to traditional values and fierce resistance to the growth of government power and world empire. No more. To win and hold high office, many have sold their souls to the very devil they were baptized to do battle with.

The party has embraced a neo-imperial foreign policy that would have been seen by the Founding Fathers as a breach of faith. It has cast off the philosophy of Taft, Goldwater, and Reagan to remake itself into the Big Government party long championed by the Rockefeller Republicans whom the conservative movement came into being to drive out of the temple. Many Republicans have abandoned the campaign to make America a colorblind society, and begun to stack arms in the culture wars.

There is no conservative party left in Washington. Conservative thinkers and writers who were to be the watchdogs of orthodoxy have been as vigilant in policing party deviations from principle as was Cardinal Law in collaring the predator-priests of the Boston archdiocese.

Conservatism, as taught by twentieth-century leaders like Robert Taft, Barry Goldwater, Ronald Reagan, and Jesse Helms is dead. Forty years after conservatives captured the party in the coup at the Cow Palace, ten years after the Republican Revolution of 1994, what do they have to show for it besides their committee chairmanships and cabinet chairs?

The GOP may be Reaganite in its tax policy, but it is Wilsonian in its foreign policy, FDR in its trade policy, and LBJ all the way in its spending policies. Pragmatism is the order of the day. The Republican philosophy might be summarized thus: "To hell with principle; what matters is power, and that we have it, and that they do not."

But principles do matter. For history teaches that if we indulge in the vices of republics and surrender to the temptation to buy votes with public money, to distract the populace with bread and circuses, to conduct imperial wars, we will destroy the last best hope of earth. And just as there came a day of reckoning for Lyndon Johnson, who delivered guns-and-butter in wartime, so, too, the chickens are coming home to roost for George W. Bush.

Back in 1960, Barry Goldwater looked about him and said in *Conscience of a Conservative* what I say today:

> I blame Conservatives—ourselves—myself. Our failure . . .
> is the failure of the Conservative demonstration. Though
> we Conservatives are deeply persuaded that our society

is ailing, and know that Conservatism holds the key to national salvation—and feel sure the country agrees with us—we seem unable to demonstrate the relevance of Conservative principles to the needs of the day.

One edit is needed in that paragraph today. We no longer "feel sure the country agrees with us." We may have lost America for good. How and where did we conservatives lose the way? How does America find the way back to the constitutional republic we were not so very long ago? Or is this just the politics of nostalgia, as the old republic is gone forever?

"Forbid it, Almighty God!" Patrick Henry said in a darker time for his country than this. I cannot believe that or accept that the old republic is beyond restoration and redemption. For even as our parents brought us through Depression and the worst war in all history without succumbing to defeatism or despair, even as our own generation persevered through forty years of Cold War, the coming generation can, if it has the knowledge and resolve, restore the republic that once was. And see us through.

That is what this brief book is about. It is about where conservatives lost the way, about where the Right went wrong, about how it came to be that a Republican-controlled capital city whose leaders daily profess their conservatism could preside over the largest fiscal and trade deficits in our history and have us mired in a Wilsonian imperial war to remake the Arab Middle East in the image of the American Middle West. And it is about a cabal that betrayed the good cause of conservatism, because, from the very beginning, they never believed in it. They had another agenda all along.

So, the purpose of this book is to retrace our steps to see where we lost the way, and rediscover the way back home to a conservative politics of principle our beloved country so transparently needs now more than ever. And so, I have written this book for the coming generation of conservatives who must be as unfulfilled with politics-as-usual as were we, when we, too, were young.

ONE

DEMOCRATIC IMPERIALISM AND THE WAR PRESIDENT

The devil begins with froth on the lips of an angel entering into battle for a holy and just cause.

—Grigory Pomerants
dissident Russian philosopher

We have crossed the boundary that lies between Republic and Empire.

—Garet Garrett, 1952

After the World Trade Center towers fell to earth on 9/11, taking the lives of three thousand Americans, *Le Monde* ran the banner "We Are All Americans." The world mourned as we buried our dead. Most of the world supported military action by the United States to punish the men who had done this and the regime that had harbored them.

Now, three years later, the United States, with little support from allies we protected through forty years of Cold War, is mired down in a guerrilla war in a nation that had nothing to do with that terror attack.

How did this happen? As Richard Weaver wrote in the title of his book *Ideas Have Consequences*, America's bloody and costly embroilment in Mesopotamia, with no end in sight, is a result of ideas George W. Bush did not bring with him to the White House but to which he was converted in the shock of 9/11.

Whose ideas are they? We shall see. But first, a little history of the conflict that broke out inside the Republican Party fifteen years ago, for the conservative crack-up began with the end of the Cold War.

When the Soviet empire started to unravel with the fall of the Berlin Wall in 1989, the Cold War that had defined America's mission came to an end. Americans began to cast about for a new foreign policy. Owen Harries of the *National Interest* invited this writer to participate in a symposium on America's role in the post–Cold War world, along with neoconservatives Jeane Kirkpatrick, Ben Wattenberg, and Charles Krauthammer.

Kirkpatrick, a former UN ambassador, held out the hope that we might become again what we had been before a half century of hot and cold war from 1939 to 1989: "The time when Americans should bear such unusual burdens (as the Cold War) is past. With a return to 'normal' times, we can again become a normal nation— and take care of pressing problems of education, family, industry, and technology."

Wattenberg, however, urged that America not come home at all but launch a global campaign to "wage democracy" all over the world.

Krauthammer's vision was even more grandiose. It should be the "wish and work" of America now, he wrote, to "integrate" with Europe and Japan inside a "super-sovereign" entity that would be "economically, culturally and politically hegemonic in the world." The old republic was to be absorbed by the new entity.

This "new universalism," wrote Krauthammer, "would require the conscious depreciation not only of American sovereignty but of the notion of sovereignty in general. This is not as outrageous as it sounds."

To some of us, it was "as outrageous as it sounds." Stunned at the call for a surrender of sovereignty to a trilateral superstate, I replied in "America First—and Second, and Third." In that essay, I advocated a noninterventionist foreign policy rooted in our history, traditions, and the wisdom of our Founding Fathers. With the Cold War over, and no mighty and ideological empire arrayed against us, we could return to a traditional foreign policy rooted in the national interest.

Under this policy, America would dissolve now-obsolete Cold War alliances and shed commitments to defend nations against a Soviet empire that no longer existed. We would pull up trip wires planted by Dulles and Acheson all over the world that were certain to ensnare us in every future war in Asia, Europe, and the Middle East, though U.S. vital interests were no longer at risk there. I urged a policy of "enlightened nationalism" and warned specifically against any Wilsonian crusade for global democracy, even then being bruited about as America's new cause in the world:

> With the Cold War ending, we should look, too, with a cold eye on the international set, never at a loss for new ideas to divert U.S. wealth and power into crusades and causes having little or nothing to do with the true national interest of the United States.
>
> High among these is the democratist temptation, the worship of democracy as a form of governance and the concomitant ambition to see all mankind embrace it, or explain why not. Like all idolatries, democratism substitutes a false god for the real, a love of process for a love of country.

Conclusion: "[T]he true national interests of the United States . . . are not to be found in some hegemonic and utopian world order."

That was the winter of 1990. That August, Iraq invaded the oil-rich emirate of Kuwait and claimed it as its nineteenth province. Kuwait had been severed from Iraq by Churchill when both were under a British mandate after World War I. "This will not stand!" thundered George H. W. Bush. Our forty-first president had found his mission.

In a masterful feat of diplomacy, he pulled together a great coalition of Arab and NATO nations. With financial support from Germany and Japan, the backing of the Security Council, the approval of Congress, and British, French, Egyptian, Syrian, and Saudi troops alongside Americans, Bush launched Desert Storm. After five weeks of air strikes, U.S. ground forces needed only one hundred hours to drive the Iraqi army out of Kuwait and up the Highway of Death to Basra and Baghdad.

At war's end, President Bush's approval rating touched 90 percent. And, in October of 1991, he went before the UN to declare that he would not be bringing U.S. troops home, but would launch a crusade to build a "New World Order." The United States would lead the UN in policing the world, punishing aggressors, and preserving the peace.

America's mission had been declared to mankind. But the American people who would have to pay in endless blood and treasure to sustain this imperial role had not been consulted.

Though elected as the heir to Reagan, President Bush had already broken with the Reagan philosophy on taxes and big government. He was now resolved to conscript America's wealth and power to launch a Wilsonian crusade to make America the policeman of the world. This was not conservatism. Thus, on December 10, 1991, I declared against him in New Hampshire and closed my announcement speech with these words:

> George Bush served bravely in America's great war. He is a man of graciousness, honor, and integrity who has given half a lifetime to his nation's service. But the differences between us now are too deep. . . .
>
> He is a globalist and we are nationalists. He believes in some Pax Universalis; we believe in the Old Republic. He would put America's wealth and power at the service of some vague New World Order; we will put America first.

Ten weeks later, I won 37 percent of the vote to Bush's 51 percent. The day after, Ross Perot declared his candidacy, and, eighteen months after his Gulf War victory parade up Constitution Avenue, the commander in chief was turned out of office with the smallest share of the vote for a president since William Howard Taft in 1912. But Bush had left a legacy. He had planted America's feet on the road to empire. Between the day he took office and the day his son followed suit, the United States invaded Panama, intervened in Somalia, occupied Haiti, pushed NATO to the borders of Russia, created protectorates in Kuwait and Bosnia, bombed Serbia for seventy-eight days, occupied Kosovo, adopted a policy of "dual containment" of Iraq and Iran, and deployed thousands of troops on Saudi soil sacred to all Muslims. In my 1999 book, *A Republic, Not an Empire,* I warned of the certainty of blowback:

> The United States has unthinkingly embarked upon a neo-imperial policy that must involve us in virtually every great war of the coming century—and wars are the death of republics . . . if we continue on this course of reflexive interventions, enemies will one day answer our power with the weapon of the weak—terror, and eventually cataclysmic terrorism on U.S. soil . . . then liberty, the cause of the republic, will itself be in peril.

In 2000, as Reform Party candidate, I repeated the warning:

> How can all our meddling not fail to spark some horrible retribution . . . Have we not suffered enough—from Pan Am 103 to the World Trade Center [bombing of 1993] to the embassy bombings in Nairobi and Dar es Salaam—not to know that interventionism is the incubator of terrorism? Or will it take some cataclysmic atrocity on U.S. soil to awaken our global gamesmen to the going price of empire? America today faces a choice of destinies. We can choose to be a peacemaker of the world, or its policeman who goes about night-sticking troublemakers until we, too, find ourselves in some bloody brawl we cannot handle.

On September 11, 2001, the "cataclysmic atrocity" occurred.

In shock and horror, America demanded retribution and George W. Bush delivered it. As effectively as his father, he pulled together a great coalition to oust the Taliban accomplices of Osama bin Laden. He won President Putin's assistance in basing U.S. forces in the former Soviet republics of Uzbekistan and Turkmenistan and President Musharraf's permission to base forces in Pakistan. He won the passive support of Iran and China and the active support of NATO. After U.S. agents enlisted the armies of the Northern Alliance and bought off dissident Pashtuns, Bush ordered the Taliban overthrown and Al Qaeda run out of Afghanistan. In three months, the war was over.

Bush then began to push the frontiers of empire far beyond where his father or Bill Clinton had left them. America now has troops in Georgia, bases in Kazakhstan, Uzbekistan, and Tajikistan, and is negotiating for bases in Azerbaijan. But while Russia, Iran, and China approved of Bush's war to oust the Taliban, they have never endorsed a permanent U.S. military presence in the heartland of Asia where even British power never penetrated at the height of empire.

SEPTEMBER 11 CHANGED Bush. As his father had found his mission when Iraq invaded Kuwait, George W. seemed to have found his when he stood in the rubble of the twin towers in Lower Manhattan. That mission: Lead America in a worldwide war on terror that would continue through his presidency and for the rest of our lives.

Nine days after September 11, Bush went before a joint session of Congress and in the most powerful address of his presidency laid down the principles and strategy America would pursue:

> Our war on terror begins with Al Qaeda, but it does not end there. It will not end until every terrorist group of global

reach has been found, stopped and defeated. . . . Every nation, in every region, now has a decision to make. Either you are with us, or you are with the terrorists. From this day forward, any nation that continues to harbor or support terrorism will be regarded by the United States as a hostile regime.

Using rhetoric that hearkened back to Christ Himself in the New Testament—"He who is not with me is against me"—Bush divided the world: "Either you are with us or you are with the terrorists."

By October, Bush had begun to expand the list of America's enemies beyond those who had had a role in 9/11 to all rogue states with a history of sponsoring terrorists, and issued this warning: "For every regime that sponsors terrorism, there is a price to be paid and it will be paid. The allies of terror are equally guilty of murder and equally accountable to justice."

He had also begun to describe the war on terror in moral terms, calling our enemies "evildoers" and "the evil ones," and telling diplomats at State, "This war is a struggle between good and evil."

For Bush, terrorists constituted not a conspiracy or a criminal gang but the very embodiment of evil. He insisted that there could be no purpose, no rationale, and no explanation for their actions apart from sheer malevolence. The "evil ones," the president said, are people who "have no country, no ideology; they're motivated by hate." For Bush this war was not, as Clausewitz would have it, an extension of politics, but a moral imperative that transcended politics. As foreign policy scholar Andrew Bacevich writes, "From the outset, President Bush looked upon that war as something of a crusade and he himself as something of an agent of divine will."

In November at Fort Campbell, home of the 101st Airborne, Bush began to describe and define the regimes that would feel our wrath:

> America has a message to the nations of the world: If you
> harbor terrorists, you are terrorists. If you train or arm a ter-
> rorist, you are a terrorist. If you feed a terrorist or fund a ter-
> rorist, you're a terrorist, and you will be held accountable by
> the United States . . .

The president had cast into the enemy camp all state sponsors
of terror as designated by the Department of State, a list that included Libya, Sudan, and Iran, though all three had passively supported our war in Afghanistan.

THE "AXIS OF EVIL"

In his State of the Union in 2002, President Bush went further,
identifying Iran, Iraq, and North Korea by name as an "axis of evil"
and delivering virtual ultimatums to all three:

> We'll be deliberate, yet time is not on our side. I will not wait
> on events, while dangers gather. I will not stand by, as peril
> draws closer and closer. The United States of America will
> not permit the world's most dangerous regimes to threaten
> us with the world's most destructive weapons.

With this threat, President Bush stunned many who had supported his leadership. What did Iran, Iraq, and North Korea have
to do with 9/11? Why was he widening the war by issuing ultimatums to Iran, Iraq, and North Korea before Al Qaeda and its collaborators had been eradicated? When had Iraq, Iran, or North
Korea threatened America with "the world's most destructive
weapons"?

By calling the three an "axis of evil," Bush consciously called to
mind Reagan's designation of the Soviet Union as an "evil empire"
and the Axis powers Nazi Germany, Imperial Japan, and Fascist
Italy. Their fate will be your fate, the president seemed to be saying
to North Korea, Iran, and Iraq.

Casting aside Theodore Roosevelt's admonition to "speak softly and carry a big stick," Bush had thundered his ultimata in the clear. "Will not permit"—here was a direct threat of war to prevent any "axis of evil" regime from acquiring atomic, biological, or chemical weapons, the "ABC weapons" of the Cold War, now referred to as "weapons of mass destruction."

The Bush threat of war upon nations that had not attacked us was unprecedented. Truman never threatened war to stop Stalin from building atomic bombs after Russia tested one in 1949. LBJ did not threaten war on China when it exploded a nuclear weapon in 1964. While it had been U.S. policy to prevent the spread of nuclear weapons, Russia, Britain, France, China, Israel, India, and Pakistan had all acquired nuclear weapons without serious retribution from the United States.

Yet Bush had put Iran, Iraq, and North Korea on notice. Should any of the three seek to enter the circle of nations possessing nuclear weapons, or the larger circle possessing biological or chemical weapons—some of which date back to World War I—they risked a preemptive strike and war to disarm them and effect "regime change" in their countries. Though the president may not have known it when he issued his ultimata, North Korea and Iran already had secret nuclear programs underway.

Still, President Bush had no authority to issue those threats. The Constitution does not empower the president to launch preventive wars. To attain Churchillian heights, Bush's speechwriters had taken him over the top. But, as events would demonstrate, Bush fully intended to go where his rhetoric was leading him.

THE WEST POINT MANIFESTO

After the president had widened the theater of conflict to include "axis of evil" nations that had nothing to do with 9/11, the coalitions he had drawn together domestically and abroad began to crumble. But the president was undeterred. In an address to the graduates at West Point on June 2, 2002, he went further, announcing a new post–Cold War mission for the armed forces of the United States:

> Our nation's cause has always been larger than our nation's defense. We fight, as we always fight, for a just peace—a peace that favors human liberty. We will defend the peace against threats from terrorists and tyrants. We will preserve the peace by building good relations among the great powers. And we will extend the peace by encouraging free and open societies on every continent.

In asserting America's duty to "extend the peace," the president was assuming a global mission no other president had ever dared assert. And, the Wilsonian rhetoric aside, America had never gone to war for any such gauzy goal as a "just peace . . . that favors human liberty."

America's wars were fought for American ends. We fought the Revolution to be rid of British rule; the War of 1812 because the Royal Navy refused to respect the rights of our seamen, and "war hawks" saw a chance to seize Canada from the hated British. We took on Mexico to keep Texas and take California. Lincoln fought the Civil War to restore the Union. We fought Spain because we wanted her out of our hemisphere. Begun to liberate Cubans, the war of 1898 ended as a colonial war to subjugate Filipinos and establish an American empire in the Pacific.

We entered World War I because the kaiser refused to respect our rights as a neutral to supply his enemies and began to torpedo our ships. We fought World War II because we were attacked at Pearl Harbor. We fought in Korea and Vietnam to prevent those nations from falling to a Communist empire whose ultimate aim was defeat of our country and the end of our way of life. We fought the Gulf War to eject Iraq from Kuwait and keep Kuwait and Saudi oil in the hands of client states.

At West Point, President Bush now rejected as obsolete the doctrines of containment and deterrence that had won the Cold War, and advocated anew an American policy of preemptive war:

> Containment is not possible when unbalanced dictators with weapons of mass destruction can deliver those weapons on missiles or secretly provide them to terrorist allies. . . . If we wait for threats to fully materialize, we will have waited too long.
>
> [T]he war on terror will not be won on the defensive. We must take the battle to the enemy, disrupt his plans, and confront the worst threats before they emerge. In this world we have entered, the only path to safety is the path of action. And this nation will act.

In dealing with terrorists the president was right. No threat will deter a suicide bomber determined to give up his life driving an airliner into the World Trade Center. But in dealing with nations, containment and deterrence had never failed us. We contained Stalin and Mao, though both had large arsenals of nuclear weapons.

Yet, with the "unbalanced dictators" of today, like Kim Jong Il, the Iranian mullahs, and Saddam, President Bush was saying, deterrence could not be relied upon to keep us secure. But why not? After all, not one of these rogue regimes ever openly or directly attacked the United States.

The president then took the Bush Doctrine a great leap forward, asserting a sovereign right to prevent any nation from ever acquiring the power to challenge the strategic supremacy of the United States:

> Competition between great nations is inevitable, but armed conflict in our world is not. . . . America has, and intends to keep, military strengths beyond challenge—thereby making the destabilizing arms races of other eras pointless, and limiting rivalries to trade and other pursuits of peace.

This was breathtaking. President Bush was saying to Beijing, Moscow, New Delhi: You may compete with us in trade, but we will not allow you to increase your strength to where it challenges America's power.

This Bush declaration—that we will brook no rival, ever again, that the future is one of permanent American hegemony—is a gauntlet thrown down to every rival and would-be world power and a challenge to lesser powers to unite against us. Had Britain adopted such a policy in the nineteenth century, Parliament would have asserted a right to go to war to prevent the United States from ever increasing its sea power to rival that of the Royal Navy.

Hoover Institution fellow Tod Lindberg called this Bush declaration of permanent U.S. superiority "sobering if not chilling."

But the president was not finished at West Point. "All nations that decide for aggression and terror will pay a price. We will not leave . . . the peace of the planet at the mercy of a few mad terrorists and tyrants. We will lift this dark threat from our country and the world."

Consider what the president is saying here. Every act of aggression, anywhere, can expect U.S. retaliation and every act of terror will bring an American reprisal. For we are responsible for "the peace of the planet." And we will lift "the dark threat" of tyranny and terror from mankind.

But when in all history has any nation been able to do this?

Israel, with a superb military and unrivaled intelligence, has been unable even to lift the dark threat of terror from Jerusalem. Not only do Hamas, Hezbollah, Islamic Jihad, the IRA, FARC in Columbia, the Basque ETA, the Tamil Tigers, and Chechen rebels employ terror, so do regimes and guerrillas all over the Third World.

Are the graduates of West Point to fight them all?

Prudence is the mark of the conservative. Where was the prudence in the president's address at West Point? Yet Bush was not done.

"Moral truth is the same in every culture, in every time, and in every place," he declared. But for one nation in a world of 190 to assert a right to define morality for all peoples for all times, and attempt to impose its code on all mankind, is a moral imperialism certain to end in calamity and tragedy.

In this most Christianized of countries, premarital sex, homosexual unions, and abortions are considered normal and moral by our cultural elites. Islamic societies reject them as immoral. Who does President Bush believe is right? At the UN, Christians cooperate with Muslims to defeat European and American progressives. Who does the president believe is on the side of "moral truth"? If moral truth is the same "in every culture, in every time, and every place," why do men yet disagree on the morality of what we did to Hamburg, Hiroshima, Dresden, and Nagasaki?

"We are in a conflict between good and evil, and America will call evil by its name," President Bush told the cadets. But in this Manichean world, which is the evil side in Chechnya, Sri Lanka, Kashmir? In a war against "evildoers," on whose side is Beijing? In Afghanistan, America was supported by Iran, Pakistan, and a Northern Alliance led by warlords guilty of mass murder. In World War II we were allied with Stalin, in the Gulf with Assad, in the Cold War with the shah and General Pinochet. America triumphed by putting "moral clarity" on the shelf and lining up allies without too-scrupulous an inspection of their humanitarian credentials. Were we acting immorally?

AT THE REAGAN Library in November of 1999, candidate Bush had repudiated the triumphalist rhetoric of the Clinton administration with all its braying about our being the "indispensable nation." "Let us have an American foreign policy that reflects American character," said Bush. "The modesty of true strength. The humility of real greatness. This is the strong heart of America. And this will be the spirit of my administration."

In a presidential debate with Al Gore, Bush had said:

One way for us to end up being viewed as the ugly American is for us to go around the world saying, we do it this way, so should you. . . . The United States must be humble . . . humble in how we treat nations that are figuring out how to chart their own course.

This was the conservative the nation had elected president.

But at West Point, humility had yielded to hubris. "The twentieth century ended with a single surviving model of human progress," the president told the cadets. "The requirements of freedom apply fully to . . . the entire Islamic world."

Here is the "founding document of a new international order with American power at its center and the spread of freedom as its aim," said columnist Lindberg. "You have heard of the Monroe Doctrine, no? . . . The West Point speech, with its liberty doctrine, will be remembered for laying out something no less consequential . . ."

By "freedom," the president means America's concept of freedom: The right to worship as we desire, write as we please, say what we will, live as we like. But Islam means "submission"—submission to the will of Allah. To Muslim believers, Christian missionaries have no right to proselytize in their land. In some Islamic countries, to attempt to convert Muslims is punishable by death. Millions reject the separation of mosque and state. *Sharia*—Islamic rules about how men and women should live—should, millions of Muslims believe, be law in all Islamic countries. Consider the reaction across the Islamic world to Salman Rushdie's blasphemous *Satanic Verses*.

If President Bush believes ours is the "single surviving model of human progress," and our ideas of freedom "apply fully to the entire Islamic world," we are headed for endless wars with an Islamic world where the faith grows militant and peoples are repelled by the social, cultural, and moral decadence they see in America and the West.

"[W]e will defend the peace that makes all progress possible," the president told the cadets.

But U.S. armed forces do not take an oath to defend "the peace that makes all progress possible." They take an oath to defend the Constitution of the United States. Yet, the president now says the armed forces of the United States, 1.4 million in number, are responsible for ending all terrorism, opposing all tyrants, preserving the "peace of the planet," and permitting no rival to challenge our supremacy, because we Americans have discovered the only path to "human progress."

THE NATIONAL SECURITY STRATEGY

On September 21, 2002, the White House issued a thirty-three-page National Security Strategy of the United States, a codification of the principles and policies enunciated at West Point. In dealing with rogue nations seeking to acquire weapons of mass destruction, the president declared, "In the new world we have entered, the only path to peace and security is the path of action. . . . we will not hesitate to act alone, if necessary, to exercise our right of self-defense by acting preemptively."

Why cannot Cuba, Libya, Syria, Iraq, Iran, and North Korea be deterred as were Stalin's Russia and Mao's China? Declared the NSS:

> Deterrence . . . is less likely to work against leaders of rogue states more willing to take risks, gambling with the lives of their people, and the wealth of their nations. . . .
>
> [O]ur enemies see weapons of mass destruction as weapons of choice. For rogue states these weapons are tools of intimidation and military aggression against their neighbors. These weapons may allow these states to attempt to blackmail the United States . . . to prevent us from deterring or repelling the aggressive behavior of rogue states.

But deterrence has worked. With the exception of Korea, 1950, where Stalin and Kim Il Sung, believing we would not fight, miscalculated, deterrence has never failed us. No rogue state has ever attacked the United States—for fear of the massive retaliation that would surely follow.

From the passage above, the Bush administration appears to fear that if nations like Iran acquire nuclear weapons, they will use them not to attack us but to curtail our freedom of action and end our dominance of their region—as Moscow's nuclear arsenal deterred U.S. intervention to effect regime change in Eastern Europe in the Cold War.

The NSS restated Bush's explicit warning: Any nation that seeks to acquire power to rival ours risks war with us. "Our forces will be strong enough to dissuade potential adversaries from pursuing a military buildup in hopes of surpassing or equaling the power of the United States."

This is the imperial edict of a superpower out to exploit its present supremacy to make itself permanent Lord Protector of the universe. And against whom is this threat directed? China and Russia, the only great power rivals to U.S. supremacy. One imagines the National Security Strategy was read closely in Moscow and Beijing.

To Gail Russell Chaddock of the *Christian Science Monitor,* the NSS was a blueprint for a "Pax Americana," "the boldest restatement of U.S. national security strategy in half a century." To Tim Reich of the *Washington Post,* it was a "watershed in U.S. foreign policy" that "reverses the fundamental principles that have guided successive Presidents for more than 50 years: containment and deterrence."

Wrote Yale historian John Lewis Gaddis in *Foreign Policy:*

> There's been nothing like this in boldness, sweep and vision since Americans took it upon themselves, more than half a century ago, to democratize Germany and Japan, thus setting in motion processes that stopped short of only a few places on earth, one of which was the Muslim Middle East.

Andrew Bacevich, foreign policy scholar at Boston University, writing of the National Security Strategy, marveled at

> . . . its fusion of breathtaking utopianism with barely disguised *machtpolitik*. It reads as if it were the product not of sober, ostensibly conservative Republicans but of an unlikely collaboration between Woodrow Wilson and the elder Field Marshal von Moltke.

Truman had introduced containment on March 12, 1947, when he declared that the United States would go to the aid of Greece and Turkey, then resisting Stalin-backed Communist rebels. He closed his speech with the historic statement: "I believe it must be the policy of the United States to support free peoples who are resisting attempted subjugation by armed minorities or outside pressures." This was the Truman Doctrine to contain the spread of Communism by aiding embattled nations along its frontiers.

Under the Truman Doctrine, we went to war in Korea. Eisenhower extended it to the Middle East. Under it, JFK and LBJ took us to war in Vietnam. The Reagan Doctrine was a "rollback" strategy under which the United States gave aid to anti-Communist rebels fighting Soviet vassal states on the periphery of empire in Nicaragua, Angola, and Afghanistan.

Conservatives credit Reagan and the Reagan Doctrine with playing a decisive role in America's Cold War victory. Yet Reagan never asserted a U.S. right to launch preemptive strikes or preventive wars on nations that had not attacked the United States.

Bush's aides believe a right of preemptive attack and preventive war is inherent in the national right of self-defense. In the missile crisis, they argue, Kennedy was prepared to attack the missile sites in Cuba rather than let them become operational. True, but the Soviet missile threat in Cuba appeared both grave and imminent. Those were nuclear missiles that could strike Washington from their Cuban bases in twenty minutes.

The Allies did intervene in Russia in 1918, after Lenin, sent across Germany in a sealed train with the approval of the German General Staff, overthrew Kerensky and signed a separate peace with the kaiser. As the Germans had helped to overthrow a fighting ally, the Western powers were within their rights to intervene to restore the allied government.

U.S., British, French, and Japanese troops were sent to aid the anti-Bolshevik rebels. But by 1919, the last champion of intervention was Churchill. Had the Allies listened to Churchill and sent veterans of the Western Front to Russia, Communism might have been strangled in its crib and the world spared the millions of murders committed by Stalin, Mao, Kim Il Sung, Castro, Ho Chi Minh, and Pol Pot.

History thus seems to justify preventive wars. Yet such a policy is alien to American tradition. Polk waited until the Mexican army shed "American blood on American soil" before asking Congress to declare war. Before calling up volunteers to march South, Lincoln waited for the attack on Fort Sumter. We did not declare war on Germany until her U-boats began to sink our ships in 1917. We did not declare war on Japan until Pearl Harbor. We did not go to war in Korea or Vietnam until those nations were under attack.

Preemptive strikes have been the war options exercised by aggressor nations like Japan at Port Arthur in 1904 and at Pearl Harbor, and Hitler's Germany against Poland. Or they have been the first resort of nations that cannot afford to lose a battle, like Israel in the Six-Day War of 1967. But preemptive strikes have never been America's way.

Yet, foreign policy scholar Walter Russell Mead says of the National Security Strategy of George Bush that it is "likely to endure as a bedrock element in American thinking in this post–Cold War world." Perhaps, but the Pax Americana it envisions may have ushered in a era of what historian Harry Elmer Barnes called "Perpetual War for Perpetual Peace."

DEMOCRATIC IMPERIALISM

In the summer of 2002, with Taki Theodora Copolous and Scott McConnell, I launched the *American Conservative,* a magazine dedicated to opposing an invasion of Iraq, for which the war drums were, by then, already loudly beating. In the first column for our biweekly, I raised a question about our coming invasion: "What comes after all the celebratory gunfire when wicked Saddam is dead?" In answering my own question, I predicted the following:

> With our MacArthur Regency in Baghdad, Pax Americana will reach apogee. But then the tide recedes, for the one endeavor at which Islamic peoples excel is expelling imperial powers by terror and guerrilla war. They drove the Brits out of Palestine and Aden, the French out of Algeria, the Russians out of Afghanistan, the Americans out of Somalia and Beirut, the Israelis out of Lebanon. . . .
>
> We have started up the road to empire and over the next hill we shall meet those who went before. The only lesson we learn from history is that we do not learn from history.

But by now the president's mind had been made up. Having named Iraq an axis-of-evil state possessing weapons of mass destruction, having laid out his doctrine of preventive war, in March 2003, President Bush ordered the invasion. In three weeks, it was over. However, in the eighteen months since, the United States has found no evidence Iraq was plotting to attack us or its neighbors, has found no evidence of ties between Saddam and the perpetrators of 9/11, and has discovered no Iraqi nuclear program or any weapons of mass destruction.

So, within months of the fall of Baghdad, the cause for which we had fought began to change as radically in Bush's rhetoric as the cause for which the Union was fighting had changed in Lincoln's rhetoric. Speaking in November of 2003 to the National Endowment for Democracy, and later at Whitehall castle in England,

Bush declared that Iraq's liberation was part of a "world democratic movement."

"The establishment of a free Iraq in the heart of the Middle East will be a watershed event in the global democratic revolution," Bush declared at Whitehall. "[O]ur commitment to the global expansion of democracy . . . as the alternative to instability and to hatred and terror is . . . the third pillar of security."

The Whitehall speech was pure Wilsonianism. We will help Iraq to establish a "democratic country in the heart of the Middle East," said Bush, because, by so doing, "we will defend our people from danger." Wilson's doctrine—only by making "the world safe for democracy" can we make America safe in the world—had been embraced by a Republican president who called himself a conservative.

But not only must Iraq embrace democracy. So, too, must Saudi Arabia, Egypt, and Pakistan, which have been laggards in joining the world democratic revolution:

> Sixty years of Western nations excusing and accommodating the lack of freedom in the Middle East did nothing to make us safe—because in the long run, stability in the Middle East did nothing to make us safe. . . . Therefore, the United States has adopted a new policy, a forward strategy of freedom in the Middle East. This strategy requires the same persistence and energy and idealism we have shown before. And it will yield the same results.

"Yield the same results"? Is Bush aware that when Jimmy Carter pressured the shah to democratize, the shah was overthrown and Iran fell to the ayatollah? Can the president believe that by hectoring and destabilizing autocracies such as Egypt, Saudi Arabia, and Pakistan, we are made more secure? Who comes to power if Mubarak goes in Cairo, the Saudi monarchy falls, or Musharraf is ousted? Previous popular revolts in the Arab world gave us and the world Nasser, Khadafi, Assad, Saddam, and the Ba'ath Party.

If President Bush's crusade for democracy leads to one-man, one-vote in Pakistan, what do we do if that nuclear-armed nation supports a return of the Taliban? Now that a countrywide insurgency has arisen against our occupation of Iraq, and the sexual abuse of the prisoners at Abu Ghraib has inflamed the Arab world against us, what do we do if the new Iraqi regime that takes power after free elections tells us to get out of their country and declares the return of Kuwait to the motherland to be as sacred to Baghdad as the return of Taiwan to Beijing?

President Bush's men may describe their call for world democratic revolution "Reaganite," but this is not what Ronald Reagan preached or practiced. Despite demands that he put pressure on autocrats to reform, Reagan got on fine with Saudi kings and Korean generals and African rulers who took America's side in the Cold War. His mission was simple and clear: Defend the country he loved against the preeminent threat and accept assistance from those who dared to stand beside us.

Reagan did call the Soviet Union an "evil empire" and declared that Communism was headed for the ash heap of history, but, like the tough union leader he once was, after he took his stand and made his case, he was ready to sit down and talk. He was tough but not bellicose. He spoke softly as he carved and carried America's big stick. Because he was confident that history and Divine Providence were on America's side, he never took precipitate or rash action.

When General Jaruzelski crushed Solidarity in Poland in 1981, Reagan refused to put the regime in default. When a Soviet fighter shot down a Korean airliner in 1983, Reagan learned that Moscow had not given the order, and let the atrocity speak for itself about the character of the regime that defended it.

When the Soviet Union deployed mobile SS-20 missiles in Eastern Europe, Reagan countered with Pershing and cruise missiles in Western Europe. But when Gorbachev agreed to take down his SS-20s, Reagan agreed to take out his Pershings. He was proud of the first strategic arms reduction treaty of the Cold War. He loved

SDI because he hated nuclear weapons. He was antiwar because he was pro-peace.

Only three times in his presidency did Ronald Reagan resort to force. When Khadafi's agents blew up the Berlin discotheque, killing one U.S. soldier and wounding twenty, Reagan's retaliation was as measured as was Jefferson's, when he, too, coped with Barbary pirates. In Grenada, Reagan swept a Soviet pawn off the board, but only after he saw a threat to American medical students. When he put Marines in Lebanon and their Beirut barracks were bombed, Reagan retaliated, but pulled the Marines out. He resisted demands to send an invasion force to avenge our 241 dead and occupy Beirut. For President Reagan saw no vital U.S. interest in Lebanon and realized he had put the Marines at risk in a civil war that was not America's war. Ronald Reagan had the courage to concede and correct a mistake—and get out.

Would Reagan have declared a policy of preventive war to keep any rival from rising to where it might challenge us? Would he have thrown over the Cold War doctrines of deterrence and containment as irrelevant to our time? Would he have called for a world democratic revolution to change regimes that did not threaten or attack his country? No one can know for certain, but I do not believe it.

As for 9/11, one cannot say with certitude how Reagan would have responded. But it is hard to believe he would have invaded Iraq without solid evidence of Saddam's involvement in 9/11 or solid proof that only an invasion would prevent an imminent attack on the United States. For, despite Reagan's reputation as a cowboy, patience, perseverance, and prudence were the hallmarks of his presidency.

"SIXTY YEARS OF Western nations excusing and accommodating the lack of freedom in the Middle East did nothing to make us safe because in the long run, stability in the Middle East did nothing to make us safe."

President Bush was hereby declaring U.S. Mideast policy since FDR to be a failure that "did nothing to make us safe"—because our allies were not democratic. But this is nonsense. In the Middle East in the Cold War, the United States had the support of the shah in Iran, presidents Sadat and Mubarak in Egypt, the Saudi royal family, and the kings of Morocco and Jordan. Does President Bush believe U.S. support of these monarchs and autocrats "did nothing to make us safe"—though we won the Cold War?

Were the policies of all eleven of his predecessors back to FDR, which prevented Soviet domination of the oil wealth of the world, really failures?

How can President Bush say we are not secure if the Islamic world is not democratic? The Islamic world has *never* been democratic. Yet, before we intervened there, our last threat came from Barbary pirates.

FREEDOM, THE PRESIDENT said at Whitehall, "must be chosen, and defended by those who choose it." Why not, then, let Islamic peoples choose or not choose it on their own timetable, and defend it themselves?

"Perhaps the most helpful change we can make is to change in our own thinking," said President Bush. It is "cultural condescension," to "assume the Middle East cannot be converted to democracy."

But if twenty-two of twenty-two Arab states are nondemocratic, this would seem to suggest that Middle Eastern soil is not particularly conducive to growing the kind of democracy that flourishes in New England. While this may be mulish thinking to the progressives at the National Endowment for Democracy, it may also be common sense. And after almost two years of war to build democracy in Iraq, perhaps it is the democratic imperialists who need to change their "way of thinking."

What support is there in history for the view that by meddling in the internal politics of foreign nations we advance our security? How would we have responded in the nineteenth century if Britain had invaded and occupied Washington until President Andrew Jackson abolished slavery and stopped his mistreatment of the Indians?

Every survey of Arab and Islamic peoples reveals that they bear a deep resentment of U.S. domination and of our one-sided support of Israel. Interventionism is not the solution to America's problems in the Middle East. Interventionism is the problem. America's huge footprint on the sacred soil of Saudi Arabia led straight to 9/11. The terrorists were over here because we were over there. Terrorism is the price of empire. If you do not wish to pay the price, you must give up the empire.

"Liberty is both the plan of Heaven for humanity, and the best hope for progress here on Earth," said Mr. Bush. Christians used to believe salvation was Heaven's plan for humanity and Jesus Christ was the way, the truth, and the life. Neoconservatives have made democracy their god. But why is George W. Bush falling down and worshiping this golden calf?

The last time we Americans heard rhetoric like President Bush's at Whitehall and the National Endowment for Democracy was the last time we were bogged down in a guerrilla war. LBJ declared that America's goal was now far loftier than saving South Vietnam. We were going to build a "Great Society on the Mekong."

Clearly, President Bush has been converted to the belief that only by making the world democratic can we ever make America secure. But our forefathers did not believe this; they did not even believe in democracy, per se. They thought they were creating a republic that would be made secure by staying out of the wars of the blood-soaked continent their fathers had left behind.

What, then, are the elements of the Bush Doctrine as enunciated in the presidential speeches and statements in the two years following 9/11?

• The war on terror is between good and evil and it will not end until we eradicate all terror networks of a global reach. Every nation must decide: Either you are with us, or you are with the ter-

rorists. Any nation that feeds or funds a group we designate as terrorist will be treated as a terrorist state, subject to attack.

• No rogue nation, especially Iran, Iraq, and North Korea, will
be allowed to acquire weapons of mass destruction. The United
States claims a right to launch preemptive strikes and wage preventive wars against any rogue regime that seeks such weapons.

• With Afghanistan and the invasion of Iraq, we have begun a
world democratic revolution that will continue until all the despotisms of the Middle East are overthrown and replaced by democracies. And this revolution will not end until the world is democratic.
We undertake this duty to mankind because we are good and our
enemies are evil, we are the "single surviving model of human
progress," and only when the world is democratic can America be
truly secure.

• No nation will be permitted, ever again, to rise to a position of
power to where it can challenge the United States, globally or re-
gionally.

Let it be said: This is utopianism. This is democratic imperialism. This will bleed, bankrupt, and isolate this republic. This over-
throws the wisdom of the Founding Fathers about what America
should be all about. This is an American version of the Brezhnev
Doctrine, wherein Moscow asserted a right to intervene to save
Communism in any nation where it had once been imposed. Only
we Americans now assert a right to intervene anywhere to impose
democracy. This is a presidential embrace of that democratist
temptation against which this writer warned the first President
Bush in that *National Interest* essay, fifteen years ago:

> How other people rule themselves is their own business. To
> call it a vital interest of the United States is to contradict
> history and common sense. And for the Republic to seek to
> dictate to 160 nations what kind of regime each should have
> is a formula for interminable meddling and endless conflict;
> it is a textbook example of that "messianic globaloney"

against which Dean Acheson warned; it is, in scholar Clyde Wilson's phrase, a globalization of that degenerate form of Protestantism known as the Social Gospel.

"We must consider first and last," Walter Lippmann wrote in 1943, "the American national interest. If we do not, if we construct our foreign policy on some kind of abstract theory of rights and duties, we shall build castles in the air. We shall formulate policies which in fact the nation will not support with its blood, its sweat, and its tears."

If prudence is the mark of the conservative, George W. Bush has ceased to be a conservative. To try "to turn democracy into a worldwide moral crusade," writes scholar-author Claes Ryn, is the mark of the "new Jacobinism," which, in its messianic zealotry, calls to mind the men of the French Revolution.

But George W. Bush did not bring these ideas with him from Crawford, Texas. Before he took his oath, he had probably rarely read or heard such democratist rhetoric before. Who put these ideas in his head? Who put these words in his mouth? Who got us into this hellish mess in Mesopotamia?

TWO

THE WAR PARTY: HIJACKERS OF AMERICAN FOREIGN POLICY

> With the end of the Cold War, what we really need is an obvious ideological and threatening enemy, one worthy of our mettle, one that can unite us in opposition.
>
> —Irving Kristol, 1996

> I don't know where the neocons came from ... Somehow, the neocons captured the president. They captured the vice president.
>
> —Gen. Anthony Zinni, USMC (ret.)
> Centcom Commander, 1998–2000

Who are they, the neoconservatives?

The first generation were ex-Trotskyites, socialists, leftists, and liberals who backed FDR, Truman, JFK, and LBJ. When the Democratic party was captured by McGovern in 1972—on a platform of cutting defense and "Come Home America!"—these Cold War liberals found themselves isolated and ignored in their own party. Adrift, they rafted over to the Republican Party and were pulled aboard as conservatism's long voyage was culminating in the triumph of Reagan. Neoconservatives were the boat people of the McGovern revolution that was itself the political vehicle of the moral, social, and cultural revolutions of the 1960s.

Kevin Phillips wrote then that a neoconservative was more likely to be a magazine editor than a bricklayer. Today, he is more likely to be a resident scholar at a public policy institute like AEI, or its clones such as the Center for Security Policy or the Project for the New American Century. Almost none came out of the Goldwater campaign, the catalyzing event of modern conservatism, or out of the business world or the military. As one wag has written, a neo-con is more familiar with the inside of a think tank than of an Abrams tank. Their heroes are the heroes of the Left: Wilson, FDR, Truman, Martin Luther King, and senators Henry "Scoop" Jackson and Daniel Patrick Moynihan.

Among luminaries of the neoconservative persuasion are Jeane Kirkpatrick, Bill Bennett, Michael Novak, and Father Richard John Neuhaus. Scholar-authors Charles Murray and James Q. Wilson are often claimed.

In numbers, it is a tiny movement, without a national con-stituency, "all chiefs and no Indians," as was said in the 1970s. And while many neocons are Jewish, most Jewish writers and intel-lectuals in America are liberals and many are among the sharper critics of neoconservatism. Even on the Right, not all Jewish writ-ers are neocons, though support for Israel is broad and deep, and no more surprising than is opposition to abortion among Catholics, Mormons, and Evangelical Christians.

"This was a movement founded on foreign policy," says Max Boot. More specifically, it was a movement originally fueled by a mounting fear that the Soviet Union was becoming a mortal threat to America and Israel. Before Israel's 1967 Six-Day War, Egypt, and Syria had been armed with Soviet weapons, as they would be for the Yom Kippur War of 1973.

In that same *Wall Street Journal* essay "What the Heck Is a Neo-con?" Boot called support for Israel "a key tenet of neoconser-vatism." It was the only tenet Boot mentioned, adding that *Commentary*, the magazine of the American Jewish Congress, is the "neocon bible."

After the U.S. defeat in Vietnam, the Soviet empire made immense strides, militarily and strategically, building up its missile force to parity with our own and rolling up South Vietnam, Laos, Cambodia, Ethiopia, Mozambique, Angola, Grenada, Nicaragua, and Afghanistan, where, for the first time since 1945, the Red Army went into combat outside the Soviet Bloc.

By 1976, "detente" had become a dirty word in conservative circles, and neoconservatives had begun to unite with the Right in organizations like the Committee on the Present Danger. We regarded one another as allies in a common cause: the Cold War. Conservatives were cradle anti-Communists. Neocons had the zeal of the convert. We were united on the proposition that Communism and the Soviet empire were the enemy. By the mid-1980s, however, prescient conservatives had sensed that these undocumented aliens now nesting in our midst did not share our traditions, beliefs, ideas, or vision. In 1986, Clyde Wilson wrote:

> The offensives of radicalism have driven vast herds of liberals across the border into our territories. These refugees now speak in our name, but the language they speak is the same one they always spoke. We have grown familiar with it, have learned to tolerate it, but it is tolerable only by contrast to the harsh syllables of the barbarians over the border. It contains no words for the things we value. Our estate has been taken over by an impostor, just as we were about to inherit.

According to Irving Kristol, the "godfather" of the movement,

> . . . the historical task and political purpose of neoconservatism would seem to be . . . to convert the Republican Party and American conservatism in general, against their respective wills, into a new kind of conservative politics suitable to governing a modern democracy.

Foremost among the traditional ideas conservatives must discard are those in the Farewell Address, Washington's admonition that we stay out of foreign wars and avoid "permanent alliances" and "passionate attachments" to nations not our own. Intervention, wars for democracy, and a passionate attachment to Israel are what neoconservatism is all about. In a 2003 essay "The Neoconservative Persuasion," Kristol, a Trotskyite in the late 1930s, drew a parallel between the United States today and the old Soviet Union:

> . . . large nations, whose identity is ideological, like the Soviet Union of yesteryear and the United States of today, inevitably have ideological interests in addition to more material concerns. Barring extraordinary events, the United States will always feel obliged to defend, if possible, a democratic nation under attack from nondemocratic forces, external or internal. That is why it was in our national interest to come to the defense of France and Britain in World War II. That is why we feel it is necessary to defend Israel today, when its survival is threatened. No complicated geopolitical calculations of national interest are necessary.

This is ahistorical and Kristol cannot be ignorant of it. When the Allies declared war on Hitler on September 3, 1939, FDR did not "come to the defense of France and Britain." He delivered a fireside chat that same night pledging there would be "no blackout of peace" in the United States.

When France fell in May–June of 1940, pleading for planes, FDR sent words of encouragement. Not until eighteen months after the fall of France did we declare war on Hitler and not until after Hitler had declared war on us. America did not go to war to defend democracy. We went to war to exact retribution from a Japanese empire that had attacked us in our sleep at Pearl Harbor. Kristol is parroting liberal myths.

In the Cold War we welcomed as allies Chiang Kai-shek, President Diem, Salazar, Franco, Somoza, the shah, Suharto, Sygman Rhee, Park Chung Hee and the Korean generals, Greek colonels, militarists in Brazil, Argentina, and Turkey, President Marcos, and

General Pinochet—because these autocrats proved more reliable friends and allies than democratists like Nehru, Olaf Palme, Willy Brandt, and Pierre Trudeau. When it comes to wars that threaten us, hot or cold, ideology be damned, we Americans are at one with Nietzsche: "A state, it is the coldest of all cold monsters."

India is democratic and two hundred times the size of Israel. Yet in India's wars with Pakistan, we tilted toward Pakistan. Why? Because the Pakistanis were allies and India had sided with Moscow. That India was democratic and Pakistan autocratic made no difference to us.

Can Kristol seriously believe we have given Israel $100 billion and taken her side in every quarrel simply because she is democratic?

Neoconservative tutoring of "the Republican Party and American conservatism" is done through publications they now control: the *Weekly Standard, Commentary, The New Republic, National Review*—and the editorial page of the *Wall Street Journal*, whose editor for three decades, the late Robert Bartley, was a patron. Though few in number, neocons wield disproportionate influence through foundations they have captured, their magazines and columns, and by networking and attaching themselves to men of power. But how did they capture the president?

THE VULCANS

Before 2000, George W. Bush seemed a tabula rasa, a blank slate on foreign policy. His father had been a congressman, U.S. ambassador to the UN, envoy to China, director of the CIA, and vice president for eight years under Reagan. But the son had no experience in foreign policy and had exhibited zero interest. In the 2000 campaign, he confused Slovenia with Slovakia, referred to Greeks as "Grecians," and flunked a pop quiz when an interviewer asked him to name the leaders of four major nations.

Yet Bush appeared an instinctive conservative. He called for a more "humble" approach toward the world than Madeleine Albright's incessant braying about our being the "indispensable nation." He was a skeptic of nation-building. He promised to "scrutinize open-ended deployments, reassess U.S. goals, and ascertain whether they can be met."

However, into his entourage there had already been insinuated a cabal that called itself "the Vulcans." Recruited by Condoleezza Rice, the best known were Paul Wolfowitz and Richard Perle. Perle's depiction of his delight at first meeting the future president reads like Fagin relating his initial encounter with the young Oliver Twist:

> The first time I met Bush 43, I knew he was different. Two things became clear. One, he didn't know very much. The other was he had confidence to ask questions that revealed he didn't know very much. Most people are reluctant to say when they don't know something, a word or a term they haven't heard before. Not him.

Thus began the tutoring of George W. Bush in Kristol's "new kind of conservative politics suitable to governing a modern democracy," just months before he assumed office as president of the United States.

Who is Wolfowitz?

In 1992, when Wolfowitz was an assistant secretary of defense, a startling document leaked from his shop. Defense Planning Guidance had been prepared by Wolfowitz and his deputy, Lewis "Scooter" Libby, for Secretary Richard Cheney. Barton Gellman of the *Washington Post* called it a "classified blueprint intended to help 'set the nation's direction for the next century . . . '"

The Wolfowitz memorandum called for a permanent U.S. military presence on six continents to deter any "potential competitors from even aspiring to a larger regional or global role." Containment and deterrence to defend the West were to yield to a new offensive strategy to "establish and protect a new order."

The Wolfowitz memo envisioned U.S. war guarantees to Eastern Europe and, wrote Gellman, "casts Russia as the gravest potential threat to U.S. vital interests and presumes the United States would spearhead a NATO counterattack if Russia launched an invasion of Lithuania."

To Wolfowitz, that Baltic republic had become a "U.S. vital interest" worth defending at the cost of war with a nuclear-armed Russia. But how could America hope to save Lithuania? Wolfowitz's plan, wrote Gellman,

> . . . contemplates a major war by land, sea and air in which
> 24 NATO divisions, 70 fighter squadrons and six aircraft
> carrier battle groups would keep the Russian Navy "bottled
> up in the eastern Baltic," bomb supply lines in Russia and
> use armored formations to expel Russian forces from
> Lithuania. The authors state that Russia is unlikely to re-
> spond with nuclear weapons, but they provide no basis for
> that assessment.

What made this scenario astonishing in 1992 was that President Bush had barely protested, a year earlier, when Gorbachev ordered his Spetsnaz troops into Vilnius. Just three weeks before the Wolfowitz memo leaked, Bush and Yeltsin had jointly declared that "Russia and the United States do not regard each other as potential adversaries."

Under the Wolfowitz Doctrine, U.S. military supremacy was to remain sufficiently dominant to deter all "potential competitors from even aspiring to a larger regional or global role." Wolfowitz had determined the United States could never again permit any nation—Russia, Germany, Japan, China, India—to rise to the status of regional power. Moreover, the Pentagon anticipated wars for purposes far beyond protecting U.S. interests.

While the U.S. cannot become the world's "policeman," by assuming responsibility for righting every wrong, we will retain the preeminent responsibility for addressing selectively those wrongs which threaten not only our interests, but those of our allies or friends, or which could seriously unsettle international relations.

Reaction was sharp. Senator Joe Biden denounced the memo as the blueprints for "a Pax Americana." Senator Edward Kennedy said the Pentagon plans "appear to be aimed primarily at finding new ways to justify Cold War levels of military spending." Disowned by the Bush I White House, the memo was seemingly forgotten. But in September 2002, with Cheney, Wolfowitz, and Libby restored to power, the Wolfowitz memo reappeared in an official document released by the White House, titled The National Security Strategy of the United States.

WHO IS RICHARD Perle?

An aide to "Scoop" Jackson, Perle has been a major player in U.S. foreign policy since the Nixon years, and through his career has had the closest of ties with the Israelis. In 1970, he was picked up on a federal wiretap discussing classified information from the National Security Council with the Israeli Embassy.

In 1996, in collaboration with Douglas Feith and David Wurmser, Perle wrote a policy paper entitled "A Clean Break: A New Strategy for Securing the Realm" for Benjamin Netanyahu. It urged Israel's new prime minister to junk the Oslo peace accords of assassinated prime minister Yitzhak Rabin and adopt a new aggressive strategy based on "the principle of preemption."

Israel can shape its strategic environment, in cooperation with Turkey and Jordan, by weakening, containing, and even rolling back Syria. This effort can focus on removing Saddam Hussein from power in Iraq—an important Israeli strategic objective in its own right . . .

In the Perle-Feith-Wurmser strategy, Israel's main enemy remained Syria, but the road to Damascus lay through Baghdad. In his own 1997 "Strategy for Israel," Feith went further and urged Netanyahu to reoccupy "the areas under Palestinian Authority control" though "the price in blood would be high." Wurmser was even bolder. A resident scholar at AEI, he urged Israel and the United States to join forces and launch a series of preemptive strikes and blitzkrieg wars from North Africa to Iran.

> Israel and the United States should . . . broaden the conflict
> to strike fatally, not merely disarm, the centers of radicalism
> in the region—the regimes of Damascus, Baghdad, Tripoli,
> Teheran, and Gaza. That would establish the recognition
> that fighting either the United States or Israel is suicidal.

Wurmser urged us to await an opportunity to launch the preemptive strikes: "Crises can be opportunities." David Wurmser published his U.S.-Israeli joint war plan on January 1, 2001, *nine months before 9/11.*

When Bush became president on January 20, 2001, Perle was named chairman of the Defense Review Board, Wolfowitz became the deputy secretary of defense, Feith the undersecretary, while Wurmser shuttled from special assistant to Undersecretary of State John Bolton, to Feith's shop at the Pentagon, to special assistant to "Scooter" Libby, now chief of staff to Vice President Cheney. Libby and Bolton echo the Wolfowitz-Perle line. According to *Ha'aretz,* in February of 2003, Bolton "said in meetings with Israeli officials that he has no doubt America would attack Iraq, and that it will be necessary to deal with threats from Syria, Iran and North Korea afterwards."

WOLFOWITZ, PERLE, FEITH, Wurmser, Bolton all belong to a clique of foreign policy specialists, academics, and writers who see U.S. and Israeli interests as identical. Arnaud de Borchgrave calls them "Washington's Likudniks," and contends they "have been in charge of U.S. policy in the Middle East since Bush was sworn into office" and have imposed a "Bush-Sharon Doctrine" on American foreign policy. But the Beltway Likud was plotting and propagandizing for war on Iraq long before 9/11.

On January 26, 1998, President Clinton received a letter urging him to use his State of the Union address to declare the overthrow of Saddam Hussein to be the "aim of American foreign policy" and to order "military action as diplomacy is failing." Should the president agree, the signers all pledged, they would "offer [their] full support in this difficult but necessary endeavor." And, they warned, "the security of the world in the first part of the 21st century will be determined by how we handle this threat."

Signing the letter were Elliott Abrams, Bill Bennett, John Bolton, Robert Kagan, William Kristol, Richard Perle, Paul Wolfowitz—and Donald Rumsfeld. Four years before 9/11, they had publicly called for an invasion of Iraq, 9/11 would be the pretext for a war they had been devising for a decade.

IN APRIL 2001, at a White House meeting called by Bush's counterterrorism chief Richard Clarke to discuss Al Qaeda and Osama, Wolfowitz scowled. "I just don't understand why we are beginning by talking about this one man bin Laden. . . . there are others that do . . . at least as much. Iraqi terrorism, for example."

When Clarke brought up Al Qaeda's role in the first World Trade Center bombing, Wolfowitz dismissed it: "You give bin Laden too much credit. He could not do all these things, like the 1993 attack on New York, not without a state sponsor."

Clarke retorted: "We've investigated that five ways from Friday and nobody [in the government] believes that. . . . It was Al Qaeda. It wasn't Saddam." And added, "As with Hitler in *Mein Kampf*, you have to believe that these people will actually do what they say they will do."

"I resent any comparison between the Holocaust and this little terrorist in Afghanistan," Wolfowitz shot back.

Paul Wolfowitz had brought his obsession with Iraq into the Bush national security councils. And in the first hours following the 9/11 attack, he would push the president to ignore Afghanistan and attack Iraq. *Time* magazine would later call him the "intellectual godfather" of the Iraq War, and the *Jerusalem Post* would name him "Man of the Year."

THE WAR DRUMMERS

Early on September 12, when Clarke returned to the White House, he was jolted:

> I expected to go back to a round of meetings examining what the next attacks could be. . . . Instead I walked into a series of discussions about Iraq. At first I was incredulous that we were talking about something other than getting Al Qaeda. Then I realized with almost a sharp physical pain that Rumsfeld and Wolfowitz were going to take advantage of this national tragedy to promote their agenda about Iraq. Since the beginning of the administration, indeed well before, they had been pressing for a war with Iraq.

By afternoon, Rumsfeld was still going on about "getting Iraq." When Colin Powell urged that they focus on Al Qaeda, Rumsfeld pushed anew for the Iraq option. Writes Clarke:

> Rumsfeld complained that there were no decent targets for bombing in Afghanistan and that we should consider bombing Iraq, which he said had better targets. At first I thought Rumsfeld was joking. But he was serious and the President did not reject out of hand the idea of attacking Iraq.

That same September 12, as Americans were still in shock, Bill Bennett told CNN we were in "a struggle between good and evil," that Congress must declare war on "militant Islam," that "overwhelming force" must be used. He cited as targets Lebanon, Libya, Syria, Iraq, Iran, and China. The *Wall Street Journal* immediately offered up a specific target list, calling for U.S. air strikes on "terrorist camps in Syria, Sudan, Libya, and Algeria, and perhaps even in parts of Egypt." Not one of these five countries or any of Bennett's six had had anything to do with 9/11.

On September 15, according to Bob Woodward's *Bush at War*, "Paul Wolfowitz put forth military arguments to justify an attack on Iraq rather than Afghanistan." Why Iraq? Because, Wolfowitz argued in the war cabinet, "attacking Afghanistan would be uncertain . . . (but) Iraq was a brittle oppressive regime that might break easily. It was doable."

On September 20, an open letter was sent to President Bush with forty signatures, among them Bill Bennett, Norman Podhoretz, Jeane Kirkpatrick, Richard Perle, William Kristol, and Charles Krauthammer. It was a political ultimatum. To retain the signers' support, Bush was told, he must target Hezbollah for destruction, retaliate against Syria and Iran should they refuse to sever ties to Hezbollah, and overthrow Saddam. Failure to attack Iraq, the signers warned Bush, "will constitute an early and perhaps decisive surrender in the war on international terrorism."

Nine days after an attack on the United States, this tiny clique of intellectuals was telling the president of the United States and commander in chief of the U.S. armed forces that if he did not follow their war plans, he would be publicly charged with a "decisive surrender" to terrorism.

Yet, Hezbollah, Syria, Iraq, and Iran had had nothing to do with 9/11. Still, the president had been warned. He must exploit the horror of that atrocity and channel America's rage into a series of wars on nations, none of which had attacked us, but all of which were hostile to Israel, or he, President Bush, would face political retribution.

"Bibi" Netanyahu, former prime minister of Israel, like some latter-day Citizen Genét, was everywhere on American television, rallying us to crush the "Empire of Terror." The "empire," Bibi informed us, consisted of Hamas, Hezbollah, Iran, Iraq, and "the Palestinian enclave."

Not only had none of these been involved in the attack but Libya, Syria, Iran, and the Palestinian Authority of Arafat—whether out of fear, opportunism, or horror—had publicly condemned the atrocities of 9/11. Sudan was cooperating with us. Nasty as these regimes might be, what had they done to justify war upon them by the United States? In a column in *USA Today*, "Whose War Is This?"—published on September 26, 2001—I warned:

> The war Netanyahu and the neocons want, with the U.S. and Israel fighting all the radical Islamic states, is the war bin Laden wants, the war his murderers hoped to ignite when they sent those airliners into the World Trade Center and the Pentagon. If America wishes truly to be isolated, it will follow the neoconservative line.

As the days after 9/11 went by, the War Party seemed desperate to get a Middle East war going before America had second thoughts. Perle warned in a *New York Times* piece that time was running out, as Saddam was getting closer to nuclear weapons:

> With each passing day [Saddam] comes closer to his dream of a nuclear arsenal. We know he has a clandestine program, spread over many hidden sites, to enrich Iraqi natural uranium to weapons grade. . . . How close is he? We do not know. Two years, three years, tomorrow even?

Moreover, to Perle there was compelling evidence Saddam had had a hand in the 9/11 attack: "Evidence of a meeting in Prague between a senior Iraqi intelligence agent and Mohamed Atta, the September 11 ringleader, is convincing." Tom Donnelly of the Project for the New American Century (PNAC) called for an immediate invasion of Iraq. "Nor need the attack await the deployment of half a million troops. . . . the larger challenge will be occupying Iraq after the fighting is over."

PNAC was echoed by Jonah Goldberg of *National Review*: "The United States needs to go to war with Iraq because it needs to go to war with someone in the region and Iraq makes the most sense." Goldberg endorsed the "Ledeen Doctrine" of ex-Pentagon official Michael Ledeen: "Every ten years or so, the United States needs to pick up some small crappy little country and throw it against the wall, just to show we mean business." Ledeen is less frivolous. In *The War Against the Terror Masters,* he identified the exact regimes America must destroy:

> First and foremost, we must bring down the terror regimes, beginning with the Big Three: Iran, Iraq, and Syria. And then we have to come to grips with the Saudis. . . .
>
> [O]nce the tyrants in Iran, Iraq, Syria, and Saudi Arabia have been brought down, we will remain engaged. . . . We have to ensure the fulfillment of the democratic revolution. . . .
>
> Stability is an unworthy American mission, and a misleading concept to boot. We do not want stability in Iran, Iraq, Syria, Lebanon, and even Saudi Arabia; we want things to change. The real issue is not whether, but how to destabilize.

Proceeding to define America's "historic mission," Ledeen wrote:

> Creative destruction is our middle name, both within our own society and abroad. We tear down the old order every day, from business to science, literature, art, architecture, and cinema to politics and the law. Our enemies have always hated this whirlwind of energy and creativity, which menaces their traditions (whatever they may be) and shames

them for their inability to keep pace. . . . we must destroy
them to advance our historic mission.

Passages like this owe more to Robespierre than Robert Taft,
and betray a streak in neoconservatism that cannot be reconciled
with any concept of true conservatism.

To the *Weekly Standard*, Ledeen's enemies list was too restric-
tive. We must not only declare war on terror networks and states
that harbor terrorists, said the *Standard*, we should launch wars on
"any group or government *inclined* to support or sustain others like
them in the future." (emphasis added)

Robert Kagan and William Kristol were giddy at the prospect of
Armageddon. The coming war "is going to spread and engulf a
number of countries. . . . It is going to resemble the clash of civilizations that everyone has hoped to avoid. . . . it is possible that
the demise of some 'moderate' Arab regimes may be just round the
corner."

Norman Podhoretz in *Commentary* even outdid Kristol's *Standard*. He called on us to embrace our destiny, a war of civilizations,
for it was George W. Bush's historic mission "to fight World War
IV—the war against militant Islam."

> The regimes that richly deserve to be overthrown . . . are not
> confined to the three singled-out members of the axis of evil
> [Iraq, Iran, North Korea]. At a minimum the axis should ex-
> tend to Syria and Lebanon and Libya, as well as "friends" of
> America like the Saudi royal family and Egypt's Hosni
> Mubarak, along with the Palestinian Authority.

Bush must reject the "timorous counsels" of the "incorrigibly
cautious Colin Powell," wrote Podhoretz, and "find the stomach to
impose a new political culture on the defeated" Islamic world. As
the war against Al Qaeda required that we destroy the Taliban,
wrote Podhoretz:

We may willy-nilly find ourselves forced . . . to topple five or six or seven more tyrannies in the Islamic world (including that other sponsor of terrorism, Yasser Arafat's Palestinian Authority). I can even [imagine] the turmoil of this war leading to some new species of an imperial mission for America, whose purpose would be to oversee the emergence of successor governments in the region more amenable to reform and modernization than the despotisms now in place. . . . I can also envisage the establishment of some kind of American protectorate over the oil fields of Saudi Arabia, as we more and more come to wonder why 7,000 princes should go on being permitted to exert so much leverage over us and everyone else.

Podhoretz credited Eliot Cohen with the phrase "World War IV." Bush was soon seen carrying a copy of Cohen's book celebrating civilian mastery of the military as exhibited by such war leaders as Churchill and Ben Gurion.

A list of the Middle East regimes that Podhoretz, Bennett, Ledeen, Netanyahu, and the *Wall Street Journal* regarded as targets for destruction by America thus included Algeria, Libya, Egypt, Sudan, Lebanon, Syria, Iraq, Saudi Arabia, Iran, Hezbollah, Hamas, the Palestinian Authority and "militant Islam." On this list is every enemy of Israel Feith and Perle identified for Netanyahu to confront or attack in "A Clean Break: A New Strategy for Securing the Realm" in 1996.

Cui Bono? Who would benefit from these endless wars in a region that holds nothing vital to America—save oil, which the Arabs must sell to us to survive? Who would benefit from a "war of civilizations" with Islam? Who, other than these neoconservatives and Ariel Sharon?

Indeed, Sharon was everywhere the echo of his American auxiliary. In February 2003, on the eve of the war, he told a congressional delegation that after the United States invaded Iraq, it was of "vital importance" that we disarm Iran, Syria, and Libya. Defense

Minister Shaul Mofaz parroted Sharon. "We have a great interest in shaping the Middle East the day after" the war on Iraq, he told the Conference of Major American Jewish Organizations. When U.S. troops occupy Baghdad, Mofaz told the American Jewish leaders, America must begin to exert "political, economic, diplomatic pressure" on Teheran.

Were the neoconservatives concerned that a war on Iraq might bring down friendly Arab governments? Not at all. They welcomed the prospect. "Mubarak is no great shakes," said Perle of Egypt's president. "Surely we can do better than Mubarak." Asked about the possibility a war on Iraq, which he had predicted would be a "cakewalk," might upend governments in Egypt and Saudi Arabia, Ken Adelman told Joshua Micah Marshall of *Washington Monthly,* "All the the better if you ask me."

On July 10, 2002, Perle brought Laurent Murawiec in to brief the Defense Policy Board. In a presentation that startled Henry Kissinger, this ex-aide to Lyndon LaRouche identified Saudi Arabia as "the kernel of evil, the prime mover, the most dangerous opponent." The United States, said Murawiec, should give the Saudis an ultimatum: Either you "prosecute or isolate those involved in the terror chain, including the Saudi intelligence services," and end all propaganda against Israel, or we invade, seize your oil fields, and occupy Mecca.

Murawiec offered a "Grand Strategy for the Middle East": "Iraq is the tactical pivot, Saudi Arabia the strategic pivot. Egypt the prize." Leaked reports of the Murawiec briefing did not indicate whether anyone raised a question as to how a billion Muslims might react to U.S. troops tromping around the Great Mosque at Mecca.

THUS WAS IT that the neoconservatives who had plotted, planned, and agitated for a war on Iraq for a decade got their war.

In 1996, Irving Kristol had written: "With the end of the Cold War, what we really need is an obvious ideological and threatening enemy, one worthy of our mettle, one that can unite us in opposition."

On 9/11 opportunity had knocked. The neoconservatives had a new "enemy . . . worthy of our mettle"—radical Islam; a new ideology—an ideology of empire; and a new doctrine—democratism, the waging of "World War IV" to advance a "world democratic revolution." They had what Richard Perle and David Frum would call "our generation's great cause."

Yet the neoconservatives could not have taken America to war on Iraq had they not persuaded Bush, Rumsfeld, Cheney, and Powell of the necessity of war. They could not have succeeded had they not been in critical posts at the Pentagon and in the vice president's office to "cherry-pick" and "stove-pipe" to the president intelligence pointing to Iraqi complicity in 9/11 and Iraqi programs to build nuclear weapons. They could not have succeeded without collaborators in the neoconservative and mainstream media.

How did they succeed? In *America Alone: The Neoconservatives and the Global Order,* Nixon-Reagan foreign policy aide Stefan Halper and Cato scholar Jonathan Clarke charge that the neoconservatives lied us into war:

> Making the case for the decade-old neoconservative objective of attacking Iraq required a web of deception: that Saddam Hussein had and intended to use WMDs; that Saddam supported al Qaeda; and that if he were not removed these weapons might be provided to al Qaeda, which would use them against the United States.

General Zinni, the former Centcom commander who had worked beside them at the Pentagon, was stunned by their arrogance and conceit:

> The more I saw the more I thought this [war] was the product of the neocons who didn't understand the region and

were going to create havoc there. These were dilettantes from Washington think tanks who never had an idea that worked on the ground.

Zinni here echoes the words of Burke on Lord North and his witless clique that plunged Britain into war on the American colonies: "Has any of these gentlemen who are so eager to govern all mankind, shown himself possessed of the first qualification towards government . . . and of the difficulties which occur in the task they have undertaken?"

Yet they succeeded. And for these imperialists of democracy, the invasion of Iraq was the first step toward realization of a vision, a vision of "World War IV," the overthrow of all "Islamo-fascist" regimes—Iraq, Iran, Syria, Sudan, Saudi Arabia, Libya, Lebanon—the tutoring of new leaders in democracy and free-market capitalism, and the admission of the newly reformed Islamic states into the world community, escorted by their neoconservative dons.

What future have they in mind for us? They no longer hide it. "People are coming out of the closet on the word 'empire,'" Charles Krauthammer told the *Boston Globe* in those salad days. "We are an attractive empire, the one everyone wants to join," added Max Boot. "[T]he truth is that the benevolent hegemony exercised by the U.S. is good for a vast portion of the world's population," wrote Robert Kagan.

What will be America's role in the new world order? Writes Kagan, "America does the bombing and fighting, the French, British and Germans serve as police in the border zones, and the Dutch, Swiss and Scandinavians provide humanitarian aid." As for Muslims in the new imperium, they are cast as Kipling's "lesser breeds without the law." But, like other subject peoples, they have begun to chafe and balk at the roles the acolytes of the new American empire have assigned to them.

"WHAT ALL THE WISE MEN PROMISED"

The War Party had promised Bush a "cakewalk," that we would be hailed as liberators, that democracy would blossom in Iraq and flourish across the Middle East, that Palestinians and Israelis would break bread and make peace. Opponents of invasion and war, like Robert Novak and this writer, denounced by *National Review* as "unpatriotic conservatives," warned President Bush that he and we might inherit an Iraq far different from the shining democracy of the neocons' vision.

On the eve of the invasion, in a six-thousand-word article "Whose War?" in the *American Conservative,* I documented and detailed the plot that had been years in the hatching, identified the plotters, and added this warning: "President Bush is being lured into a trap baited for him by these neocons that could cost him his office and cause America to forfeit years of peace won for us by the sacrifices of two generations in the Cold War."

AND SO IT came to pass that the neocons captured a president and may yet destroy his presidency. Eighteen months have now elapsed since the fall of Baghdad. At the time of this writing, the cost of the war is at $200 billion and rising, with close to 900 U.S. dead and many thousands wounded and maimed. America has been shamed by the obscene cruelties of Abu Ghraib and is now doubtful of the wisdom of having gone to war. As Iraq appears to be careening toward chaos and civil war, Bush must be muttering with Melbourne, "What all the wise men promised has not happened and what all the damn fools said would happen has come to pass." Yet, like the Bourbons of old, the neoconservatives seem to have learned nothing and forgotten nothing.

In February 2004, Charles Krauthammer was still rhapsodizing triumphantly at the annual AEI dinner that we Americans have "acquired the largest-seeming empire in the history of the world."

We are the world's "unipolar power . . . the custodian of the international system." We have "global dominion."

"This is a staggering new development in history, not seen since the fall of Rome," Krauthammer ranted on. "Even Rome is no model for what America is today." As Francis Fukuyama writes, passages such as these suggest that Krauthammer has become "strangely disconnected from reality."

"Reading Krauthammer," says Fukuyama, "one gets the impression the Iraq war . . . had been an unqualified success, with all of the assumptions and expectations on which the war had been based fully vindicated." Yet it has been anything but an unqualified success.

THESE, THEN, WERE the men and ideas behind the greatest strategic blunder in forty years, a mistake more costly than Vietnam. Yet the halcyon days of the War Party may be over and the neoconservative hour in American politics may be coming to an end. For rather than seeking new Middle East wars to fight, President Bush and Secretaries Rumsfeld and Powell seem to be looking for an exit ramp out of the Mesopotamian morass.

Moreover, the neoconservative role in hyping the case for war has been exposed, as has the existence and membership lists of the tiny cabal. Americans are also coming to understand that for all their bombast about "unipolar moments," "benevolent global hegemony," and "American empire," there are limits to our power—and we are approaching them.

Big-budget deficits are back, the national debt is soaring again, and the active-duty army, only 480,000 strong, is stretched thin. There is grumbling in reserve and guard units about too many tours, too far from home. Backing away from his "axis of evil" rhetoric, Bush declared in his 2004 State of the Union, "We have no desire to dominate, no ambitions of empire." Even if the president were to be persuaded to attack another of the Arab or Islamic regimes on the hit list of the neoconservatives, he could not now, without a direct attack on our own country or its citizens, win the authority from Congress. Nor does it appear he intends to try.

THE LEGENDARY U.S. military thinker Colonel John Boyd once described strategy as appending to oneself as many centers of power as possible and isolating one's enemy from as many centers of power as possible. This was the strategy pursued brilliantly by the president's father in the Gulf War. He persuaded Russia and China to sign on in the Security Council, Germany and Japan to finance the war, Egypt and Syria to send soldiers, Britain and France to help fight it. By giving everyone a stake in victory—call it imperial bribery if you will—Bush I lined up the whole world against Iraq. As did George W. Bush, brilliantly, in Afghanistan.

But what neoconservatives are about is the antithesis of strategy. They do not want to narrow America's list of enemies to those who attack us. They want to broaden the theater of war and multiply our enemies, to escalate "the Firemen's War" into a war for American hegemony. Should Bush adopt their strategy, it would be us against the Islamic world with Europe neutral and Asia rooting for our humiliation. Thus, it needs to be said: It is vital to the defeat of Al Qaeda, the security of our homeland, and our critical interests in an Arab world of twenty-two nations and an Islamic world of fifty-seven nations from Morocco to Malaysia that we not let our war on terror be conflated and morphed into the neoconservatives' war for empire. If we do, we will lose our war, isolate America, and bankrupt our republic.

"Often clever, never wise," was Russell Kirk's final verdict on the neocons. As scholar Claes Ryn writes, in temperament, they are often the antithesis of conservative and call to mind the Jacobins of the French Revolution:

> [O]nly great conceit could inspire a dream of armed world hegemony. The ideology of benevolent American empire and

global democracy dresses up a voracious appetite for power. It signifies the ascent to power of a new kind of American, one profoundly at odds with that older type who aspired to modesty and self-restraint.

The neoconservatives are marinated in conceit, and their hubris may yet prove their undoing. And ours as well. For as Burke wrote to the prideful rulers of the British Empire at the apex of their ascendancy,

> Among precautions against ambition, it may not be amiss to take precaution against our own. I must fairly say, I dread our power and our own ambition; I dread our being too much dreaded. . . . We may say we shall not abuse this astonishing and unheard of power. But every other nation will think we shall abuse it. It is impossible but that, sooner or later, this state of things must produce a combination against us which may end in our ruin."

THREE

IS ISLAM THE ENEMY?

> You can resist an invading army; you cannot resist an
> idea whose time has come.
>
> —Victor Hugo

On the eve of World War II, the Islamic world from Morocco to
Malaysia was under the rule of the European empires, and to that
world few paid notice. For the fate of mankind was about to be de-
cided by the Axis powers—Nazi Germany, Imperial Japan, Fascist
Italy—and Stalinist Russia along with the democracies France,
Britain, and the United States.

Yet in 1938, a perceptive British Catholic looked south and east
and saw Islam stirring. "It has always seemed to me . . . probable,"
wrote Hilaire Belloc, "that there would be a resurrection of Islam
and that our sons or our grandsons would see the renewal of that
tremendous struggle between the Christian culture and what has
been for more than a thousand years its greatest opponent." Belloc
was prophetic. Islam is rising again to shake the twenty-first century as it did so many previous centuries.

OUT OF THE DESERT

Six hundred years after the death of Christ, the Mediterranean,
the mare nostrum of Graeco-Roman civilization, was a Christian

lake. The western and eastern empires had been converted. In *The Great Heresies,* Belloc described the sudden appearance of Islam in Europe:

> By A.D. 630 all Gaul had long been Catholic. The last of the Arian generals and their garrisons in Italy and Spain had become orthodox. The Arian generals and garrisons of northern Africa had been conquered by the orthodox armies of the Emperor.
>
> It was just at this moment, a moment of apparently universal and permanent Catholicism, that there fell an unexpected blow of overwhelming magnitude and force. Islam arose—quite suddenly. It came out of the desert and overwhelmed half our civilization.

Mohammed was a merchant living in obscurity in Mecca, the city of his birth. Historians today place him with Jesus and St. Paul as one of the three most influential men in history. The religion he founded has more followers than Catholicism and is the largest and fastest-growing on earth.

Mohammed was driven by two ideas: submission to Allah, the one true God, and the moral elevation of his people. As he gathered converts, those who followed him were called Muslims, or "those who have submitted to the will of Allah."

As Mecca's merchants began to view his doctrines as subversive, and the populace became enraged by his attacks on their idols, Mohammed was forced to flee in 622 (the Hejira) to Yathrib, later renamed Medina—or City of the Prophet. There the first mosque was built, and 622 became Year 1 of the Muslim calendar. In Medina, Mohammed became both law-giver and leader, and, after permitting raids on Meccan caravans, went to war. In A.D. 630, he returned to Mecca in triumph and destroyed the idols, but kept the black stone of the Ka'aba as the sign of the true God.

THE RELIGIOUS PRECEPTS of Islam are simple. Muslims, Christians, and Jews are all children of Adam and Abraham, and the God of Judaism and Christianity is God. But, though Jesus was the last and greatest prophet, he was not God. Mohammed, writes Belloc,

> . . . gave to our Lord the highest reverence, and to our Lady also for that matter. On the day of judgement (another Catholic idea which he taught), it was our Lord, according to Mohammed, who would be the judge of mankind, not he, Mohammed. The Mother of Christ, Our Lady, "the Lady Miriam" was ever for him the first of womankind.

But Mohammed rejected the Incarnation.

In Islamic theology, paradise awaits all faithful Muslims, especially those who die in jihad, or holy war against the infidel. A horrible hell awaits the damned. In its moral teachings, Islam accepted slavery and polygamy, but four wives was the limit. Pork and alcohol were forbidden.

There are "Five Pillars" of Islam. One must believe that there is no God but Allah and Mohammed is His prophet. Alms must be given to the poor. Every Muslim, after prostrations and ablutions, must turn to Mecca five times a day in prayer. During the holy month of Ramadan, fasting must begin at dawn and continue to dusk. Every Muslim with the means must make a pilgrimage to Mecca once in his lifetime.

Sharia is the body of religious laws and duties, and all Muslims, regardless of race, tribe, or rank, constitute the *ummah*, or fellowship of the faithful. There is no priesthood in Islam and no sacraments. Imams or teachers lead the faithful in daily prayer at the mosque.

Belloc believed Islam to be a Christian heresy whose strength lay in its "insistence on personal immortality, the Unity and Infinite Majesty of God, on his Justice and Mercy (and in) . . . its insistence on the equality of human souls in the sight of their Creator." He called it a Reformation religion with parallels to "the Protestant—Reformers—on Images, the Mass and Celibacy." Another Catholic writer, Joe Sobran, has a similar explanation for the appeal of early Islam and its astonishing growth:

> Islam is a simple religion, easily understood by ordinary people. Its commandments are rigorous but few. When it conquered, its subjugated people often felt more liberated than enslaved, because it often replaced burdensome old bureaucratic governments with relatively undemanding regimes— and low taxes. As long as its authority was respected, Islamic rule was comparatively libertarian. It offered millions relief from their traditional oppression . . . no Muslim could be a slave.

Toward its Christian and Jewish subjects, Islam adopted a policy of "tribute or the sword." Religious peoples who lived by the "Book," i.e., sacred writings such as the Old and New Testament, were not forcibly converted, but they had to pay a tax. The churches and monasteries thus endured in the lands conquered by Islam, though Christians were cut off from their brethren in Europe and under social pressure to convert.

There was no separation of mosque and state in Islam. The caliph was both religious and political leader. It was over the right of succession to the prophet that the schism between Shiites and Sunnis arose that endures to this day. From the succession struggles came the dynastic divisions, with the Fatamites ruling in Cairo, the Umayyads in Damascus, and the Abassids in Baghdad.

Yet, there was a core unity among Muslims. All read the words of the prophet in Arabic, the only language authorized for the Koran. With one book, one language, one faith, one caliph, and one commercial empire in the Mediterranean basin, the Islamic world was united, despite the rivalries of the petty states that arose. As Belloc observed, one can also speak of an Islamic culture, for "what the scholars of Baghdad did soon became the common property of their confreres at Cordova."

CHRISTENDOM AND ISLAM

"Islam from the start has been a religion of conquest," writes J. M. Roberts, author of *A History of Europe*. Indeed, from birth, Islam was a fighting faith, its adherents driven by an unconquerable will to subdue the infidel and bring all mankind into submission to Allah.

By Mohammed's death in 632, western Arabia was Islamic, and on his deathbed, the prophet had reputedly instructed his heirs— "Let there not be two religions in Arabia."—to expel all Christians and Jews from this sacred land, the Hejaz. The edict was carried out by his second successor, Caliph Umar. Within a few years, the Arabian Peninsula had been united by the Rashidun caliphs, and Islamic warriors had spread the faith across three continents.

Umar marched on foot behind his soldiers when the Muslims captured Jerusalem, and he ordered the protection of the Christian sites. Within a century of Mohammed's death, the armies of Islam had overrun Syria, Palestine, Egypt, North Africa, Portugal, and Spain. Half of the old Roman Empire and Christian world had been conquered.

But at Poitiers, in the heart of France, in 732, one hundred years after the death of the prophet, the Islamic tide crested and broke. The warriors of Islam were defeated by "the Hammer of the Franks," Charles Martel, in one of the decisive battles of history. Had Islam triumphed, Christianity might have been extinguished in Europe as it was in the cities of Augustine and Athanasius.

As Bernard Lewis writes, from its inception, Islam saw Christianity as its great rival and adversary:

From an early date, Muslims knew that there were certain differences among the peoples of the House of War (Dar al

Harb). Most of them were simply polytheists and idolaters, who represented no serious threat to Islam and were likely prospects for conversion. The major exception was the Christians, whom Muslims recognized as having a religion of the same kind as their own, and therefore as their primary rival in the struggle for world domination—or, as they would have put it, world enlightenment. It is surely significant that the Koranic and other inscriptions on the Dome of the Rock, one of the earliest Muslim religious structures outside Arabia, built in Jerusalem between A.D. 691 and 692, include a number of anti-Christian polemics: "Praise be to God who begets no son, and has no partner," and "He is God, one, eternal. He does not beget, nor is He gotten, and He has no peer."

In the Persian and Byzantine Empires, the warriors of Islam found the same hollowness they had encountered in Visigoth Spain. Byzantine lands were overrun, and the Persian Empire conquered within a dozen years of Mohammed's death. But the stout defense of Emperor Leo III halted Islam at the Bosphorus and saved Constantinople for Christianity. The soldiers of Islam retired over the Taurus Mountains and, for three hundred years, Asia Minor remained a Byzantine province and the Balkans remained Christian.

BY A.D. 750, the Umayyads had given way to the Abassids, and the caliphate moved from Damascus to Baghdad. There it would remain until 1258, when Mesopotamia, modern-day Iraq, was overrun by the Mongols and the Baghdad caliphate was abolished.

In the West, the conquests of Islam had not ended at Poitiers. In the ninth century, soldiers of Islam overran Sicily, Sardinia, and Corsica. In 846, a naval expedition from Sicily entered the Tiber, and Islamic soldiers sacked Rome and profaned the tombs of the apostles. Pope Leo IV built a wall around St. Peter's and the Vatican palace, an enclosure corresponding to today's Vatican City. From its eastern shore to its western exit at Gibraltar, the Mediterranean was now dominated by a faith and civilization hostile to Christianity. Half of all Christendom had been lost and Christian commerce was swept from the Inland Sea.

NOT FOR TWO and a half centuries after the sacking of Rome did the counterattack begin. In 1095, at a church council in Clare-mont, France, Pope Urban II rose to preach the First Crusade. Its goal: Jerusalem and the Holy Sepulcher that had held the body of Christ. "Those who deride this as a Christian objective have lived too long in books and under lamps," writes Catholic historian War-ren Carroll.

> Real men and women, as distinct from scholarly abstrac-tions, have homes which they love. Jesus Christ was a real man. He had a home. He loved it. His followers (and) wor-shipers who came after Him loved the land and places He had loved and trod, simply because He had loved and trod-den them. Utterly convinced that He is God, they could not believe it right that any people not recognizing Him as God should rule his homeland.

In 1099, led by Godfrey of Bouillon and Raymond of Toulouse, the Crusaders captured the Holy City. Offered the title "King of Jerusalem," each refused to wear a crown of gold in the city where Christ had worn a crown of thorns.

Muslims regard the crusades as wars of Christian aggression. But a majority in Palestine was probably still Christian in 1095, and had as much right to the land as their conquerors. "[T]he common assumption that the Crusades were an act of unprovoked Christian aggression" is false, writes Carroll. Before 1095, "all the aggression had been Muslim. The Muslims were the original and continuing attackers and conquerors of Christian territory." The First Crusade was "a just war conducted for a deeply spiritual pur-pose though often seriously flawed in its execution."

If Mecca were overrun today by infidel armies, would not Muslims be justified in conducting a jihad to liberate their holy city? Would devout Muslims be ashamed of such a war, or apologize for having waged it?

No RECORD REMAINS of Urban's epochal address. But it is said that this former monk from Cluny was extraordinarily eloquent in his native French as he rallied the martial spirit of his audience to redirect it from feudal conflicts to a nobler cause. The pope spoke of a holy war to reunite Christians and recapture a land of milk and honey from Seljuk Turks who preyed on Christian pilgrims. Perhaps Urban saw in this first crusade a way to end the schism that had lately separated the eastern church from Rome. To all Crusaders who died repentant, Urban offered a plenary indulgence. When he finished speaking, the congregation stood as one and roared, *"Deus vult!"*—God wills it!

Volunteers for that First Crusade far exceeded papal expectations.

Another view of the Crusades is held by our multicultural elite, who charge that these were wars of Christian aggression whose signature was pillage and massacre. Speaking at his alma mater, Georgetown University, ex-President Clinton suggested that 9/11 may have been payback for the crimes of Godfrey and Raymond.

> Those of us who come from various European lineages are not blameless. In the First Crusade, when the Christian soldiers took Jerusalem, they first burned a synagogue with three hundred Jews in it, and proceeded to kill every woman and child who was Muslim on the Temple Mount. The contemporaneous descriptions of the event describe soldiers walking on the Temple Mount, a holy place to Christians, with blood running up to their knees. I can tell you that story is still being told today in the Middle East, and we are still paying for it.

A massacre did occur in Jerusalem in 1099, but the same fate befell the Christian knights and their wives and children when the last crusader castle at Acre fell to the Mameluks. Nor have we heard many apologies for that massacre. And why Americans, whose first president was a Mason that did not take office until 1789, should be massacred in 2001, for the crimes of a crusade preached by a French pope in 1095, Clinton did not explain.

While the First Crusade triumphed, later crusades failed. In 1187, Jerusalem fell to Saladin, and Richard the Lionhearted failed to retrieve the Holy City. It would not be retaken by soldiers from Christian Europe until British general Allenby marched in in 1917. Acre, the last of the Crusaders' coastal fortresses, fell in 1291.

BY THE END of the thirteenth century, the Baghdad caliphate had been overrun and abolished by the Mongols. Swept westward, ahead of these Mongol hordes, was a nomadic tribe of Turks who settled in the northeast corner of Anatolia. Known as Osmali, from the name of their chieftain, Osman, they came to be known in the West as Ottoman Turks.

Brave and fanatic, they brought new energy to Islam. Their armies soon leapt the Bosphorus, entered the Balkans, overran Bulgaria, and in 1389 defeated the Serbs at Kosovo. Ottoman Turks now displaced Arabs as rulers of Islam. And among their Christian subjects, they imposed the blood tax. One boy of every five was taken from his parents, raised as a Muslim, and indoctrinated in fanatic loyalty to the sultan. These would become the *yeni cheri* (new troops), or Janissaries. The blood tax was ruthlessly enforced.

In 1453, the Ottoman ruler Mehmet the Conqueror besieged and captured Constantinople, resurrecting the old eastern Roman empire as a Muslim empire. Christians were permitted to practice their faith only if they paid a special tax to the caliph. They did, and they persevered.

In 1520, the Turkish drive into Europe was renewed. In 1521, Suleiman the Magnificent captured Belgrade. In 1526 he defeated the Hungarian knights and slew King Louis II on the field at Mohacs. In 1529, Suleiman laid siege to Vienna. Unsuccessful after three weeks, his army ravaged the countryside, and Budapest became a Turkish province.

ISLAM'S LONG RETREAT

When the Abassids had captured Damascus, an Ummayad prince had fled to Spain to establish Ummayad rule there. This began the Golden Age of Islam in the Iberian Peninsula. Cordova was made the capital of Muslim Spain and became the most populous city in Europe and the greatest in cultural and intellectual achievements. But, by the time of the Crusades, the Islamic tide had begun to recede in the West. The Muslims had already been expelled from Sicily when, in 1492, Ferdinand and Isabella drove the last of the Moors out of Spain. The *reconquista* was complete, Grenada was gone, Spain was Catholic again.

A series of sea battles now ensued between Suleiman's fleets and those of the Holy Roman Emperor Charles I for dominance of the Mediterranean. Not until their deaths would the issue be decided.

In 1570, after Suleiman captured Cyprus and threatened Malta and Crete, the last Christian strongholds in the eastern Mediterranean, Pius V sent out a call for a last great crusade. Genoa, Venice, and Spain responded, providing warships for a Christian fleet to be commanded by the illegitimate son of Charles I, Don Juan of Austria.

On October 7, 1571, this Catholic prince, using superior cannon and tactics, destroyed or sank most of the 273 Ottoman ships, killing twenty thousand sailors and soldiers and liberating thousands of Christian slaves who had been impressed to man the oars.

This was Lepanto, the last great sea battle between Christian and Islamic fleets, and is recalled in all its pageantry and romance by G. K. Chesterton. In the movement of his verse, one hears the march of feet and the beat of drums as the Last Crusade begins:

> Dim drums throbbing, in the hills half heard,
> Where only on a nameless throne a crownless prince has stirred,
> Where, risen from a doubtful seat and half attainted stall,
> The last knight of Europe takes weapons from the wall,
> The last and lingering troubadour to whom the bird has sung,
> That once went singing southward when all the world was young.
> In that enormous silence, tiny and unafraid,
> Comes up along a winding road the noise of the Crusade.

In the Ottoman archives, there is a terse report of Lepanto by the commander of the Turkish ships, Kapudan Pasha. It consists of two lines: "The fleet of the divinely guided Empire encountered the fleet of the wretched infidels, and the will of Allah turned the other way." In histories of the empire, writes Bernard Lewis in *What Went Wrong?*, "the battle is known simply as *Sıngın*, a Turkish word meaning a rout or crushing defeat."

After Lepanto, the naval power of the Ottomans withered and died. The enemies of Christendom were reduced to piratical raids on Europe's commerce by Barbary corsairs operating from North Africa. The battle of the Mediterranean was over.

THE FINAL OTTOMAN drive into Europe came in the east, ending in a second siege of Vienna. On September 11, 1683, the Hapsburg imperial capital was rescued by King John Sobieski of Poland. Wrote an Ottoman chronicler of the time: "This was a calamitous defeat, so great that there never has been its like since the first appearance of the Ottoman state."

Turkish power now began its long retreat from Europe.

To drive the Ottomans off the continent, Pope Innocent XI formed a Holy League. Venice, Poland, and Russia joined, as for a time did the Sun King, Louis XIV. In 1686, Budapest was recaptured; in 1688, Belgrade; in 1689, Bosnia, though the Turks managed a brief recapture of the Serb capital when the Christian powers fell to fighting one another. But the Ottoman Empire was no longer a predator in Europe. It was the prey.

In 1695, Czar Peter the Great seized Azov on the north coast of the Black Sea. Catherine the Great consolidated his conquests. Following a series of battles in 1768–1774, the Ottomans were forced to cede Azov, guarantee better treatment for Balkan Christians, open the Bosphorus and Dardanelles to Russian ships, and permit Russia to become protector of the Christian churches in Istanbul.

In 1798, the Islamic world was rudely awakened to its weakness and retardation when the young general Napoleon invaded and occupied Egypt. It was not Egyptians or Ottomans who forced Napoleon to withdraw, but the warships of Admiral Horatio Nelson that destroyed the French fleet in the Battle of the Nile.

IN THE EARLY nineteenth century, the Ottoman grip on the Balkans began to slip. A Greek rebellion in 1821 in which British poet Lord Byron would lose his life in 1824, and where the Ottomans introduced Arab troops, led to a mediation effort by Britain, France, and Russia. When the Turks rejected it, the combined fleets of the three powers sank a Turco-Egyptian naval squadron at Navarino.

Czar Nicholas I then declared war on the Turks and with help from Serbia fought his way almost to Istanbul. He compelled the sultan to grant greater independence to Greece and autonomy to Serbia and the Rumanian principalities of Wallachia and Moldova. Nicholas began to call the sultan "the sick man of Europe" and openly to covet the invalid's estate.

The Ottomans were saved by the British and French who feared the rising power of Russia more than the receding power of the Turks. When the czar went to war with the Ottoman Empire in 1853, Britain and France sent ships and men through the Dardanelles to fight in the Crimea. Russia was defeated. But the price Britain and France exacted from the Ottoman Turks was a grant of greater independence to the principalities that would become Rumania. Napoleon III now consolidated control of Algeria. From there in 1881, the French mounted a military expedition into Tunisia, forcing its Muslim ruler to submit to a protectorate.

ANOTHER RUSSO-TURKISH war in 1877–78 resulted in another crushing defeat for the Ottoman Empire. Only British and Austrian intercession at the Congress of Berlin prevented Alexander III from imposing harsh and humiliating conditions. But London and Vienna demanded compensation. Britain won the right to occupy Cyprus, and Austria the right to administer Bosnia and Herzegovina. The sultan was compelled to recognize the independence of Rumania, Serbia, and Montenegro.

The Ottoman Empire was being steadily stripped of its Arab and Balkan subjects. In 1882, the Royal Navy bombarded Alexandria, and British troops occupied Egypt, establishing a protectorate over what was a nominal Ottoman dependency. In 1884, the European scramble for Africa began. More Muslims fell under Western rule.

In 1908, Austria annexed Bosnia and Herzegovina. In 1911, Italy decided to get in on the kill and annex the North African provinces of Tripoli and Cyrenaica. The Young Turks declared war and sent Enver Pasha to do the fighting, but with insufficient troops. Italy defeated the Turks, annexed Tripoli and Cyrenaica, and was given administration of the Dodecanese in the Aegean. But for Istanbul, worse was to come.

With half its army tied down in North Africa, the Ottoman Empire suddenly confronted a new threat from a Balkan League formed by King Ferdinand of Bulgaria that included Serbia, Greece, and Montenegro. The new Balkan nations wanted their own bites out of the carcass of the dying empire that had ruled them for centuries. To the astonishment of Europe, they defeated the Turks. In 1913, another war broke out in the Balkans among the victorious nations over how to share their spoils.

On June 28, 1914, Gavrilo Princip, a Serb nationalist, determined that Serbia would expand at the expense of the now-tottering Hapsburg Empire, assassinated the Austrian archduke and his wife in Sarajevo. In five weeks, Europe had plunged into a four-year bloodbath in which Serbs would lose proportionately more men than any other nation. But Princip's act of terrorism succeeded. It had sparked the war that would bring about the collapse of both the Hapsburg and Ottoman Empires and give birth to a Serb-led kingdom that would incorporate Montenegrins, Bosnians, Croats, Albanians, Macedonians, and Hungarians.

Only at Gallipoli in 1915, the battle that cost First Lord of the Admiralty Winston Churchill his post, did Ottoman Turks inflict a major defeat on an Allied army. In 1917, General Allenby led a Christian army into Jerusalem for the first time in eight centuries, as Lawrence of Arabia led the revolt that liberated Arab lands from centuries of Ottoman rule.

But Lawrence's promises to his Arab warriors were dishonored. The British and French empires divided Syria, Lebanon, Palestine, and Iraq between themselves and accepted League of Nations mandates to rule them. Even more humiliating for the Arabs was the November 1917 declaration of Lord Balfour that "His Majesty's Government looks with favor upon the establishment of a homeland for the Jews in Palestine . . ."

Consider what had become of one of the world's oldest and greatest empires in a single century. In 1800 the Islamic Ottoman Empire spread across three continents. But by 1919, after the Allies finished carving up the world at Versailles, Morocco was divided between Spain and France. Algeria and Tunisia were ruled by

France. Libya was an Italian colony. Egypt and Sudan were British protectorates. Lebanon and Syria had been mandated to France by the League of Nations. Palestine, Transjordan, Kuwait, and Iraq had been mandated to Great Britain. Aden and the east coast of Arabia were under British rule, and in Persia British influence was dominant. Only in Yemen and the Hejaz were Arab Muslims independent of the West.

In Turkey itself, Ataturk had abolished the caliphate that symbolized the unity of the faithful and made the nation a secular state.

THE RESURRECTION OF ISLAM

Though Versailles had enlarged the British and French Empires, the Great War had wounded them psychologically and physically. Three-quarters of a million British soldiers had perished. French losses were almost double that. And the genie was now out of the bottle, for that grave-digger of empires, Woodrow Wilson, had arrived in Paris preaching the gospel of "self-determination" for all peoples.

His secretary of state, Robert Lansing, was quick to realize the far-reaching consequences: "The phrase [self-determination] is simply loaded with dynamite. It will raise hopes which can never be realized. . . . What a calamity that the phrase was ever uttered! What misery it will cause!"

Soon after the guns fell silent on the Western Front, there were rumbles of rebellion in Egypt and India. The Western empires held on in North Africa and the Middle East until 1945, then, suddenly, all the Arab and Islamic peoples were rising to demand independence.

In 1948, the British quit Palestine. In 1952, army colonels seized power in Cairo. King Farouk was told not to come home. In 1958, the monarchy in Iraq was overthrown and young King Faisal's body dragged through the streets. By 1962, when Algeria won its war of independence, Morocco and Tunisia had already been cut loose. In 1969, King Idris of Libya was ousted by twenty-seven-year-old Colonel Khadafi. In 1974, the emperor of Ethiopia was dethroned and murdered. The pro-Western shah of Iran fell in 1979. Thus, a few decades after the Allied victory in World War II, the Western empires had vanished from the Islamic world. Uneasy lies the head that wears a crown today in the Middle East.

YET, AFTER TWO generations of independence, it is difficult to identify a single Arab or Muslim state in the Middle or Near East that can be called a successful nation by Western standards.

For half a century, Egypt has been ruled by soldiers: Nasser, Sadat, Mubarak. Poverty is rampant, and Cairo depends on tourism and U.S. aid. Turkey has undergone several military takeovers and has had nineteen bailouts from the International Monetary Fund (IMF). Iran is run by mullahs twice repudiated in popular elections. Saudi Arabia depends on the United States for its defense and on oil for virtually its entire national income.

Following defeat in the Gulf War and the U.S.-British invasion of 2003, Iraq is occupied. Algeria remains torn by a civil war between fundamentalists and the army that has taken one hundred thousand lives. Morocco's monarchy is shaky. Libya is still ruled by Khadafi. Sudan is the heart of darkness. Jordan, 60 percent Palestinian, is among the poorest nations in the region, despite continuous Western aid. The emirate of Kuwait and the sheikdoms of the Gulf are rich, but remain strategic dependencies of the United States.

Remove oil and the total exports of the twenty-two Arab states are comparable to Finland's. Their combined GDP is less than that of Spain. Poverty remains pandemic and prosperity limited to the privileged few.

Not only do the Arab nations remain far behind the First World in living standards, industry, and technology, they have been left in the dust by Taiwan, South Korea, and Singapore, which, half a century ago, were more impoverished. Only the countries of the sub-Sahara have failed more visibly than the nations that once made up the heartland of the greatest civilization on earth.

The oil riches of the region have been largely squandered in wars and dissipation. Great as they are, they no longer provide a rising standard of living for the exploding populations that are becoming radicalized by the endless calls of the imams for jihad.

Politically, with the overthrow of the pro-Western monarchs, the Arab nations first tried nationalism and socialism. Egypt's Nasser, exemplar of both, presided over the greatest debacle in modern Arab history, the Six-Day War. All who followed Nasser's lead, from Khadafi, to Assad in Syria, to Saddam Hussein, failed to build successful nations.

Wherever one looks at the Arab world, one sees dictators, generals, kings, sheiks, ayatollahs, or presidents-for-life, threatened by assassins and backed by secret police. From Morocco to Pakistan there is not a successful republic. The closest approximation is Turkey, a non-Arab nation, the founding father of which, Kemal Ataturk, separated mosque and state and sought to construct his country on a Western model.

In 1979, with the revolution of the Ayatollah Khomeini, the first modern Islamist regime arose in Iran. A political system rooted in Sharia and run by mullahs was established. Sudan and Afghanistan followed. All failed. The Taliban were routed by the Americans and Northern Alliance, Sudan remains in the grip of a civil and tribal war that has cost two million lives, and Iranians have voted twice to reject the mullahs.

As practiced in Iran, Sudan, and Afghanistan, Islamism has failed. As an ideology, it has none of the broad mass appeal that the twentieth century rebellions against Western imperialism have had among the young. Iran has been unable to export its revolution. Where Islamist politicians attain power in elections, as in Turkey, they move to moderate their positions. In the West, posters of the ayatollah are unlikely to replace those of Che Guevara in student dorms.

The Islamic world has only two ways left to confront modernity: the way of Khomeini and the way of Kemal. The struggle in the future is between Islamism and secularism, between the ayatollahs and imams on one side and the Westernized politicians and soldiers on the other. Peoples of the region shift allegiances back and forth between them. Turkey is today a secular state beset by Islamist fervor among it young. Iran is an Islamist state resisting the lures of secularism to its young.

The Arab nations have also failed militarily. Five times they have been defeated by a small nation of five million Jews. Unable to confront the United States or Israel directly, Islamic and Arab radicals have opted for the weapon of the weak, terrorism.

WHAT WENT WRONG?

When one looks back over history, it seems indisputable that Islam gave birth to a civilization that was superior to the Christian West for eight centuries from the death of Mohammed to the discovery of America. Bernard Lewis writes:

> For many centuries the world of Islam was in the forefront of human civilization and achievement. In the Muslims' own perception, Islam itself was indeed coterminous with civilization, and beyond its borders there were only barbarians and infidels. . . .
>
> In the era between the decline of antiquity and the dawn of modernity, that is, in the centuries designated in European history as medieval, the Islamic claim was not without justification.

Warren Carroll agrees. While Christian nations remained largely illiterate, Islam spread "for seven hundred years, until it had mastered the Balkans and the Hungarian plain, and all but occupied Western Europe itself through its early material and intellectual superiority." Yet it was the Christian nations that discovered the New World and found the sea routes around the Ottoman Empire to the East Indies, China, and Japan, over which missionaries and merchants sailed and, soon after, the soldiers and civil servants followed to manage the new empires.

One of the great questions of history is why Islamic civilization began to fail so rapidly after the defeats at Lepanto and Vienna. Why was it not only superseded but conquered and colonized by the West? Why did it fall backwards? For a millennium, Muslims had looked on Europeans as the Romans looked on the Germanic tribes, as barbarians. One hundred years before Yorktown, the Ottoman Empire was superior in arms. But in the eighteenth and nineteenth centuries, Islamic civilization was eclipsed by the West.

Some argue that the Islamic faith prevented Ottoman civilization from advancing in arms, science, technology, industry, communications, ships, and governance. But how can Islam be the cause of the decline of that world, when Islam was, for a thousand years, the faith that sustained the most advanced culture and civilization on earth? Separation of church and state creates a more liberal society, but religion-based regimes are not necessarily failures. The Catholic Spain of Isabella was a great nation as was the Protestant England of Elizabeth I. Christian Democratic parties in Europe succeeded after World War II.

Rather than look within themselves for the answer to "What went wrong?" Islamic leaders, writes Lewis, looked outside and demanded to know "Who did this to us?" And just as African regimes blame long-departed European colonial powers for present failures, Arab and Islamic peoples blame the Mongols, the Turks, the Jews, the British, or the Americans.

Yet amid these many humiliations of Arab and Islamic peoples by European powers have come triumphs of war. In the last half century, Arab and Islamic rebels have inflicted stinging defeats on their European occupiers. Algerian insurgents used terror to drive out the French. A single jihadist, driving a truckload of explosives, killed 241 Marines in their barracks and brought about Reagan's retreat from Beirut. An ambush in Mogadishu killed eighteen of the best-trained soldiers in the U.S. Army, wounded scores, and forced a U.S. withdrawal from Somalia. Two daring Islamic warriors steered a motorboat up to the USS *Cole* in Aden harbor, stood, saluted, and ignited their explosives, killing nineteen sailors and almost sinking a billion-dollar warship.

The Afghan mujahedeen used U.S. weapons and a willingness to die for Allah and their country to inflict on the Soviet Union the only defeat in its history, which brought about the collapse of an empire and the death of a superpower. Hezbollah sent an Israeli army that had not lost an Arab war out of Lebanon with its tail between its legs.

WHY DO THEY HATE US?

When the terrorists of 9/11 drove those planes into the twin towers of the World Trade Center, the Pentagon, and the field in Pennsylvania, Americans were shocked at how many in the Islamic world said, "The Americans had it coming!"

What had we done that any should take satisfaction in the massacre of three thousand of our people? Why did demonstrators from Palestine to Pakistan support the Taliban? Why do millions in that world admire Osama? Why do Islamic radicals hate us so they are willing to commit suicide if they can take some of us with them? They cannot defeat or destroy the United States. Are they mad?

"Why do they hate us?" Americans asked after 9/11. President Bush professed himself shocked even by the implications of the questions. "I am," he declared,

> . . . amazed . . . that in some Islamic countries there is vitri-
> olic hatred of America. . . . I'm amazed that there's such
> misunderstanding of what our country is about that people
> would hate us . . . like most Americans, I just can't believe
> [it]. Because I know how good we are.

When others probed for a deeper answer, they were charged with "blaming America first," parroting enemy propaganda, trying to place responsibility on our own country for what the murderers had done to us.

We were attacked, declared *National Review* on its cover, "because we are powerful, rich and good." Our enemies "hate our democracy, our liberal markets, and our abundance and economic opportunity, at which the terror attacks were clearly directed," said Jack Kemp.

"They hate what they see right here in this chamber: a democratically elected government," President Bush told Congress. "They hate our freedoms: our freedom of religion, our freedom of speech, our freedom to vote and assemble and disagree with each other."

Americans for Victory Over Terrorism, a subsidiary of Empower America, declared in its statement of principles: "The radical Islamists who attacked us did so because of our democratic ideals, our belief in, and practice of, liberty and equality."

With due respect, these answers insult the intelligence of a second-grader. Did the Japanese attack us at Pearl Harbor because we were free, rich, good, and had low marginal tax rates? What is it about us Americans that we so often lack for what the poet Robert Burns said was the greatest gift the gods can give us, "to see ourselves as others see us."

We are not hated for who we are. We are hated for what we do. It is not our principles that have spawned pandemic hatred of America in the Islamic world. It is our policies.

Nothing justifies the mass murders of 9/11. Nothing. Nor need we hear out the extended plea bargains of those who slaughtered our countrymen. They deserve the rough justice they are receiving. But now that the Taliban have gone down, bin Laden is in hiding, and Iraq is occupied, we need to reflect on why Islamic peoples despise the United States so much they wish to see us dead or gone. If we wish to avert a clash of civilizations, from which we have nothing to gain, we need to listen to what they say—not to what we say—about America.

In the indictment of the Muslim world, these are our crimes:

1. We preach democracy and human rights, yet prop up dictators and oligarchies who oppress Islamic peoples and steal and squander their wealth.

2. By moving thousands of U.S. soldiers, especially women soldiers, onto the sacred soil of Saudi Arabia, we have insulted Arab honor and defiled the land on which sit the holiest sites of Islam. As Ian Buruma and Avishai Margalit, the authors of *Occidentalism: The West in the Eyes of Its Enemies,* write, "true Wahhabi believers, such as Osama bin Laden . . . view the presence of American women soldiers in Saudi Arabia as an act of defilement. To him and his followers, it is as if the Americans were sending their temple prostitutes to defend the unmanly rulers of Saudi Arabia."

3. America's neopagan culture—alcohol, drugs, abortions, filthy magazines, blasphemous books, dirty movies, hellish music—is a satanic lure that corrupts the morals of Islamic children.

4. Americans use a hypocritical double standard in dealing with Arabs and Israelis. We embargoed and blockaded Iraq, which cost the lives of tens of thousands of Iraqi children, because Saddam defied UN resolutions. Yet we give Israel all the aid Sharon demands to defy UN resolutions, seize Arab land, and deny Palestinians rights that America professes to champion.

5. We attacked, invaded, and occupied a prostrate Arab nation that did not attack us, did not want war with us, and could not resist us, on the pretext that Iraq had played a role in the 9/11 horrors and was building weapons of mass destruction to attack us. These were lies to cover up our greed to control the oil wealth of Iraq, destroy a defiant Arab nation, and erect an American empire in the Middle East.

To millions of Muslims, we are the "evil empire."

EVEN TO DETAIL this indictment is, to some outrageous and unpatriotic. Yet, as we are the new Rome, we are never going to be

loved, and it seems quintessential stupidity not to try to compre-
hend what it is that motivates those who hate us so much they ap-
plaud the killing of our innocent countrymen.

Know thy enemy, know thyself, in a thousand battles, a thousand victories, wrote Sun Tzu. If we must fight these people, we
have to know why they hate us, and we delude ourselves if we believe that 9/11 happened because we are "good." Evil as these massacres were, they were neither senseless nor irrational. They were
purposeful acts of terror to wound, humiliate, and provoke us into
reprisals that may yet bring on the war of civilizations for which Al
Qaeda plots and prays.

By attacking and occupying an Arab nation that had no role in
9/11, no plans to attack us, and no weapons of mass destruction,
we played into bin Laden's hand. We have given Muslims from
Morocco to Malaysia a unifying cause and recruiting slogan:
"Drive the Americans out of Iraq!"

To understand our enemies, we should read their words. In a
1998 article in *Foreign Affairs,* "License to Kill," Bernard Lewis
disclosed and dissected a declaration of war against America, published in London in an Arab newspaper. Lewis described this "Declaration of the World Islamic Front for Jihad Against the Jews and
the Crusaders" as a "magnificent piece of eloquent, at times even
poetic Arabic prose."

The author was Osama bin Laden, then being sought in the
bombing of our embassies in Kenya and Tanzania. Osama's declaration began by citing the most militant passages of the Koran, and
asserted that Americans are the Crusaders reincarnated.

> Since God laid down the Arabian peninsula . . . no calamity
> has even befallen it like these Crusader hosts that have
> spread in it like locusts, crowding its soil, eating its fruits,
> and destroying its verdure; and this at a time when the na-
> tions contend against the Muslims like diners jostling
> around a bowl of food. . . .

For more than seven years the United States is occupying the lands of Islam in the holiest of its territories, Arabia, plundering its riches, overwhelming its rulers, humiliating its people, threatening its neighbors, and using its bases in the peninsula as a spearhead to fight against the neighboring Islamic peoples.

Here then is the first charge against us: We are a Christian empire plundering Arab wealth and trampling with infidel feet on the sacred soil of the Hejaz. Osama next charged that America was preparing a new war to destroy the Iraqi people and humiliate all Muslims, in collusion with Israel.

Despite the immense destruction inflicted on the Iraqi people at the hands of the Crusader-Jewish alliance and in spite of the appalling number of dead, exceeding a million, the Americans nevertheless . . . are trying once more to repeat that dreadful slaughter. It seems that the long blockade following after a fierce war, the dismemberment and destruction are not enough for them. So they come again today to destroy what remains of this people and to humiliate their Muslim neighbors. . . .

While the purposes of the Americans in these wars are religious and economic, they also serve the petty state of the Jews, to divert attention from their occupation of Jerusalem and their killing of Muslims in it.

These crimes represent a "declaration of war by the Americans against God, his Prophet and the Muslims," wrote Osama. Thus, jihad against America becomes the duty of every Muslim.

Not all Muslims accept this. But of the one billion Muslims in the world, tens of millions do, including millions in Saudi Arabia, Jordan, Kuwait, Egypt, and Pakistan—and among the 5 to 6 million in France and the 10 million Muslims in Britain, Germany, Italy, Spain, and the other nations of the European Union. At the close of his declaration of war on the crusader Americans, Osama issued his fatwa:

> To kill Americans and their allies, both civil and military, is an individual duty of every Muslim who is able, in any country where this is possible, until the Aqsa Mosque [in Jerusalem] and the Haram Mosque [in Mecca] are freed from their grip and until their armies, shattered and broken-winged, depart from all the lands of Islam, incapable of threatening any Muslim.
>
> By God's leave, we call on every Muslim who believes in God and hopes for reward to obey God's command to kill the Americans and plunder their possessions wherever he finds them and whenever he can. Likewise we call on the Muslim ulema and leaders and youth and soldiers to launch attacks against the armies of the American devils and against those who are allied with them from among the helpers of Satan.

In his declaration, Osama sought to identify himself both with the cause of the purification of the Islamic world and with the Arab populist and nationalist causes—ridding the Middle East of America's puppet regimes, expelling Israel from Arab land, ending the looting of the wealth of Arabia, and standing beside persecuted Iraqis.

To defeat bin Laden and crush Al Qaeda, U.S. strategy should have been to narrow the conflict and isolate them from every Arab and Islamic center of power, as we did in Afghanistan, when Libya, Iran, Pakistan, and even Sudan supported us. Instead, listening to the neoconservatives, Bush invaded Iraq, united the Arab world against us, isolated us from Europe, and fulfilled to the letter bin Laden's prophecy as to what we were about. We won the war in three weeks—and we may have lost the Islamic world for a generation.

A Pew Research survey, a year after the invasion, found that 31 percent of Turks, 46 percent of Pakistanis, 66 percent of Moroccans, and fully 70 percent of Jordanians believed that suicide bombings of U.S. troops in Iraq were justified. In all four countries, the people believed that Iraqis were worse off after the invasion. Every Islamic country polled reported huge majorities wishing the Iraqis had put up stiffer resistance. Bin Laden was viewed favorably by 45 percent in Morocco, 55 percent in Jordan, 65 percent in Pakistan. Only 7 percent of Pakistanis had a favorable view of President Bush.

Seventy-one percent of the Palestinians said they trust Osama to "do the right thing," a rating higher than Arafat. Negative feelings about the United States and President Bush are at historic highs across the Islamic world.

Osama and his imitators have fertile ground to plow. And, with his fatwa, his call to kill Americans, we have no option but to pursue and finish him and his fanatic disciples before they kill more of us. Yet, we are on notice. Osama is saying exactly what the enemies of the Western empires said through the twentieth century. The price of your occupation, the price of your empire in our world, is terror. The Islamic terrorists of 9/11 were over here because we were over there. We were attacked by suicide bombers in New York for the same reason that our Marines were attacked by a suicide bomber in Beirut. We took sides in a religious civil war, their war, and they want us out of that war.

The fifteen hijackers from Saudi Arabia did not fly into the World Trade Center to protest the Bill of Rights. They want us off sacred Saudi soil and out of the Middle East.

The questions for us are these: Is a huge U.S. military presence in the Arab and Islamic world the way to win the war Arab and Islamic terrorists have launched against us—or is that a principal cause of the war? Is a permanent imperial presence in that part of the world worth the price of repeated acts of terrorism against us? Is a U.S. army killing insurgents in Iraq eliminating more enemies than it is creating? Is there anything over there—oil, bases, empire—worth risking an atomic bomb on U.S. soil? We must address that question, for if ever these terrorists get hold of a nuclear weapon, they will try to smuggle it into the United States. And detonate it.

WHO, EXACTLY, IS THE ENEMY?

Who, then, is America's enemy in this "war on terror"? And what is needed to defeat him? Is the enemy Islam? Were that true, the odds in our favor would be less than in the Cold War. For, unlike Leninism, which lasted but seven decades, Islam is fourteen hundred years old and it is not dying, it is exploding. "While the 22 Arab states currently have 280 million people, soaring birthrates indicate that by 2020 they will have 410 to 459 million," writes Thomas Friedman.

Islam is the fastest growing faith in Europe. As the churches and cathedrals of Europe empty out, the mosques are filling up. Islamic populations are surging due to immigration and higher birth rates. Muslims have begun to exercise a veto over European support for U.S. policy in the Middle East. While the Eurocide of the continent is not caused by Islam, Islam stands to become the beneficiary. In the United States, Muslims, though only 1 percent of the population, are surging in confidence and making converts.

The adversary with which Islam has the greatest difficulty coping today, the enemy stealing its children, is no longer Christianity. It is the MTV culture, America's secular faith of freedom, individualism, consumerism, and hedonism. Let a hundred flowers bloom and let the good times roll.

As Soviet ideologists divided the world into a "zone of peace" where Communism had triumphed and a "zone of war" outside the domain, Islam divides the world into the "Dar al Islam," the world of Islam, and the "Dar al Harb," the world of war where the infidel rules. Almost everywhere the Islamic world rubs up today against the Dar al Harb—the Philippines, Indonesia, southern Thailand, Kashmir, Xinjiang Province, the old Soviet republics of Central Asia and the Caucasus, Chechnya, Kosovo, Bosnia, Macedonia, Palestine, Lebanon, Sudan, Nigeria—there are what Harvard Professor Samuel Huntington calls "bloody borders." Islamic warriors battle Indians, Chinese, Russians, Serbs, Israelis, and Christians in jihads where the weapon of choice is terror.

"As had been true throughout its history, the expansion of Islam is not peaceful," writes scholar and strategist William Lind. "More Christians are being martyred today than at the height of the Roman persecutions, and most of them are dying at the hands of Islam."

To defeat a faith you need a faith. While Islamic warriors appear willing to die to drive infidels out of the Islamic world, Westerners appear indifferent to the persecution of Christians in the Islamic world. While Muslims are full of grievance, Westerners are full of guilt. We preach the equality of all faiths. Where Islam is dominant, it rejects equality, for it holds there is but one true faith. Islam is assertive, the West apologetic—about Crusaders, conquerors, and empires.

But Islamic fundamentalism is not an imminent or grave threat to America. Nor are U.S. combat divisions designed to defeat a fighting faith. If Islam is rising and its sons are prepared to die to enlarge the Dar al Islam and use terror to drive us out of their world, can we defeat it? No other Western empire did.

If a clash of civilizations is coming, the West is unchallenged in wealth and weaponry. Yet, wealth did not prevent the collapse of Europe's empires, nor did awesome weaponry prevent the collapse of the Soviet empire. Rome was mighty, Christianity weak. Christianity endured and prevailed. Rome fell.

America's enemy then is not a state we can crush with sanctions or an enemy we can defeat with force of arms. The enemy is a cause, a movement, an idea. Writes Michael Vlahos,

> The terrorist network is a ring of military subcultures that represents a much larger political movement within Islam, one that is nothing less than a civilization-wide insurgency against the established regimes of Sunni Islam. The "terrorists" are merely fighters in this jihad. Millions of sympathizers and supporters play active, even critical roles in the movement. While most perhaps are passive, they are nonetheless loyal adherents.

Adds Daniel Pipes, "The enemy is militant Islam." Yet, counters Vlahos, for us to declare war on militant Islam would pose grave problems:

> If the United States were to suggest that it is waging war against militant Islam, Islam as a whole might interpret this as a declaration of war against all Muslims. . . . [P]olitical needs have forced the United States to publicly limit the scope of the war. *Can we defeat an enemy that we are afraid to name?*

President Bush has taken pains to assure the Islamic world that Islam is a "religion of peace" and not America's enemy. When CNN anchor Lou Dobbs suggested that our enemies were "Islamists," he was attacked. Can we defeat an enemy that we are afraid to name?

The jihadists have allied themselves with the most popular causes and tapped into the most powerful currents in their world: anti-Zionism, Palestinian nationalism, anti-imperialism, anti-Americanism, and the felt need of devout Muslims to purify the Dar al Islam of a corrupting Western culture they believe is a fatal narcotic to the faith of their young. And in waging these struggles, Islamists have millions of well-wishers among the Muslim faithful.

The war into which we have plunged in Iraq and Afghanistan, then, is a civil-religious war to decide who shall rule in the Islamic world. Governments of men who are part of America's world. Or regimes of True Believers sworn to purge their world of Zionists, infidels, Christians, and collaborators. Today's struggle for the hearts and minds of Muslims and Arabs is between Ataturk and the Ayatollah.

FOUR

UNWINNABLE WAR?

> Terrorism is the war of the poor, and War is the
> terrorism of the rich.
>
> —Sir Peter Ustinov

President Bush has been clear about why we must fight the War on Terror, but less so about exactly who our enemies are. For, unlike Hitler's Germany or Hirohito's Japan, terrorism is not a nation, a regime, or an army. Terrorism is a tactic, a technique, a weapon that fanatics, dictators, and warriors have resorted to through history. If, as Clausewitz wrote, war is the continuation of politics by other means, terrorism is the continuation of war by other means. Writes historian Daniel Pipes:

> Terrorism is a military tactic employed by different groups
> and individuals around the world for different ends. To speak
> of a "war on terrorism" is a little like speaking about a war on
> weapons of mass destruction. One needs to know who owns
> or is deploying these weapons, and for what reason.

Harper's Lewis Lapham is equally dismissive of the idea of fighting a "war on terror." "Like an Arab jihad against capitalism, the American jihad against terrorism cannot be won or lost; nor does it ever end. We might as well be sending the 101st Airborne Division to conquer lust, annihilate greed, capture the sin of pride." Adds columnist William Pfaff, "It was a fateful mistake for Bush to have declared his 'war against terrorism,' after Sept. 11, 2001. That made it a war that can't be won."

To Zbigniew Brzezinski, declaring a war on terror after 9/11 made about as much as sense as it would have for Britain and France, after Hitler's lightning invasion of Poland, to have declared war on blitzkrieg.

What is terrorism? At a Jerusalem Conference in 1979, terrorism was defined as the "deliberate, systematic murder, maiming and menacing of the innocent to create fear and intimidation to gain political or tactical advantage . . ." In his National Strategy Statement of 2002, President Bush defined terror as "premeditated, politically motivated violence perpetrated against innocents." He added: "No cause justifies terrorism."

Benjamin Netanyahu, whose brother was killed in the July 1976 raid on Entebbe to rescue Israeli hostages held by terrorists, wrote:

> Terrorism is defined by one thing and one thing alone . . . by the nature of the act. Terrorists systematically and deliberately attack the innocent. . . . They intentionally cross the lines that define the conventions of war that have been developed in accordance with basic morality to try to limit and regulate conflict. They willfully try to kill as many innocent civilians as they can. And this is never justified regardless of the cause. Terrorism is always criminal.

Yet, foreign policy scholar Michael Vlahos argues that terms like "terrorism" and "terrorist" are loaded labels applied by besieged regimes to delegitimize enemies:

> "Terrorism" was first used in 1795, during the so-called Reign of Terror, when British commentators labeled the legitimate government of France as "terrorist" (from the French *terroriste*). The objective here was to delegitimize the French Republic by describing its behavior as uncivilized

and therefore no better than criminal. Of course most of the old-line monarchies in Europe were already at war with France and had failed to overthrow the new republic in battle. So wags like Edmund Burke were hard at work looking for other ways to strip the Sans-Culottes of legitimacy. This is not to say that Robespierre was a model political leader, but simply to show how the word terrorism was first used as it is still used, to place an enemy "beyond the pale."

While Burke was no "wag" and Robespierre had earlier used the term "terror" himself, Vlahos is correct that, through the twentieth century, governments applied the label "terrorists" to criminalize insurgents and justify a refusal to address their demands. "We do not negotiate with terrorists!" is the standard response of embattled rulers.

Thus when President Bush declared War on Terror, Russia branded the Chechen rebels terrorists. Beijing applied the label to Muslim Uighurs seeking autonomy in Xinjiang. India applied it to Islamic rebels fighting to wrest control of Kashmir from New Delhi. Sharon declared Arafat a "terrorist," i.e., a man with whom no Israeli can negotiate, though Arafat had negotiated with four of Sharon's predecessors and shared a Nobel Peace Prize with two of them, Yitzhak Rabin and Shimon Peres.

Is terrorism evil? Certainly. But when Churchill ordered his secret services "to set Europe ablaze," the methods Allied agents used were the sabotage of trains, assassination of German pilots and military officers, bombing of buildings, and execution of collaborators. The French Maquis and Italian partisans did the same. To the Allies, they were heroes fighting a just war, and the stories of their exploits are now legend.

After the war the tactics used against Japanese and Germans were used by Zionists against the British, by the Viet Minh and Algerian FLN against the French, and by Mandela's ANC against the white government of South Africa.

If the cause is just in Western eyes, Western leaders appear more tolerant of the methods used and the allies who are welcome. In ousting the Taliban, America was supported by Iran, Sudan, and Libya. The State Department had listed all three as state sponsors of terror. The Northern Alliance that provided most of the invading forces that overran Kabul was led by warlords steeped in blood.

In the Gulf War, America welcomed the Syrian troops of Hafez al Assad, who had massacred perhaps twenty thousand rebel Moslems in Hama. Did Bush's father ally us with one terrorist, Assad, to defeat another, Saddam?

It would not be the first time. To defeat Hitler, FDR partnered with Stalin, architect of what author Robert Conquest calls the Great Terror. Richard Nixon went to China and toasted the greatest state terrorist of them all, Mao Tse-tung—in words written for him by this author. Even his most savage critics hailed Nixon's opening to China as an act of statesmanship. "If you harbor a terrorist, you are a terrorist," President Bush told Congress, to the applause of our Saudi ally then giving sanctuary to Idi Amin.

Something else needs to be said about terrorism. As the *Toronto Star*'s Thomas Walkom writes, terrorism often succeeds:

> History demonstrates two dirty little secrets about terrorism, neither of which governments are anxious to admit. The first is that terrorism is almost impossible to prevent—unless its root causes are seriously and systematically addressed. The second is that, quite often, terrorists get what they want.

THE ROOTS OF TERRORISM

Even before the Romans put Carthage to the sword, terrorism has been with us. In our time, there seem to be four categories:

1. State terror is the *ultima ratio* of rulers such as Lenin, Stalin, and Mao to coerce the obedience of subject masses. "Shoot one and

intimidate a thousand," Stalin reputedly said. In the *Melian Dialogues*, Thucydides relates how the Melians, the allies of Sparta, refused to yield to the demands of the Athenians, who, for reasons of state and to send a message to all resisters, put every Melian man to the sword and sold their women and children into slavery.

2. Revolutionary terror is the weapon of the powerless and stateless to wound and enrage regimes they are too weak to confront with arms.

3. War terror was the methodology of Scipio Africanus in Carthage and the Red Army in its rampage across Europe. "War against civilians has been a feature of the Western military tradition since the Romans razed Carthage," writes Michael Ignatieff. Adds Walkom: "Terror is an old strategy in warfare—from the medieval European practice of placing the heads of captured enemies on pikes to the savage raids against women and children that characterized the French-English frontier wars of 18th-century Canada."

4. Anarchic terror is the seemingly nihilistic and senseless slaughter of the innocent. It has been called symbolic terror, an act of shocking violence to make a dramatic statement. "The act of terrorism is very often a potent instrument of self-expression, rather than just a means toward some political end," wrote Malraux in *Man's Fate*.

The term originated in the French Revolution. Historian Stanley Loomis traces the onset of the Reign of Terror to June 2, 1793, the day Marat's mob invaded the National Convention in the Tuileries and evicted twenty-two Girondists who went to the guillotine, and its end to July 27, 1794, 9 Thermidor, the day Robespierre was overthrown and quickly guillotined.

After Marat had been assassinated and Danton beheaded, Robespierre gained control of the Committee on Public Safety. There, he began to use charges of treason to send enemies to the Revolutionary Tribunal, which had been ceded absolute power to determine guilt and impose sentence. To go before the tribunal meant death, often by day's end. By holding the threat of a charge of treason over members of the committee, Robespierre and his agents St. Just and Couthon leveraged the committee to control the National Assembly.

The Committee of Public Safety and Revolutionary Tribunal were the first instruments of state terror in modern times—a regime using a threat of summary execution to cow rivals and coerce the obedience of subjects. This situation would not be replicated until Robespierre's great disciple seized power in Petrograd in 1917.

Whence came the moral sanction for the Reign of Terror? Who prepared the ground? The men of the Enlightenment. There was Voltaire, who signed off his letters with the command *"Ecrasez l'infame!"*—"Wipe out the infamy!"—i.e., the church; and Diderot, author of the *Encyclopédie,* who wrote, "Mankind will not be free until the last king is strangled with the entrails of the last priest." Then, there was Rousseau who inspired Robespierre: "Man was born free but everywhere he is in chains."

Church and crown were the twin tyrannies that held mankind in chains. Hence, king, queen, the parasite aristocracy of Versailles, and the bishops and priests who held the people in thrall by claiming to be the intermediaries of God, all must be eradicated. Else the people will never be free.

"The King was beheaded and priests and nuns in hundreds, perhaps thousands, expiated the sins of the Inquisition," writes British historian D. W. Brogan. The September Massacres began with the priests.

Even the great democrat Thomas Jefferson seemed to sanction terror. Long before the fall of the Bastille, he wrote: "What signify a few lives lost in a century or two? The tree of liberty must be refreshed from time to time with the blood of patriots & tyrants. It is its natural manure."

Jefferson's words echoed in France's National Assembly. "The tree of liberty only grows when watered by the blood of tyrants," declaimed Bértrand Barere. That innocent men and women were being murdered by the Revolution, Jefferson did not deny. Yet he believed the Revolution was so entwined with a glorious future for all mankind it must not be lost, no matter its excesses. In the most condemned passage Jefferson ever penned, he wrote to a friend:

> The liberty of the whole earth was depending on the issue of the contest, and was ever such a prize won with so little innocent blood? My own affections have been deeply wounded by some of the martyrs to this cause, but rather than it should have failed, I would have seen half the earth desolated. Were there but an Adam and Eve left in every country & left free, it would be better than it is now.

This is the sentiment not of a statesman but of a sans-cullotte. The great end justifies the ghastly means.

When the Revolution overthrew altar and throne, it overthrew the moral code of Christianity and wrote a new code for the new age. First and greatest commandment in the new dispensation: Whatever advances the Revolution is moral; whatever imperils the Revolution is immoral and must be eradicated, without remorse. And the revolution awed its contemporaries. Said Metternich: "Having seen what was done in the name of brotherhood, if I had a brother, I should call him cousin."

And if God does not exist and the church is a monstrous fraud to deprive people of their freedom, who decides right and wrong?

Answer: The republic now decides. The republic now commands the loyalty once rendered to the king and all may be sacrificed to secure the republic. As the God of the Old Testament exercised sovereign power to incinerate Sodom, the republic asserts a sovereign right to punish Lyon. Writes Loomis:

> Lyon, the second largest city in France, was put to the sword. In "batches" numbering in the hundreds, citizens

were dragged to the plain of Brotteaux outside the gates of the city where they were put to death by cannon fire, by bayonets and by clubs. Hecatomb followed hecatomb. The bodies of the dead were tossed into the Rhone. "Let their bleeding corpses strike terror on both banks of the river as they drift toward the cowardly city of Toulon."

Robespierre practiced state terror, the Jacobin means to the end of absolute power. But the category that concerns us is revolutionary terror, the terror of the alienated, the desperate, the dispossessed, the fanatic, the stateless—the terror of 9/11. This vintage, too, has a venerable pedigree.

REVOLUTIONARY TERROR

By the late nineteenth century, many of Russia's idealistic young had become alienated from the autocracy of Alexander II who had freed the serfs as Abraham Lincoln was issuing his Emancipation Proclamation. A few sought to change Russia by going out to the peasants, the *narod,* to convert them to a revolution to create an egalitarian, socialist, democratic Russia. But the peasants of Russia were blood-and-soil people, marinated in centuries of Orthodoxy, and they turned the missionaries of revolution into the czar's secret police. "The socialism of the West bounces off the Russian masses like a pea off a wall," lamented one revolutionary.

Failure to convert the peasantry opened the minds of the radicals to a gospel of redemptive violence preached by such veteran revolutionaries as the charismatic Mikhail Bakunin, of whom historian W. Bruce Lincoln writes:

Bakunin's personal dedication to the cause of revolution was worldwide. He fought on the barricades of Paris in February 1848 and hastened to pursue revolution's red flags in

Berlin, Frankfurt, and Prague before year's end. After two years in Saxon and Austrian prisons, he was extradited to Russia in 1851 and exiled to the remote eastern regions of Siberia only to launch a daring escape that carried him down the Amur River, to Japan, San Francisco, across the Isthmus of Panama, to New York and then on to London where he joined his friend and fellow radical Herzen.

"What a man!" Paris's prefect of police exclaimed of Bakunin. "On the first day of the Revolution, he is a perfect treasure; on the second he ought to be shot!"

"Bakunin preached destruction so long as there was anything left to destroy," wrote his biographer E. H. Carr. "He preached rebellion—even when there was nothing left to rebel against."

His great rival was Marx. Where Bakunin was an anarchist who wanted to destroy the state, Marx was a socialist who wanted to destroy capitalism. Where Bakunin insisted the revolution could come at any moment from an explosion in some reactionary European state, Marx declared that revolution could come only from the proletariat and only after the workers had been organized and trained. With the crushing of the Paris Commune in the *année terrible,* as Victor Hugo called 1871, Bakunin appeared to have been proven wrong. "We reckoned without the masses, who did not want to be roused to passion for their own freedom," the disconsolate anarchist wrote his wife.

After losing control of the First International to Marx, the old revolutionary died in despair in 1876. But his gospel had been heard. Russia's rebellious young began to call themselves *narodniki,* to identify with the peasantry, and to imbibe deeply of Bakunin's dogmas and those of the even more fanatic Sergei Nechaev, the author of the *Catechism of a Revolutionary:*

The revolutionary is a doomed man. He has no interests, affairs, feelings, attachments, property, not even a name that he can call his own. Everything in him is absorbed by one exclusive interest, one thought, one passion—the revolution. . . . He has severed all ties with laws, decorum, all the generally accepted conditions and morality of this world. He stands as its relentless enemy and, if he continues to live in it, then it is only in order to be more certain of its destruction. . . . Day and night he must have but one thought, one single goal— merciless destruction. Striving only for this aim, coldly and tirelessly, he must be prepared to perish himself and to destroy with his own hands all that hinders its realization.

Nechaev was a scoundrel and murderer who spent the last decade of his life in the dungeon of the Peter and Paul Fortress, but, in the 1870s, the seeds he and Bakunin planted began to sprout in the souls of the young.

Enter Vera Zasulich. A young woman with a deep sense of justice, on January 28, 1878, Zasulich set out to avenge the flogging of a student on the orders of General Trepov, the military governor of St. Petersburg. Posing as a petitioner, Zasulich asked to see Trepov, and, when brought before him, pulled out of her muff a snub-nosed revolver known as a "bulldog" and shot him. Though she had fired only one of six bullets in the chamber and only wounded Trepov, Zasulich calmly laid the pistol down and offered no resistance when the general's aides arrested her.

As historian Virginia Cowles describes it, the Zasulich trial was the sensation of St. Petersburg. The greatest trial lawyer in Russia, Petr Aleksandrov, undertook her defense, aided by the knowledge that Trepov was widely hated for his cruelty. Rising in her own behalf at the trial, an emotional Zasulich declared:

I did not find—indeed I could not find—any other way to bring attention to this situation . . . I could see no other way. . . . It is terrible to raise one's hand against a fellow human being, I know, but I concluded that this had to be done.

When the jury returned a verdict of "not guilty," the courtroom exploded with cheers and stamping feet. "Many great lords and ladies from high society," wrote the minister of war in his diary, "were in ecstasy at the court's verdict." One who did not rejoice was Leo Tolstoy. Deeply troubled at the verdict, the great novelist wrote a friend the following day:

> The Zasulich business is no joking matter. This madness, this idiotic capriciousness that has suddenly seized hold of people is significant. These are the first signs of something that is not clear to us. But it is serious. The Slavophil madness was the precursor of war, and I am inclined to think that this madness is the precursor of revolution.

Tolstoy's foreboding proved justified. Zasulich's exoneration had decanted the demon of terrorism in Russia. In 1879, in the small town of Lipetsk, a tiny organization was formed that called itself *Narodnaya Volya*, The People's Will. With thirty members, this was, writes Richard Pipes, "the source of all modern terrorist groups" from the Tupamaros of Uruguay to Italy's Red Brigades to Germany's Baader-Meinhof Gang to America's Weathermen. Adds Pipes:

> The People's Will organization was the first to consider the enemy to be the whole system, and by system I . . . emphasize it meant not only autocracy, but also capitalism, religion, law and everything else which kept the body politic intact. They had no particular hostility towards Alexander II personally; some of them indeed admired him for liberating the serfs. But he was regarded as an essential part of an inherently evil system, and had to be destroyed.

The *narodniki* declared their belief in the justice of revolutionary violence. "The bomb was to be the Messiah," wrote Barbara Tuchman. High officials were soon being cut down by assassins, and plots against the czar uncovered. Three years after Vera Zasulich shot General Trepov, one of those plots, led by another young woman, would succeed.

Sophia Perovskaya was the daughter of a governor general of St. Petersburg, and is thus described by the historian Edward Crankshaw: "Tiny, flaxen-haired, almost doll-like with pink and white cheeks and pale blue eyes, she was a revolutionary to the bone. . . . Sophia loathed and detested the whole social and militaristic set-up in which she had been born. She hated her bully of a father." In *The Romanovs* Virginia Cowles tells her story.

Every day, for weeks, Perovskaya stood outside the Winter Palace to observe the comings and goings of Alexander II. She noted that it was the czar's habit to ride out on Saturdays to visit the Grand Duchess Ekaterina.

When her lover was arrested, Perovskaya feared their plot would be exposed and decided to act at once. She stationed four accomplices, each with grenades of nitroglycerine, along the only two routes the czar could take on his return to the palace. She then planted herself within sight of all four, so she could signal with her handkerchief which way Alexander was coming. As the czar had headed off to visit the grand duchess, Sophia concluded he would return along the Catherine Canal Embankment.

When Alexander's bomb-proof carriage, a gift from Napoleon III, turned onto the embankment, Perovskaya's first assassin hurled his bomb. The explosion was heard across St. Petersburg and instantly killed two Cossacks and three horses. The czar was unhurt. As he stepped down from his carriage to see what could be done to aid the wounded, a relieved police officer said, "Thank God Your Majesty is safe."

"Rather too soon to thank God!" shouted a second terrorist as he hurled his bomb at the czar's feet.

The second explosion shook the windows of the Winter Palace. By now the snow was crimson. The Emperor half-lay, half-sat, with his back to the canal railings. His face was streaming with blood, his abdomen torn open, his legs shattered. "Quickly! Home to the Palace to die!" he muttered and lost consciousness.

The Czar Liberator was dead. Liberalism was finished. And, as several of the regicides bore Jewish names, pogroms swept Russia. On 3 April 1881, the surviving plotters, Sophia Perovskaya among them, were hanged in Semenovsky Square.

To mark the sixth anniversary of Alexander II's assassination, a cell of students committed to the principles of The People's Will plotted the assassination of Alexander III, with nitroglycerine grenades packed with two hundred tiny metal balls, and hollowed-out dictionaries filled with dynamite.

Among them was Alexander Ulyanov. "I do not believe [merely] in terror," Ulyanov had declared. "I believe in systematic terror."

The plan was to have assassins stalk the czar during his walk along the Nevskii Prospect between the Winter Palace and Kazan Cathedral. But a careless letter written by one of the plotters wound up in the hands of the *Okhrana,* the czar's secret police. Three of the would-be assassins were arrested carrying bombs. Among those rounded up was Ulyanov. At his trial, Ulyanov admitted he belonged to the party of The People's Will and had prepared the bombs. Addressing the court, Ulyanov defined the terrorism with which our world has become so well acquainted:

> Terror is that form of struggle that has been created by conditions of the nineteenth century. . . . It is the only form of defense to which a minority, strong only in terms of spiritual strength and in its knowledge of the rightness of its beliefs, can resort against the physical strength of the majority.

Alexander Ulyanov was hanged with four others in May of 1887. His brother Vladimir was seventeen at the time. Three decades later, Vladimir, now known to the world as Lenin, would order the execution of the son of Alexander III and his entire family.

The story of Vera Zasulich and General Trepov, and the legend of the *narodniki*, would live on in the hearts of revolutionaries. In 1954, in *Odyssey of a Friend,* Whittaker Chambers, who had delivered up Alger Hiss, wrote:

> I came to Communism under the influence of the anarchists. . . . But, above all, I came under the influence of the Narodniki. . . . It has been deliberately forgotten, but, in those days, Lenin urged us to revere the Narodniki—"those who went with bomb or revolver against this or that individual monster." . . . I remained under the spiritual influence of the Narodniki long after I became a Marxist. . . . I never threw it off. I never have. It has simply blended with that strain in the Christian tradition to which it is akin.

Chambers wrote of how his moral bond with the *narodniki* and the inspiration he drew from their deeds made him beloved of his Bolshevik comrades:

> I remember how Ulrich, my first commander in the Fourth Section, once mentioned Vera Zasulich and added, "I suppose you never heard that name." I said, "Zasulich shot General Trepov for flogging the student, Bogomolsky, in the Paviak prison." And I remember the excited smile with which he answered. . . . "That is true but how did *you* know that?" For the spirit of the Narodniki, all that was soldierly and saintly in the revolution, found its last haven, O irony!, in the Fourth Section (one purpose of the Great Purge was to kill it out once for all.)

"Soldierly and saintly."

Thus did Chambers describe the attempted assassination of Trepov. Yet in that unpunished crime, Tolstoy saw that a moral Rubicon had been crossed in Russian history, and would lead to revolution. Zasulich had fired a single shot to avenge the flogging of a student. But those who came after her would accept that the innocent might have to die with the guilty. The grenades hurled at Alexander II ended not only his life but the lives of twenty-two others. The *narodniki* had embraced a new morality.

Were the czars tyrants? To Russians they were rightful rulers. But to radicals, and to Jews whose families had suffered in pogroms and who believed the czars knew and had approved, they were tyrants whose assassination was richly deserved. Here is D. W. Brogan on how Western liberals viewed the Romanovs in the late nineteenth century:

> The permanent underground war against Tsardom had now the sympathy of most of Liberal Europe and America. Assassination was, as Bacon said of revenge, "a kind of wild justice." And was there not cause enough for revenge? "Who Can be Happy and Free in Russia?" a famous tract inquired and the answer of the western world was "Nobody."
>
> Mark Twain suggested, more or less seriously, that the ideal place to start a model republic was Siberia, for its inhabitants had been, for generations, carefully chosen for courage, independence of mind and intelligence. That most of the prisoners in Siberia were of the same type as filled Sing Sing and Dartmoor was not generally appreciated.

What was the purpose of these acts of revolutionary terror? To demystify the state, writes Richard Pipes, to show the people the regime was not an invulnerable monolith, to cause it to lash out at its wounding. And terrorism was contagious. For these terrorist acts in defiance of death ignited fires in the minds of men like Chambers who, alienated from the world, wished to dedicate their lives to a cause greater than themselves.

Revolutionary terror has many ends. To wound a detested regime. To expose its vulnerability. To enter a blood claim to the leadership of a cause. To awe and inspire by the drama of the deed. To goad a state into reprisals that ravage its reputation for justice, rip away its legitimacy, and force people to choose sides. To attain immortality.

Revolutionary terror was the weapon of Al Qaeda on 9/11. And like almost all such acts of terror, it is a symptom of the disease, not the disease itself. September 11 appears to us an unvarnished act of evil. And indeed it is. But that must not blind us to the fact that behind the act of evil lay a political purpose: To shock the world, wound the United States, provoke America into lashing out in retribution against the Islamic world, and to draw the United States into a war against Islam in which America, like the imperial powers before her, will be driven out of the Middle East and Islamic world. Bin Laden cannot be such a fool as to believe America would not wield the "terrible swift sword" of retribution. His act of terror was designed to provoke America into blind rage, and his act of terror may have succeeded beyond his wildest expectations—in Iraq.

While 9/11 was an act of mass murder for which payment must be made, we make a terrible mistake if we do not reflect upon the motives and agenda of these Islamic warriors, and think how best to avoid playing the role they have assigned to us in their bloody drama.

Looking back, the journalist John Judis believes that 9/11 "is not the first phase of a new stage" of world history but "the last phase of an old stage. . . . Al Qaeda and bin Laden represent the reductio ad absurdum of the anticolonial revolts that shook Asia, Africa, and Latin America during the twentieth century."

Judis's point is well taken. In the twentieth century, revolutionary terror was the weapon of the IRA, the Irgun, the Stern Gang, Algeria's FLN, the Mau Mau, the MPLA, PLO, Black September, the Basque ETA, the Red Brigades, the Baader-Meinhof Gang, the Red Army, Hezbollah, Islamic Jihad, Hamas, the Al Aksa Martyrs Brigade, SWAPO, ZANU, ZAPU, the Tupamaros, Shining Path, FARC, the ANC, the Viet Cong, the Huks, Chechen rebels, Tamil

Tigers, the Weather Underground, Symbionese Liberation Army, FALN, and its predecessor, the Puerto Rican Nationalist Party that attempted to assassinate President Truman and shot up the House floor in 1954, to name but a few.

"THERE ARE NO INNOCENT BOURGEOIS"

As Alexander Ulyanov was mounting the scaffold, the legend of the *narodniki* was spreading West. The anarchists would follow Bakunin rather than Marx and they, too, would fail. But their shocking crimes and the bristling defiance with which they went to scaffold and guillotine and before firing squads riveted, even as it revolted, Western societies.

On February 5, 1895, the anarchist Vaillant, who had thrown a nail bomb from the gallery onto the floor of the French Assembly, went to the guillotine, shouting "Long live anarchism." Just seven days later, writes Barbara Tuchman in *The Proud Tower,* Vaillant "was avenged by a blow of such seemingly vicious unreason that the public felt itself in the midst of a nightmare."

Emile Henry chose as the target of his bomb the Café Terminus on the Gare St. Lazare where Parisians came to enjoy a glass of beer after work. Henry's bomb killed one and wounded twenty. At trial, he was asked by the judge why an anarchist who claimed to be at war against the state, in the name of the people, would bomb a café that was filled with innocent people. Henry's retort: "There are no innocent bourgeois."

ANARCHISM LEAPT ACROSS the Atlantic and its greatest success came in America. On September 5, 1901, as President McKinley stood in a receiving line at the Buffalo Exposition, he was shot and mortally wounded by the Polish-American anarchist Leon Czolgosz. McKinley's successor, Theodore Roosevelt, in his message to Congress on December 3, 1901, declared in words anticipating President Bush: "Anarchism is a crime against the whole human race and all mankind should band against the Anarchist."

But all mankind did not. Western intellectuals have romanticized what the poet Shelley called the "tempestuous loveliness of terror." Writes D. W. Brogan:

> The anarchist outbreaks in the eighties and nineties were taken as signs of the sufferings of the poor, as rebukes to the callousness of the rich. No one approved of the assassination of the Empress Elizabeth of Austria, but was there not something in the slogan of her assassin, "He that does not work, neither shall he eat."? All revolutionary creeds were mixed up together; all were equally romantic if wrong-headed. The Goddess of Revolution whom Disraeli's romantic revolutionaries had toasted as "Mary Anne" was worshiped vicariously by many men of letters. Men like Oscar Wilde might announce that they sympathized with those Christs that die upon the barricades.

Adds Walter Laquer, "Terrorists have found admirers and publicity agents in all ages."

> No words of praise are fulsome enough for these latter-day saints and martyrs. The terrorist (we are told) is the only one who really cares; he is a totally committed fighter for freedom and justice, a gentle human being forced by cruel circumstances and an indifferent majority to play heroic yet tragic roles: the good Samaritan distributing poison, St. Francis with a bomb.

To Laquer, "such a beatification of the terrorist is grotesque." Yet even Stalin's Great Terror in the 1930s, in which a million perished of the tens of millions who would fall to Soviet Communism, had apologists in the West: "You cannot make an omelette without breaking eggs."

And, today, Saudi ambassadors in London write poems about female suicide bombers in Palestine and even Osama and the murderers of 9/11 have millions of admirers in the Islamic world.

WARS OF NATIONAL LIBERATION

In the twentieth century, revolutionary terror was first employed during the Boxer Rebellion of 1900. Fanatics, determined to cleanse China of foreign domination, massacred Christian converts, assaulted and murdered foreign diplomats, and, bent upon slaughter, besieged their compound in Peking. British, French, German, Russian, and Japanese troops, with six thousand U.S. Marines, took fifty-five days to march from the coast to Peking to relieve the diplomatic missions. The Boxers were put down ruthlessly and the dowager empress forced to pay a huge indemnity to the imperial powers.

The first use of revolutionary terror against a Western power by a Christian people was Ireland's war of independence.

On Easter Monday 1916, while Britain was fighting for its life in France, two thousand Irish rebels seized the General Post Office in Dublin, and other public buildings. The rebels had conspired with the Germans, and a weapons shipment had been intercepted off the Irish coast on Good Friday. The conspirators were seen by Britons and many of their own countrymen as traitors stabbing in the back the Mother Country and the British army, in which thousands of their Irish kinsmen had enlisted.

Met by apathy and ridicule and facing superior British firepower, the rebels capitulated in a week. Had their leaders been sentenced to long prison terms, the incident would have been over. But at this point, the British government enraged at what it saw as wartime treachery and treason, "committed perhaps its greatest blunder in seven centuries of dealing with Ireland," writes Irish historian Kenneth Neill.

In a sweeping roundup, 3,500 Irish were imprisoned. Many had no role in the rising. Then, fifteen rebel leaders, including cultural nationalist Patrick Pearse and labor leader James Connolly, were sent before firing squads. Instantly, fifteen martyrs to Irish independence had been created to be immortalized by Yeats:

> I write it out in a verse—
> MacDonagh and MacBride
> And Connolly and Pearse
> Now and in time to be,
> Wherever green is worn,
> Are changed, changed utterly:
> A terrible beauty is born.

Earlier in 1916, Pearse had written: "Bloodshed is a cleansing and a sanctifying thing, and the nation which regards it as the final horror has lost its manhood." MacBride had fought the British in the Boer War and married Maud Gonne, the legendary lady who had rejected Yeats's proposal of marriage but inspired his poetry. As Jill and Leon Uris relate,

> Faithful to the cause to the end, John MacBride was in Jacob's Biscuit Factory during the Easter Rising, a mere second in command to Thomas MacDonagh. There seemed to be no reason to execute MacBride except that the British still remembered the Boer War. At Stonebreaker's Wall he made a last lovely defiance when offered a blindfold. "It's not the first time I've looked down their guns, Father," he told the attending priest.

Out of such stuff are legends made, and one man's traitor becomes another's martyr. The British were within their rights to execute the rebels. But was it wise? History suggests not, that it was a classic example of retribution that does not stifle a revolution but spreads it. The blood of martyrs, after all, has been the seed of rebellion as well as of the church. In contrast to the blunder of 1916, British statesmen had elected not to execute a greater menace. Rather than send Napoleon before a firing squad, Britain exiled him to St. Helena's, an honorable and wise act even the defeated French could acknowledge.

WHEN THE REBELS of the Easter Rising were executed, the Home Rule Party of John Redmond that supported the British war effort and urged Irishmen to enlist was finished, replaced in Irish hearts by the new party of independence Sinn Fein (Ourselves Alone). And though many more Irish civilians than rebels or British soldiers had been killed in the rising, the executions had put the bungling conspirators into the pantheon of Irish freedom fighters where they remain unto this day.

Do they belong there? To Tim Pat Coogan, author of *The Easter Rising,* the Irishmen, alongside whom his father fought, were following a "physical force tradition." To conservative John Derbyshire, the Irish "physical force tradition" is "Irish fascism," the Easter Rising its "beer-hall putsch," and Coogan a "propagandist for the politics of the ambush and the car bomb." As for Pearse, he was a "sinister fantasist" and "atrocious" poet who got what he deserved. For Irish to celebrate the rising, writes Derbyshire, reveals a flaw in their national character.

IN MARCH OF 1918, London blundered again. Prime Minister Lloyd George declared his intent to impose conscription on Ireland to make up for British losses on the Western Front. Sinn Fein, the Home Rule Party, and Catholic bishops united in an Irish Anti-Conscription League. Lloyd George withdrew his proposal but the damage was done. In the "Khaki Election" of December 1918, the Home Rule Party of Charles Stewart Parnell won but six seats in Parliament. The separatists swept seventy-nine, and the twenty-seven not then in exile, prison, or hiding set up an independent Dáil Eireann in Dublin.

On the first day the Dáil met in January 1919, Irishmen ambushed an ammunition lorry in County Tipperary, killing two constables. These were the first shots fired in the war of independence. For two and a half years, the British and the Irish Republican Army would fight a war of terror and reprisal.

"Flying columns" would assemble and attack isolated police barracks, or ambush lorries full of British soldiers, disband, and disappear into the population. Assassination and ambush were its tactics, demoralizing a British army that then sent in veterans of the Western Front. The "Black-and-Tans" took out their frustration and rage on civilians by burning towns and much of the city of Cork. Yet, so successful were they in crushing the rebellion that Michael Collins told a British official in the July 1921 peace negotiations, "You had us dead beat. We could not have lasted another three weeks."

Still a confident imperial power in 1921, the British had nearly won the century's first war of national liberation against the empire.

Compared with later such wars, Ireland's war of independence was not a bloody affair. It resulted in only about 18 deaths in 1919, 282 in 1920, as well as 82 in Ulster's sectarian riots, and 1,086 in 1921 before the truce. Nearly half of the victims were soldiers or police. Historian Lawrence James describes how the Irish rebels saw themselves and how they were seen by the British.

> The IRA volunteer was a patriot, convinced that the moral rightness of his cause, a united republican Ireland, released him from obedience to normal codes of human behavior. His enemies saw him as a cold-blooded murderer. Particularly horrific killings were answered by reprisals against a civilian population which was tainted with guilt by association. Most notorious of these spontaneous acts of revenge was after the IRA shot dead twelve British officers in their billets on 21 November 1920, alleging they were intelligence agents. That afternoon a detachment of Auxies fired into a crowd at a Dublin football ground, claiming they were an-

swering IRA fire; twelve spectators were shot or crushed in
the panic.

This would be the pattern for wars of liberation in the twentieth
century. The Irish rebels believed their dream—a nation of their
own—justified the only means they believed could win their independence. The British, who saw soldiers and loyal civil servants
murdered in the streets, reacted with a savagery that created new
martyrs, forcing Irish men and women to choose between kinfolk
and country.

By 1921, both British and Irish had had enough. A truce was
called for midsummer. Peace negotiations began. The Irish delegation left for London to face the victor of Versailles, Lloyd
George, and his colonial secretary, Winston Churchill. Britain's
final offer, which Collins, the brilliant and courageous Irish military commander, accepted, was for an Irish Free State—with restrictions. Ireland was to remain a British dominion, like Canada,
continue to host British naval bases, and swear allegiance to the
Crown. And Ireland's six northern counties with Protestant majorities were to remain independent of Dublin, a permanent part
of Great Britain.

Collins returned to a country bitterly divided over the treaty he
had brought home, and the fighting hero of the war of independence now faced charges of treason. As David Fromkin wrote in his
1975 *Foreign Affairs* article, "The Strategy of Terrorism,"

> Michael Collins was a romantic figure who captured the
> imagination of all Ireland as long as he was an outlaw; but
> when he sat down to make peace, he was seen by many in a
> much different light. As he signed the Irish Treaty of 1921
> on Britain's behalf, Lord Birkenhead remarked to Collins, "I
> may have signed my death-warrant tonight"; to which
> Collins replied, "I may have signed my actual death-
> warrant." Eight months later Michael Collins lay dead on an
> Irish roadway with a bullet through his head.

In the civil war that followed the peace Collins brought home, far more Irish would die than in the three years of the war of independence. The revolution devours its children.

About the Irish rebellion, it needs be said: terror succeeded. The ambushes and assassinations of police, soldiers, and collaborators brought savage reprisals by the Black-and-Tans, the public reaction to which tore away the last bonds of Irish loyalty to king and country. T. E. Lawrence, who had led the Arab uprisings against the Turks in the Great War, had warned his countrymen: "You can't make war upon rebellion."

To imperial diehards this was the counsel of defeat. Sir Henry Wilson decried the Anglo-Irish Treaty as a "cowardly surrender to the pistol" and declared the empire "doomed." "We must either clear out or govern." In June 1922, Sir Henry was assassinated by IRA gunmen. They were apprehended and hanged, but, by now, Ireland was lost to the empire.

Yet Wilson was right. If the British lacked the ruthlessness to crush a rebellion, the empire was doomed. Rebels everywhere took heart from the IRA victory. Many would adopt its tactics. What the Irish war had shown was that terror triggers reprisals, which attract sympathy and new recruits to the rebellion. Once the British concluded they had lost the loyalty of the Irish, they lost the will to fight on or to hold on to Ireland—and let go. James describes the bewilderment of veterans of the Somme in coping with the flying squads of IRA gunmen:

> Urban and guerrilla warfare was still a novelty in 1919. Its rules perplexed soldiers used to being able to recognize their opponents and led to a widespread feeling of impotent rage. This was expressed by General Sir Nevill Macready in his memoirs: "The British Government never recognized the term 'guerrilla warfare,'" he wrote. "Had they done so the task of the soldier would have been infinitely easier." He could, for instance, have shot every man found armed but not in uniform.

One sees today in the faces and conduct of Israeli soldiers, forced to deal with a rebellious Palestinian people who hate them, the same impotent rage felt by the British veterans of the Western Front.

TERROR OUT OF ZION

By 1945, the Jewish resistance in Palestine had begun to use terror tactics. The Stern Gang specialized in assassinations. In 1944, the gang gunned down British minister of state, Edward Lord Moyne, in Cairo. In his eulogy in the House of Commons, Churchill expressed his revulsion:

> A shameful crime has shocked the world and affected none more strongly than those like myself who, in the past, have been consistent friends of the Jews and constant architects of their future. If our dreams for Zionism should be dissolved in the smoke of revolvers of assassins and if our efforts for its future should provoke a new wave of banditry worthy of the Nazi Germans, many persons like myself will have to reconsider the position we have maintained so firmly for such a long time.

Chairman Chaim Weizmann of the British Zionist Federation echoed Churchill: "In the eyes of all men of goodwill, our movement is sinking to the level of gangsterism." Weizman's condemnation came a month before what French author Dominique Lapierre describes as the "first massive terrorist political action in modern history."

The Irgun had been formed in 1945 to force the expulsion of the British from Palestine. It initially restricted itself to destroying property, but, as Fromkin writes, "terrorism generates its own momentum, and before long the killing becomes deliberate."

On July 22, 1946, after a phoned warning to which no one paid heed, Irgun agents ignited seven milk cans containing 350 kilos of TNT inside the headquarters of the British Mandate for Palestine, the King David Hotel. Ninety-one Brits, Arabs, and Jews were killed and forty-six injured in the explosion.

In April 1948, a month before Israel declared independence, the Irgun and Stern Gang attacked the village of Deir Yassin on the road to Jerusalem. The Arabs in Deir Yassin were peaceful and lived on friendly terms with their Jewish neighbors. What occurred there was a massacre. Children were murdered. Pregnant women had their bellies slit open. Bodies were dumped into the village well. The atrocity at Deir Yassin enraged David Ben Gurion and gave him the moral authority to crush the Irgun. He ordered the Haganah, the Israeli army, to attack the *Altalena,* the ship the Irgun was using to bring Jewish refugees to Palestine. Yet Zionist terror had worked.

Because of the Irgun massacre at Deir Yassin, six hundred thousand Arabs fled the Palestinian territories the UN had set aside for a Jewish state, ensuring a Jewish majority in the new nation. "Though terror alone did not create the State of Israel," writes Michael Ignatieff of the Kennedy School of Government at Harvard, "terror was instrumental and terror worked." The Irgun, writes Fromkin,

> . . . played a big part in getting the British to withdraw. Its ingenuity lay in using an opponent's own strength against him. It was sort of jujitsu. First the adversary was made to be afraid, and then, predictably, he would react to his fear by increasing the bulk of his strength, and then the sheer weight of the bulk would drag him down.

Six months after Israel's declaration of statehood, the Stern Gang assassinated Count Bernadotte, the Swedish UN mediator who had been sent to Palestine to resolve the war.

With a state of their own, Israelis would deal with Arab terrorism far more ruthlessly than the British had dealt with theirs. In October of 1953, after Arab infiltrators murdered a young Israeli woman, Susan Kanias, and her two small children, Israel sent a commando unit into the village of Kibya. The commandos blew up the buildings in which terrified Palestinian women and children were hiding, killing sixty-nine.

The leader of that commando unit? Ariel Sharon, a future prime minister. The leader of the Stern Gang? Yitzhak Shamir, a future prime minister. The leader of the Irgun? Menachem Begin, a future prime minister. In both storied uprisings of the twentieth century, the Irish and Israeli wars of independence, terrorism was used, and those who used it are today national heroes in the pantheons of their people.

THE BATTLE OF ALGIERS

Seeing how the Zionists had driven the British out of Palestine, the Arabs and Berbers of the Algerian FLN adopted the same tactics, planting bombs in markets and movie theaters. Writes UPI's Martin Walker:

> The National Liberation Front of Algeria fought French rule with a ruthless terror campaign, using Arab women dressed as fashionable young Frenchwomen, to place bombs in cafes, dancehalls, and cinemas. The French fought back ferociously, and in the battle of Algiers, General Jacques Massu's battalion of paratroopers broke the FLN network in the casbah, or Arab quarter, with ruthless interrogations and the widespread use of torture.

Massu won the Battle of Algiers, but the means he used ensured France's defeat in the war. Reports of reprisals and torture by the paras disgusted public opinion, brought down governments, and undermined the will to fight. In 1958, General DeGaulle returned to power and began the negotiations that led to independence in 1962. Half a million Algerians and French died in the eight-year war, a far longer and bloodier struggle than the Irish and Israeli wars of independence put together.

For France, the key to victory was not to lose the loyalty of the Arab population. But that loyalty began to die in Algerian hearts when Paris replaced French Muslim troops in Algeria with French European troops, and started to treat all Berbers and Arabs as potential suspects. Racial profiling, while a successful tactic, proved a disastrous strategy. By treating the French *"pied noirs"* differently from the Arabs, France made the Algerian Arabs realize they were a separate people. As more and more Arabs identified with the cause of independence and joined the rebellion, the FLN escalated to guerrilla war and appealed to a world by now converted to anti-colonialism from the high ground that this was not a civil war but a people's war of national liberation. Writes Fromkin:

> From the French point of view all had become hopeless; for no amount of force can keep an unwilling population indefinitely in subjugation. Even though the FLN had written the script, the French, with suicidal logic, went ahead to play the role for which they had been cast.

To Ignatieff, the lesson of the battle of Algiers is not that "terror never works" but that "indiscriminately brutal acts of counterterror rarely succeed."

WAR TERROR

Churchill described the American Civil War as the last war fought between gentlemen. But the authors of two recent books on the South and secession, Charles Adams and Thomas DiLorenzo, describe a war different from the one of which Churchill wrote so glowingly.

According to author Adams, in 1861, every West Point graduate was familiar with the rules of conduct for fighting a just war that had existed since the Middle Ages, and prohibited making war on civilians. The U.S. Army commander, General Halleck, had written his famous Order No. 12, outlawing the wanton destruction of private property:

> The inevitable consequences are universal pillage and a total relaxation of discipline; the loss of private property, and the violation of individual rights . . . and the ordinary peaceful and noncombatants are converted into bitter and implacable enemies. The system is, therefore, regarded as both impolitic and unjust, and is coming into general disuse among the most civilized nations.

To British military historian B. H. Liddell Hart, the code of civilized warfare in Europe for two hundred years was first broken by Lincoln with his policy of directing the destruction of civilian life in the South. Lincoln's "policy was in many ways the prototype of modern total war," wrote Hart.

Generals Sherman and Sheridan were first to cross the forbidden frontier. What Sherman did with the burning of Atlanta and in his march to the sea, what Sheridan did with the burning of the Shenandoah, was to inflict suffering on the women and children Confederate soldiers had left behind. Yet Lincoln never objected. Rather, he conveyed to Sheridan the "thanks of the Nation and my own personal admiration and gratitude . . ."

While Lincoln was hailing Sheridan, a sergeant in Sheridan's army had another view of what he and his fellow soldiers were doing to the valley towns of Dayton, Harrisonburg, and Bridgewater:

> The whole country around is wrapped in flames, the heavens are aglow with the light therefrom . . . such mourning, such lamentations, such crying and pleading for mercy I never saw nor never want to see again, some were wild, crazy mad,

some cry for help while others would throw their arms around Yankee soldiers and implore mercy.

Another Union officer, writes DiLorenzo, described the refugees of Sheridan's fires thus: "Hundreds of nearly starving people are going north. Our trains are crowded with them. They line the wayside. Hundreds more are coming . . . so stripped of food that I cannot imagine how they escaped starvation."

Grant told Sheridan to make such a wasteland of the Shenandoah that a crow flying over the valley would have to carry its own rations. These Union generals made the slaughter of farm animals, the burning of barns and crops, the looting and torching of cities, legitimate acts of war, leaving the civilians, in Sherman's words, with only their eyes to weep with.

According to Adams, Sherman, given command by President Grant of the army in the Plains wars against the Indians, sent the White House a letter that gave meaning to his dictum "War is hell": "We must act with vindictive earnestness against the Sioux, even to their extermination, men, women, and children. Nothing else will reach the root of this case."

Sheridan, sent out to do the fighting, would conclude: "The only good Indians I ever saw were dead." By life's end, "Uncle Billy" Sherman would call for a massacre of all American Indians as the "final solution to the Indian problem," a phrase that would resonate in the twentieth century.

Ending slavery, however, and reuniting the Union, gave to William Tecumseh Sherman retrospective absolution for the war crimes he knew full well he had committed: "[I]n the beginning, I, too, had the old West Point notion that pillage was a capital crime, and punished it by shooting."

Not all Union generals were Sheridans and Shermans. As Adams writes, Union general Don Carlos Buell resigned from the army in protest: "I believe the policy and means with which the war was being prosecuted were discreditable to the nation and a stain on civilization." The hero of Little Round Top, Joshua Chamberlain, was also disgusted. He wrote his wife in 1864: "I am willing to fight men in arms, but not *babes in arms.*"

But terror tactics succeeded, and Sherman's is now a famous name while Buell's is forgotten.

IN WORLD WAR II, perhaps the greatest single act of Allied war terror was the fire-bombing of "the Florence of the Elbe." An undefended city of 630,000, in February of 1945, Dresden was packed with hundreds of thousands of desperate refugees fleeing the Red Army.

As the *Washington Post*'s Ken Ringle wrote on the fiftieth anniversary of the raid, "if any one person can be blamed for the tragedy at Dresden, it appears to have been Churchill."

Before leaving for Yalta, Churchill ordered Operation Thunderclap, the use of Allied air power to "de-house" German civilians to make them refugees so they would clog the roads over which German soldiers had to move to stop the winter offensive of the Red Army. It was British Air Marshal Arthur "Bomber" Harris who put Dresden on the target list. As Ringle describes the first night of the raid, 770 Lancaster bombers arrived over Dresden around ten p.m. In two waves three hours apart, 650,000 incendiary bombs rained down on Dresden's narrow streets and baroque buildings, together with another 1,474 tons of high explosives.

The morning after the Lancasters struck, five hundred American B-17s arrived over Dresden in two waves, with three hundred fighter escorts to strafe fleeing survivors.

The fires burned for seven days. More than 1,600 acres of the city were devastated (compared to 100 acres burned in the German raid on Coventry) and melting streets burned the shoes off those attempting to flee. Cars untouched by fire burst into flames just from the heat. Thousands sought refuge in cellars where they died, robbed of oxygen by the flames, before the buildings above them collapsed.

Novelist Kurt Vonnegut, one of twenty-six thousand Allied prisoners of war in Dresden who helped clean up after the attack, remembers tunneling into the ruins to find the dead sitting upright in what he would describe in *Slaughterhouse-Five* as "corpse mines." Floating in the static water tanks were the boiled bodies of hundreds more.

Estimates of the dead in the Dresden firestorm run from 35,000 to 250,000. Even Churchill acknowledged what it had all been about: "It seems to me that the moment has come when the question of bombing of German cities *simply for the sake of increasing the terror, though under other pretexts,* should be reviewed." (emphasis added)

BEGUN BY THE British, air terror was perfected by the Americans. A few weeks after Dresden, General Curtis LeMay's B-29s went into action over Tokyo. Nicholas von Hoffman describes what happened:

> On March 9, 1945, 179 American bombers, armed with incendiary bombs intended to torch the wood-and-paper Japanese capital appeared over Tokyo, a city with population density of 135,000 per square mile. All went according to plan. Tokyo was consumed by fire so ferocious that the heat boiled the water in the lakes and ponds, cooking those who fled to safety there like human lobsters. Official American figures put the death toll for that night's raid at 87,000 people. Nobody knows what the true number is.

What is the moral difference between burning alive 87,000 people with incendiary bombs from five miles up—and burning to death 187 Czechs in a barn at Lidice?

In the documentary *Fog of War,* former Defense Secretary Robert McNamara, who worked with Lemay on the plans to incinerate Japanese cities, says the general came to the conclusion that "if we'd lost, we'd be prosecuted as war criminals; and I think he was right. Lemay, and I, were acting like war criminals."

Six months after Tokyo, Harry Truman ordered atom bombs dropped on Hiroshima and Nagasaki, killing an estimated eighty thousand in the first strike on August 6 and forty thousand in the second on August 9. Truman dropped the bombs to force Japan to surrender. Had we not, it is said, half a million U.S. soldiers, sailors, and airmen might have died in the planned invasion of the Home Islands. Asked if he agonized over the decision to burn alive a hundred thousand Japanese civilians, Truman replied: "I never gave it a second thought."

If war terror is the deliberate slaughter of noncombatants, to break the will of an enemy, were not Dresden, Tokyo, Hiroshima, and Nagasaki war terror on a monumental scale?

SUICIDE BOMBERS

If Rimbaud's time was "the time of the assassins," ours is the time of the terrorist, from Mohammed Atta and his eighteen accomplices to the suicide bombers of Jerusalem. Yet famous suicides have been canonized in legend and myth.

In the Old Testament, the warrior-hero Samson, blinded by his own folly, used his strength to move the pillars and bring the roof of the temple down on the Philistines. Kamikaze pilots gave up their lives for Japan and the emperor to cripple and sink U.S. warships moving toward the Home Islands. Even today the Japanese honor their memory. But the most famous act of collective suicide in the annals of war occurred almost two thousand years ago.

In A.D. 73, nine hundred of the Jewish zealots who had risen against Rome had retreated into the fortress of Masada, a thousand feet above the desert floor near the Dead Sea. As the Romans prepared to scale the cliffs, the defenders resolved not to be taken alive, and committed mass suicide. Two women and three children survived. Atop Masada today, the soldiers of Israeli armored divisions take their oath of allegiance.

Was Masada a moral act? Or was it a Jonestown? Did all the women and children there assent to their deaths? Or did some resist and have to be put to death? Would the zealots who slew their own wives and children have balked at blowing up the wives and children of the Roman soldiers?

THE CANONIZATION OF TERRORISTS

While we condemn terror, it will be used again and again. For terror often triumphs. Sherman and the Union armies crushed the South, setting it back a century. But they were victorious, they freed the slaves, and they are lionized. Hiroshima and Nagasaki convinced the emperor that unconditional surrender was preferable to the alternative. The IRA, the Irgun, the Stern Gang, the Viet Minh, the FLN, the Mau Mau, the ANC all used terror and all prevailed. And innocent blood shed in the revolution is quickly washed away in the exhilaration of victory.

The FLN's Ben Bella became the first president of Algeria. Jomo Kenyatta, Kikiyu leader of the Mau Mau, became the father of his country, Kenya, and the "grand old man" of Africa. Yitzhak Shamir became prime minister, as had Menachem Begin, his predecessor, who would go on to win the Nobel Prize for Peace. So would Nelson Mandela, who went to prison in 1964 for the bombing of trains and whose ANC was famous for "necklacing" enemies, i.e., cutting off their arms and draping a gas-filled tire around their necks, which was set ablaze to the laughter of the mob. Today, Mandela is perhaps the most respected political figure on earth. Arafat, too, shares a Nobel Prize for Peace and aspires to be the first president of Palestine.

The body of the Communist state terrorist Ho Chi Minh is honored in Hanoi. Saigon is now Ho Chi Minh City. The remains of the tyrant responsible for the deaths of perhaps 30 million Chinese lie in a crystal sarcophagus in Tiananmen Square. The waxen body of Lenin, the archterrorist and the brother of the terrorist who attempted to assassinate Czar Alexander III, lies in a mausoleum in the heart of Red Square.

D. W. Griffith's classic *Birth of a Nation* portrayed the Klan as gallant and heroic. Geronimo, the Indian chief who murdered pioneer women and children, was lionized in a Hollywood film. *Michael Collins* is the title of a film starring Liam Neeson, in which Collins is portrayed as an Irish hero fighting for freedom. In *State of Siege,* the 1973 film based on the kidnapping and murder of a U.S. aid official in Uruguay, his Tupamaro executioners are portrayed as sensitive and principled.

Terrorism often succeeded in the twentieth century, and, when it did, the ex-terrorists achieved power, glory, and immortality, with streets, towns, and cities named for them. And America today recognizes every regime to come out of these wars where terrorism was a common tactic.

Indeed, consider two home-grown American terrorists.

In August 1831, in the Tidewater area of Virginia, Nat Turner led a slave rebellion which, before it ended with sixteen convicted and hanged, and Turner hanged and skinned, women, children, and babies were clubbed, stabbed, or axed to death.

In *The Americans: A Social History of the United States,* J. C. Furnas described Turner as a "psychotic," "the poor twisted creature," "a paranoid slave preacher and cunjur man [who] led his superstition-fuddled followers to kill fifty-five whites or all sexes and ages in an aimless terrorizing of Southhampton County in the southeastern corner of Virginia."

This was the judgment of history until 1966, when William Styron published *The Confessions of Nat Turner,* a "meditation on history" about the August days when Turner's band of slaves tried to butcher every white woman and child in a thirty-mile swath from Turner's farm to the county seat of Jerusalem.

Styron, wrote Clifton Fadiman of Random House, has "dramatized the intermingled miseries, frustrations—and hopes—which caused this extraordinary black man to rise up out of the early mists of our history and strike down those who held his people in bondage.

"The dynamic interplay of Nat Turner's desperate, obsessed mind and the obdurate, incomprehensible social system against which he pits that mind's full resources," Fadiman goes on, "all this is handled not only with ingenuity but with a kind of brooding compassion." A compassion, one notes, Nat and his crazed killers never showed the terrified women and children they slaughtered. But modernity often forgives the sins of terrorists because of the nobility of the cause they served. *The Confessions of Nat Turner* was a Book of the Month Club selection and winner of the Pulitzer Prize.

John Brown, too, qualifies as an American revolutionary terrorist. In "Bleeding Kansas," he murdered Southerners in reprisal for the killing of Northerners. Then he came east to start a slaves' rebellion. In his conspiracy, Brown was aided by the men author Otto Scott calls "the Secret Six," including Ralph Waldo Emerson. With their money, Brown acquired carbines, pistols, spears, pikes, cartridges, powder, and percussion caps to arm the slaves he believed would rise up when he seized the arsenal at Harper's Ferry.

After taking hostages, Brown fought a brief battle with U.S. Marines led by Colonel Robert E. Lee. Captured, he was hanged under the watchful eye of a cadet battery of the Virginia Military Institute under the command of professor of artillery Major Thomas J. Jackson. Jackson wrote to his wife that Brown behaved on the scaffold "with unflinching firmness." On the day of Brown's execution, bells tolled in the North. Church services and public meetings were held to glorify his deeds and sanctify his cause, the abolition of slavery. He would become a martyr and, singing the battle hymn—"John Brown's body lies a'mouldering in the grave / But his soul goes marching on"—Union troops invaded and ravaged the South. Stephen Vincent Benét's epic poem is titled *John Brown's Body*.

One man's terrorist is another man's freedom fighter.

WHY TERRORISM SUCCEEDS—AND FAILS

Empires, republics, dictators, rebels, revolutionaries, anarchists have all used terror, and terrorism has helped to win wars, consolidate tyranny, expel colonial powers, and advance national independence. In the twentieth century, revolutionary terror has both succeeded and failed.

The IRA, Irgun, Viet Minh, Algerian FLN, ZANU and ZAPU in Rhodesia, the ANC in South Africa, Hezbollah in Lebanon, used terrorist tactics and succeeded in expelling the ruling power. Filipino Huks and the Malay guerrillas of the MCP, Italy's Red Brigades, Germany's Baader-Meinhoff Gang, the Basque ETA, the Tupamaros in Uruguay, Shining Path in Peru, the Puerto Rican FALN, the Weathermen, and Black Panthers all failed. Why?

Because in Ireland, Palestine, Indochina, Algeria, Rhodesia, South Africa, and Lebanon, the rebellions had put down roots among the people. Imperial powers that violate Jefferson's dictum that all just powers arise from the consent of the governed seem most vulnerable in our modern era.

A government that reflects the will of the people can, with patience and perseverance, defeat movements that resort to terror tactics. And, while democracies are the societies most vulnerable to terror attacks, they are also, due to their openness and freedom, the most resilient in fighting back. For they are sustained by the people.

Crucial to defeating a terrorist movement is the way a government responds. As the ultimate battle is for hearts and minds, an overreaction can be fatal. Britain's response to the Easter Rising—hanging the rebel leaders—and France's response to FLN terror—the roundups, reprisals, and torture—advanced the revolution. Massu's victory in the Battle of Algiers is a textbook case of an imperial power winning a battle and losing the war.

Terrorists are picadores and matadors. They prick the bull until it bleeds and is blinded by rage, then they snap the red cape of bloody terror in its face. The bull charges again and again until, exhausted, it can charge no more. Then the matador, though smaller and weaker, drives the sword into the soft spot between the shoulder blades of the bull. For the bull has failed to understand that the snapping cape was but a provocation to goad it into attacking and exhausting itself for the kill.

But this is sobering news for the American imperium. For while the United States is a republic, autocracy is a better description of the regimes we support in the Middle East and Central Asia. Our dominance of that region and our reflexive support of Israel are universally resented. Also, to devout Muslims, as to devout Christians, our popular culture appears as decadent and toxic. Muslims look on our cultural exports the way patriotic Chinese regarded Britain's imposition of the opium trade on their people.

Our problem in this vast region is that tens of millions of Arab and Islamic peoples have now concluded they want us out, the Israelis gone, and pro-Western autocrats overthrown. And growing numbers are willing to die to bring this about. Support for Osama is widespread. Support for the Palestinian intifada is universal. Islamists who fight us in the name of these goals are swimming with a powerful current.

Moreover, while Arab armies have rarely defeated a Western army, Arab and Islamic revolutions that employ terror tactics against Westerners have rarely failed. They effected the ouster of the French from Algeria, the British from Palestine, the United States from Beirut, the Israelis from Lebanon, the Soviets from Afghanistan. Why should Islamic revolutionaries not think the same can be done to the Americans in Iraq and to the kings, sultans, and sheiks of Morocco, Jordan, Saudi Arabia, Oman, and Kuwait?

And if Iraqi insurgents and Islamic warriors are willing to die indefinitely to drive us out of that country and their world, the probability is that they will one day succeed.

FIVE

CROUCHING TIGER, HIDDEN DRAGON

China is a sleeping giant. Let it sleep, for when it awakes it will shake the world.

—Napoleon Bonaparte

As America fights the small wars of democratic imperialism in the Near and Middle East, in the Far East, a power is rising that may prove a far greater challenge to the United States in the twenty-first century. In Asia, China is the rising power, America the receding one.

But, in coming to terms with China, Americans should recall their own history. For between our past and China's present there are parallels.

Before 1900, U.S. history is the story of a relentless and often ruthless drive to expel the French, British, Mexicans, Russians, and Spanish from our country and continent and establish U.S. hegemony over the hemisphere, then over the Pacific all the way to the coast of China.

Between 1754 and 1763, Americans helped push the French back over the Alleghenies, then out of North America. In 1781, we drove the British out. In 1810, Madison seized West Florida while Spain and Britain were preoccupied with Napoleon. In 1812, egged on by "war hawks" like Calhoun and Clay, Madison tried to grab British Canada. In 1818, Jackson took Florida in a lightning raid, and Secretary of State John Quincy Adams swindled Madrid out of the peninsula.

In 1823, Monroe told Europe that its days of collecting colonies in the Americas were over. In 1836, we tore Texas from Mexico. In 1845, Tyler annexed Texas. When an enraged Santa Anna tried to reclaim his lost province, Polk took the northern half of his country. In 1865, Johnson sent General Sheridan and a Union Army to the Rio Grande to persuade Napoleon III to get his army out of Mexico. In 1867, Seward took Alaska off the czar's hands, then annexed Midway.

In 1898, McKinley evicted Spain from Cuba and annexed Puerto Rico, Hawaii, Guam, and the Philippines. It took three years to subdue the Filipino resistance. And so, as the last of the imperial powers, we arrived at the coast of China. There, we declared an Open Door and marched with the Europeans and Japanese to Peking to crush the Boxer Rebellion of 1900.

In 1945, the United States reduced the Japanese empire to ashes to become the hegemonic power in Asia. This was the apex of U.S. power. But more swiftly than the American tide had risen, it began to recede. In 1949, the United States suffered a historic disaster with the loss of China to communism, though the way Mao saw it, China had at last "stood up."

Now, the Chinese tide began to rise. The Maoists quickly consolidated Manchuria and invaded Tibet.

In June of 1950, North Korea invaded the South and almost drove the Americans off the peninsula. MacArthur counterattacked at Inchon, destroyed the North Korean army, and drove to the Yalu. Mao intervened massively to preserve his North Korean buffer state. The cost to China? A million dead. An armistice was struck in 1953.

In 1959, the Tibetans rose up against the Han Chinese and Maoist rule, and an estimated 1.2 million perished over a dozen years, with six thousand monasteries, temples, and cultural and historic buildings and their contents destroyed.

In 1962, China attacked India and annexed the Aksai Chin region of Kashmir. In 1969, she clashed with Russia over islands in the Amur and Ussuri Rivers. In 1974, China seized the Paracels from an embattled South Vietnam. In 1979, she fought Vietnam over control of Cambodia. In 1992, she asserted sovereignty over the Paracel and Spratly island chains, and in, 1994–95, occupied Mischief Reef inside the exclusive economic zone of the Philippines. The Chinese now have a naval base there. In 1998, she took back control of Hong Kong after 150 years of British rule. Macau, under Portuguese sovereignty since 1887, passed to Beijing in 1999.

China has now begun to displace U.S. influence in Thailand and Burma. She has been an enabler of both the Pakistani and North Korean nuclear and missile programs and has begun to extend her influence westward. With Russia, Kazakhstan, Kyrgyzstan and Tajikistan, China has formed the Shanghai Cooperation Group to counter U.S. strategic penetration of Central Asia and to reconstruct the Silk Road to the oil of the Caspian and Near East.

With a growth rate of 8 percent, a capable and energetic population of 1.3 billion, the silent allegiance of millions of "overseas Chinese" from Singapore to San Francisco, a history of having been the world's foremost civilization and Middle Kingdom between heaven and earth, China is determined to become again the first power on earth.

What America and China must avoid is the fate of Wilhelmine Germany and the Britain of George V, when the world's rising power and receding power stumbled into a thirty-year war that destroyed both.

THE MATURATION OF MAOIST CHINA

Not until the death of Mao in 1976 did the madness of his revolution burn itself out in the Great Proletarian Cultural Revolution. During that pogrom, scores of thousands of intellectuals were mobbed, murdered, or sent to the countryside to be "reeducated."

But when the Great Helmsman passed away, the fever passed. Under the guidance of Chou En-lai and Deng Xiaoping, China set Marxist dogma aside and began to take the capitalist road.

"It does not matter whether the cat is black or white," said Deng, "as long as it catches mice." American, Japanese, and European businessmen were invited in to build factories to exploit the inexhaustible pool of Chinese labor and to produce for export to the world. China is not the same nation it was when Air Force One brought Richard Nixon to Beijing in 1972.

The Beijing regime remains authoritarian and brutal. It still forces abortions on women who defy its edicts about the number of children they may bear. Its leaders continue to suppress religious and political dissent, to treat the nationalists and separatists of Tibet and Xinjiang as terrorists, and to encroach upon the border territories Beijing regards as eternally Chinese. China still executes more "criminals" than any other regime. But China is today as different from Mao's China as Putin's Russia is from Stalin's Russia. While Mao risked war with the United States in 1950 and with the Soviet Union in 1969, since his death, Beijing has avoided any clash with a great power. China's vision is to displace U.S. hegemony in Asia and become the first power on earth. Her obsession is Taiwan.

CHINA'S AMBITIONS, TO be discovered in the statements of her military and in her actions, appear as follows:

• Convert her two hundred-mile Exclusive Economic Zone and the skies above into national territory that no nation's planes or vessels may transit without permission. Thus, the repeated interference with U.S. planes and ships.
• Assert sovereignty over the Spratlys and all submerged reefs and uninhabited islands in the South China Sea and extend her territorial waters one thousand miles south to Indonesia and the Philippines. Foreign vessels, including U.S. warships, would tra-

verse these waters at the sufferance of Beijing. Ultimate objective: convert the South China Sea into a Chinese Chesapeake Bay.

• Effect the slow detachment of Siberia from Moscow by moving emigrants across the Amur and Ussuri Rivers into these vast depopulated lands that belonged to China before 1860, even as Mexicans are moving back into former Mexican territories in the American Southwest.

• Expel U.S. bases from Kazakhstan, Kyrgyzstan, and Tajikistan and bring the ex-Soviet republics neighboring China into Beijing's orbit.

• Restore Taiwan to Beijing, by force if necessary. This would add mightily to China's prestige and economic power and put her air and naval forces on an unsinkable aircraft carrier athwart Japan's oil lifeline. The deployment of five hundred missiles opposite Taiwan can have but two purposes: Intimidate Taipei into surrendering its autonomy, or attack and break Taiwan before the United States can intervene.

• Ultimately, eject U.S. power from the Western Pacific back to Hawaii, Midway, and Guam. "[As for the United States,] for a relatively long time it will be absolutely necessary that we quietly nurse our sense of vengeance. . . . We must conceal our abilities and bide our time." So the vice commandant of China's Academy of Military Sciences was quoted in 1996.

Other strategists have been quoted as saying that by 2020, China intends to dominate the Western Pacific "out to the second island chain." This would include not only Taiwan, but Japan and the Philippines.

THE BONE IN BEIJING'S THROAT

During the Cold War, Khrushchev referred to West Berlin, a free city encircled by the Red Army, as the "bone in our throat." Taiwan is the bone in Beijing's throat. The regime and people believe Taiwan is part of China and will fight rather than lose the island forever. Should Taipei declare independence, China has made clear it will bring Taiwan back the way Lincoln brought the South back to the Union.

Yet, Beijing's claim to the island that China ruled for only four years in the twentieth century is by no means unchallengeable.

China ceded Formosa to Japan at the end of the Sino-Japanese War in 1895, and Tokyo ruled the island for half a century until her defeat in 1945. America turned Formosa over to its ally Chiang Kai-shek. But with the triumph of Mao's armies in 1949, Chiang and two million Nationalists fled to Formosa. There they established the Republic of China on Taiwan. The U.S. 7th Fleet protected the island.

Chiang ruled Taiwan until his death and was succeeded by his son. Under both men and their successors, Taiwan has evolved into a robust free-market economy, one of the "tigers of Asia." It has become a full-fledged democracy where native Taiwanese, 90 percent of the population, have grown increasingly independent and unwilling to submit to Beijing's rule.

For China, however, Taiwan's return is a matter of honor. No declaration of independence would be accepted, any more than the secession of South Carolina would have been accepted by Andrew Jackson.

THE U.S. POSITION ON TAIWAN

The U.S. position on Taiwan is ambiguous.

In the 1950s Eisenhower provided the Nationalists with air-to-air missiles that enabled them to sweep Chinese MIGs from the skies over the strait. He sent eight-inch howitzers to Quemoy and Matsu when those tiny islands were under fire from the mainland. The howitzers were capable of firing nuclear shells. The Maoists got the message. The shelling ceased.

For two decades after the triumph of Mao's revolution, China and the United States remained isolated from one another. But in 1972, Nixon made his historic journey to Peking. And in the Shanghai Communique, negotiated by Henry Kissinger, the United States addressed the "crucial question obstructing the normalization of relations":

> The United States acknowledges that all Chinese on either side of the Taiwan Strait maintain there is but one China and that Taiwan is a part of China. The United States Government does not challenge that position. It reaffirms its interest in a peaceful resolution of the Taiwan question by the Chinese themselves. With this prospect in mind, it affirms the ultimate objective of the withdrawal of all U.S. forces and military installations from Taiwan. In the meantime, it will progressively reduce its forces and military installations on Taiwan as the tension in the area diminishes.

The communique said nothing about the Taiwanese people, the vast majority on the island, few of whom had any desire to be ruled by Beijing. Yet, as long as he remained in office, Nixon maintained the U.S. embassy in Taipei and the treaty commitment to defend the Republic of China.

Jimmy Carter, however, severed diplomatic relations with Taiwan, terminated the security treaty, and recognized the People's Republic as the sole legitimate government of China. A firestorm ensued, and Congress passed the Taiwan Relations Act. The TRA mandates a U.S. policy "to maintain the capacity of the United States to resist any resort by force or other forms of coercion that would jeopardize the security, or the social or economic system, of the people of Taiwan."

Reagan reaffirmed the Shanghai Communique—that Taiwan was a part of China—and agreed to cut back arms sales to the island. In a Joint Communique in 1982, the United States declared that it

> . . . does not seek to carry-out a long-term policy of arms sales to Taiwan, that its arms sales to Taiwan will not ex-

ceed, either in qualitative or in quantitative terms, the level of those supplies in recent years . . . and that it intends to reduce gradually its sales of arms to Taiwan, leading over a period of time to a final resolution.

While this writer, among others, opposed the Shanghai Communique and the more far-reaching Carter and Reagan concessions, that does alter reality. The pass has been sold. The cat cannot be walked back. The day when Taiwan might have declared independence with U.S. support is gone.

AFTER TIANANMEN SQUARE, U.S. policy toward Beijing began to stiffen. There was a cutoff in arms sales by the United States and the European Union. President George H. W. Bush sold F-16s to Taiwan. In 1996, when Beijing test-fired missiles toward Taiwan, Clinton ordered two carrier battle groups to the region to show American resolve.

During that crisis, a Chinese official told Chas Freeman, then a U.S. diplomat in China, that if Americans loved Los Angeles they had best not interfere. China, the official was warning the United States, might resort to nuclear weapons to effect the return of the island to the mainland. In that 1996 crisis, the rest of Asia stood aside as though it had no stake in a U.S.-China clash over Taiwan. In any confrontation with the mainland, Taiwan can expect help from no other quarter than the United States.

When Clinton visited China, he acceded to Beijing's demand that he recite the "three nos." There would be, Clinton said, *no* U.S. support for Taiwan's independence, *no* U.S. recognition of an independent Taiwan, and *no* U.S. endorsement of Taiwan's entry into any international organization.

Soon after Bush II took office, an EP-3 reconnaissance plane flying over the South China Sea was forced down on Hainan Island by a Chinese fighter pilot who crashed into it. Secretary of State

Powell apologized to the Chinese. But President Bush later blurted out, when asked whether America would use all her power to protect the island, that he would do "whatever it took to help Taiwan defend herself."

In 2003, a diplomatic clash occurred. In a fight for reelection, Taiwan's president Chen Shui-bian had a bill enacted calling for a referendum whereby the Taiwanese could vote to demand that Beijing remove the missiles on its side of the strait.

Beijing was enraged. PLA Major General Peng Guangqian was quoted as saying, "Taiwan leader Chen Shui-bian will be held responsible if a war breaks out across the strait, and separatists on the island will be treated the same way war criminals are dealt with elsewhere in the world."

During a visit to Washington by Premier Wen Jiabao, President Bush—in the sharpest language a president has ever used on a president of Taiwan—rebuked Chen for holding the referendum. Bush did not mention the five hundred missiles targeted on the island. Even the *Washington Post,* in an editorial titled "Mr. Bush's Kowtow," thought the president had gone too far in groveling before Beijing and lashing out at a friend for holding a peaceful referendum.

Looking back over the half century since Chiang's army fled the mainland, two realities emerge. America has been Taiwan's only true friend, and the U.S. commitment to the island grows weaker each decade.

THE BALANCE OF POWER

Is China a strategic threat as great as was the former Soviet Union in the Cold War? Certainly not yet. Moscow had an army and armored forces larger than the United States, a navy of submarines and surface ships that prowled the world's oceans, bombers and missiles that could have delivered thousands of nuclear warheads on American soil. China has nothing remotely comparable today.

Still, China is conducting the most rapid military buildup in Asia since Japan in the 1930s. Her power is growing, and Beijing could visit immense damage on U.S. bases and forces in the Far East. While we have one hundred thousand men and women under arms in the Asia-Pacific region, China has twenty-three times that number. In recent years, the PRC

- Has become the third nation to put a man in space.
- Has deployed twenty Dong Feng ICBMs that can hit Hawaii and the West Coast of the United States.
- Has run up the second largest military budget on earth, between \$50 and \$70 billion.
- Has conducted mock missile strikes on U.S. bases in Korea and Japan, using road-mobile CSS-5 missiles with a range of 1,300 miles, and silo-based CSS-2 missiles with a range of 1,900 miles. China seems to be warning that any attack on its forces by the 7th Fleet in a clash over Taiwan will be answered with counterstrikes on U.S. forces from South Korea to Guam.
- Has deployed over 500 DF-11 and DF-15 missiles across from Taiwan and plans to increase the number to 650. Both missiles are nuclear-capable and Taiwan is defenseless against them. This is the most daunting conventional missile threat in the world today. When Moscow attempted to intimidate Europe by targeting mobile SS-20s against NATO, Reagan responded by deploying Pershing and cruise missiles in Western Europe targeting the Warsaw Pact. Neither Taiwan nor the United States has made a comparable response to the Chinese missile buildup.
- Has acquired almost 300 Sukhoi Su-27 fighters and Su-30 fighter-bombers, the latter of which are to be equipped with supersonic antiship missiles with ranges up to 200 miles. These fourth-generation Russian fighters and fighter-bombers are more than a match for the badly outnumbered U.S. air superiority fighters currently based on Okinawa.

• Has purchased two Sovremenny-class Russian destroyers armed with supersonic Sunburn antiship missiles, designed by Moscow to sink Aegis cruisers and aircraft carriers, and twelve long-range Kilo-class diesel submarines with cruise missiles. China is also developing her own nuclear submarines. These vessels are being purchased with the carriers *Nimitz, Truman, Kennedy, Lincoln,* and *Reagan* in mind.

• Has purchased and copied the French Exocet antiship missile.

• Is developing laser weapons to blind U.S. satellites, and radar satellites to see through clouds to keep U.S. ships in her sights.

China appears to be buying the weapons to fight and win a naval war. And there is only one fleet out there. Richard D. Fisher, an expert on China's armed forces, warns of this scenario in a clash over Taiwan.

> The Chinese are not going to let us fight a Taiwan war in classic American style; we take twelve months to build up our overwhelming superiority. It will be a lightning war during a period of maximum U.S. diversion elsewhere. The few F-15s or even the single carrier battle group in Japan that we manage to send—provided they survive PLA special forces and 5th column attacks—will be overwhelmed by what the PLA is now buying. . . .

In the *Atlantic Monthly* in 1998, Paul Bracken, author of *Fire in the East,* wrote that America's forward engagement strategy in Asia, with its reliance on U.S. bases in South Korea and Japan, amounts to an "American Maginot Line" in a world of ballistic missiles.

Our bases in Asia, because they are naked to missile attack, he writes, are becoming hostages against U.S. action. Missile strikes against such "soft targets" could wreak havoc, destroying air fields, fuel dumps, and weapons and ammunition depots, rendering the bases useless.

"With forty-five missiles," writes Bracken, "China could virtually close Taiwan's ports, airfields, waterworks, and power plants, and destroy the oil-storage facilities of a nation that needs continual replenishment from the outside world." Thus, by firing one in ten of its missiles now targeted on Taiwan, Beijing could paralyze the island.

THE ENABLERS

Three nations have been indispensable to the modernization of China's arsenal: Russia, Israel, and the United States. From Russia, China is buying fourth-generation aircraft, destroyers, submarines, antiship missiles, and the technology for medium-range ballistic missiles.

According to *Washington Times* reporter Bill Gertz, China has bought from Belarus a chassis for the SS-20, the Soviet mobile missile whose sudden appearance in Eastern Europe impelled Reagan to deploy nuclear-armed Pershing and cruise missiles in Western Europe.

According to Gertz and Richard Fisher, Israel has provided China with

• Technology for battlefield laser weapons to shoot down missiles.

• Technology for the U.S. Patriot antimissile missile.

• AWACS technology, specifically the Phalcon phased-array radar.

• Lavi fighter technology now used in China's J-10 attack planes.

• STAR-1 cruise missile technology that incorporates U.S. stealth technology.

• The Python, an Israeli stepchild of the Sidewinder we gave to Tel Aviv. The Chinese fighters that intercepted our EP-3 over the South China Sea, one of which requested permission to shoot it down, were armed with Pythons.

• The Harpy drone that flies over enemy radar sites for hours until they lock on to the unmanned vehicle. Then the Harpy releases a bomb that follows the electronic radar waves back to the site and explodes.

"This [Harpy] is only an offensive weapon, and in the Taiwan Strait, is a particularly threatening device," says Fisher. "Its only purpose is to take out Taiwan's electric eyes and ears and to make Taiwan vulnerable to Chinese missiles and bombs." Fisher also notes that China has exploited information from the Patriot to enable its own missiles, opposite Taiwan, to evade Patriot interception. Our friends on Taiwan, staring across the strait at five hundred Chinese missiles, rely on Patriots for their survival.

Why does Israel sell U.S. weapons technology to a Chinese regime that could one day use it against democratic Taiwan? "When the customer is interested," writes Israeli scholar Yitzhak Shichor, "it [is] difficult for the Ministry of Defense to abort or prevent an Israeli arms transfer to whatever country for whatever reason."

The Pentagon has not protested publicly, and the administration and Congress appear too timid to confront the Israelis.

Where does China get the hard currency to pay Israel and Russia? From its huge trade surplus with the United States. When one considers that Beijing covets Russia's Far East, sends missile technology to Israel's enemies, menaces America's friends on Taiwan, and uses profits from its trade with us to buy weapons to target U.S. troops, ships, planes, and even our homeland, all three nations may one day rue their avarice.

In 1995, President Clinton lifted export restrictions on supercomputers to China. Beijing went on a "buying spree," snatching up forty-six. Believed purpose: Help China develop warheads for a mobile missile to give her the ability to strike the U.S. West Coast. So reported Jeffrey Gerth in a *New York Times* story to which the official reaction was yawning indifference.

HOW CHINA SEES US

But if the Chinese buildup appears alarming, even ominous to us, consider how we must appear to the Chinese.

When the Red Army went home from Europe, and the Soviet Union broke apart into fifteen nations, did the United States, victorious in the Cold War, dissolve its alliances and bring American troops home?

We did not. Rather, we seized upon our "unipolar moment" to extend NATO to Russia's borders, rubbing her face in her defeat. We then bombed her ancient ally, Serbia, for seventy-eight days, until Belgrade surrendered Kosovo province that had belonged to her for many centuries longer than South Carolina belonged to Mr. Lincoln's Union. During that bombing campaign, we sent a laser-guided missile into the communications and code room of the Chinese embassy in Belgrade. To many Chinese, this was no accident.

In the Gulf War, the Balkan wars of the 1990s, and Operation Iraqi Freedom, China saw a twenty-first-century military in action. The United States was able to see its enemies from space and attack them from drones, from planes invisible to radar, and from cruise missiles fired from ships and aircraft hundreds of miles away. U.S. fighter planes, tanks, artillery, satellites, carriers, and Stealth bombers are generations ahead of any weaponry China possesses.

Not only has the United States modernized its military since the end of the Cold War, it has strengthened its alliances with Japan, South Korea, the Philippines, Australia, and Thailand, occupied Afghanistan, restored its ties to Pakistan, formed a warm relationship with India, sent a warship to visit Vietnam, established bases in the old Soviet republics in Central Asia that border on China, created a partnership with Putin's Russia, and kept up satellite surveillance of China and air and naval reconnaissance off her coast. Clinton sent carriers to support Taiwan in 1996, and President Bush has pledged to do "whatever it took" to defend the island.

If the Chinese are denouncing U.S. "containment" and "American hegemony," do they not have a point? Is this not the stated goal of neoconservatives like William Kristol and Robert Kagan, when they write in the *New York Times,* "The United States must make it clear in both word and deed that we will contain China's strategic ambitions"? How would we react to Chinese bases in Mexico, Cuba, British Columbia, and Nova Scotia "to fight terrorism"? How would we respond to Chinese reconnaissance flights off our coasts and Chinese naval patrols in the Gulf of Mexico?

If China's hawks see in America a superpower resolved to encircle, contain, and deny her her rightful place in the sun, are they wrong? Is this not declared U.S. policy in the National Strategy Statement?

How would we have reacted had Great Britain in the nineteenth century published a national security strategy asserting a British right to prevent America from ever building fleets large and powerful enough to challenge Royal Navy dominance of the Atlantic and Caribbean?

According to John J. Tkacik Jr. of Heritage Foundation, a prominent Chinese scholar has charged in one of China's most respected foreign-policy journals that "the United States uses the fight against terrorism as an opportunity to pursue its hegemonic strategy and hegemonism is carried out under the cover of antiterrorism." Considering how we launched a preemptive war on Iraq to disarm it of weapons it did not have, does that scholar not have an argument?

If Beijing believes America intends the replacement of its regime with a democracy more receptive to U.S. "benevolent global hegemony," is it wrong? Is regime change in China not an end goal of President Bush's "world democratic revolution"?

U.S. SUPERIORITY

Rising powers move almost by nature to fill vacuums left by failing ones.

After World War I, the British and French Empires annexed the African, Middle Eastern, and South Pacific colonies of the Ottoman and German Empires. Japan annexed the kaiser's Pacific possessions north of the equator. With the defeat of Germany and Japan in 1945, and the collapse of the British and French Empires, Americans and Russians inherited their estates and the duties that went with them.

With the disintegration of the Soviet empire and breakup of the Soviet Union, China has begun to displace Russian power and influence in Asia and to assume Russia's role of balancing off U.S. power in Asia. This is natural and normal and no cause for hysteria.

While China's military buildup, especially the missiles targeted on Taiwan and U.S. bases, seems ominous, China presents no mortal threat. Beijing may have 3,400 military aircraft, but, as former Cato scholar Ivan Eland writes, only 100 are fourth-generation Russian fighters, while America's more than 3,000 aircraft are all fourth-generation (F-14s, F-15s, F-16s, F-18C/Ds) or fifth-generation (F-22s and F-18E/Fs). China's pilots lack the training and experience of U.S. pilots. To China's twenty Don Feng rockets targeted on America, the United States could put thousands of warheads on China, if, God forbid, a war between us went nuclear.

Where we spend $40 billion a year on research and development of modern weapons and $60 billion on procurement, China spends 10 percent of that. China has a few Kilo submarines and Sovremenny destroyers with antiship missiles, but they would not survive the first hours of battle with the U.S. Navy. They cannot hide from Aegis ships and spies in the sky and space and cannot stop precision-guided bombs and missiles. In nuclear weapons, bombers, ballistic missile submarines, ICBMs, aircraft carriers, helicopters, the U.S. military dwarfs China in the quality and quantity of its weapons. America can project power globally. China cannot.

CONFLICTING VIEWS

About China's growing power, there are two fundamental views. The benign one is rooted in the classical liberal belief in the salvific power of free markets and free trade. Briefly, it is this: The Chinese are like us in that they seek for themselves and their children what Americans want—freedom and the good life. Treated with respect, invited into the family of nations to compete fairly in the global economy, China's leadership will channel the nation's energies into peaceful pursuits. As China's standard of living rises, a middle class will emerge to press for greater freedom, property rights, and a rule of law. Gradually, this middle class will bring an end to the Communist Party's monopoly of power and create a bourgeois nation in the image of Japan and the other free nations of Asia. Thus we will have on the mainland an awakening giant with which the world can live in peace.

To realize this vision, the United States has been China's patron for decades. We supported World Bank loans to Beijing. We opened up our markets to Chinese goods by granting her Most Favored Nation (MFN) trade status. We escorted China into the World Trade Organization (WTO). We accepted a trade relationship in which America buys 10 percent of China's GDP, while China purchases two-tenths of 1 percent of ours. We take 30 percent of China's exports. China takes only 2.5 percent of ours. We permit tens of thousands of Chinese students to study in the United States. We have treated China's leaders as partners, even as friends.

This is the rationale for strategic engagement. Yes, China is ruled by ruthless men with long rap sheets, but compared with the regime of the Great Helmsman and the Gang of Four, China's leadership is benign and its behavior improving. U.S. policy is succeeding.

THE DARKER VIEW is this. China is ruled by men full of grievance and resentment over the humiliation of their country by the imperial powers from the Opium Wars to the Boxer Rebellion to the Japanese conquest to America's isolation of China until 1972. While China's rulers may have set aside Maoist ideology, they have replaced it with a virulent form of nationalism and racial chauvinism unseen since the 1930s. A revered Mao remains in his crystal sarcophagus in Tiananmen Square where China gave its answer to peaceful democratic reform in 1989. Beijing is resolved to be patient and avoid a clash with the United States until she is ready. She is biding her time and building her strength for the long struggle and final showdown with U.S. hegemony in Asia. And that showdown is almost certain to climax in a shooting war between us.

In this view, the Chinese are indeed like Americans, but more like the Americans of the late nineteenth century, who were full of patriotic and nationalistic fire to drive the Spaniards out of our hemisphere than the self-indulgent Americans of today.

What if the hawks are right? What if China's long-term goals involve the showdown and war that, some of her strategists and generals write, is inevitable? What will be said of the generation that gave Beijing a trillion dollars in trade surpluses with which to buy the weapons to dominate Asia and expel the Americans from the Western Pacific?

IS A WAR INEVITABLE?

As China is the one nation with the size, population, ideology, and power to contest the United States for hegemony in Asia, is war inevitable?

Answer: No more inevitable than was war between Germany and Great Britain in 1914. Neither today nor tomorrow does there appear to be any grievance between us so great as to justify war. War is possible. But whether it comes will depend upon China and upon us.

China today does not threaten any vital U.S. interest. Even her annexation of Taiwan would not threaten us. Should Beijing establish her hegemony over the South China Sea, how would that imperil the United States? If South Korea and Japan were to follow the Philippines and ask us to close our bases, how would that threaten our survival as a great, free, and independent republic? While it might mean the end of our Asian hegemony, it would not mean the end of the United States.

From the U.S. vantage point, war with China would be suicidal folly. There is no conceivable gain that could justify the risks such a conflict would entail for our country, or the damage that could be done.

From China's standpoint, war with America would be a disaster. China would lose a naval war in the strait and be humiliated. Should she attack U.S. bases in Japan, Korea, and Guam with chemical or nuclear weapons, terrible retaliation would follow. Beijing must know this. Even during the years of madness under Mao, China did not risk war over Taiwan. She fought only to keep us off the Yalu in Korea and only after British spies confirmed that Truman would not use on Chinese troops the atomic bombs he had used on Japanese cities.

However, because reason argues that a war between us would be folly for both does not mean war cannot come through miscalculation. Historians today question the wisdom of Britain's secret commitment to go to war against the kaiser's Germany on behalf of France and Russia, when the latter were the greater rivals of the empire. That did not stop Asquith and Sir Edward Grey from taking Britain into a war in 1914 that caused 750,000 British casualties. Its benefits? A bagful of African and Middle East colonies the empire would be forced to disgorge after a second world war that would bring socialism to England, Stalinism into the heart of Europe, and an end to the British Empire. The March of Folly is the history of the great powers.

But a desire to avoid war does not argue for appeasement. America should instead use her immense leverage with China to steer her off her current course—or cease subsidizing her soaring growth.

WEAKNESSES OF THE MIDDLE KINGDOM

In the eternal struggle among nations for primacy, there is always a basic question: Whose side is time on? In the nineteenth century, time was on the side of the Americans in the struggle for preeminence with the Mother Country. In the Cold War, time was on our side as well. Khrushchev's boast "We will bury you!" was empty. And time may be on our side in the rivalry with China for preeminence in Asia and the Western Pacific.

Having reviewed China's strengths, let us consider her weaknesses.

First, the regime's legitimacy and moral authority are in question. Originally, the monopoly of power held by Mao's party was rooted in its claim to have reunited the nation and restored her to greatness, and to be the spear point of revolution of the oppressed peoples of the planet in the climactic Marxist struggle against the capitalist West. But that struggle we call the Cold War is over. Marxism was defeated. Beijing is no longer command post of world revolution. She is another nation-state, albeit a great one.

Indeed, in 1989, as Communist regimes were falling like dominoes across Eastern Europe, China's Communist Party seemed to have lost the mandate of heaven and to be at imminent risk of being overthrown. Only tanks in Tiananmen Square saved the regime.

With the raison d'être of its monopoly of power gone, the party must now justify that monopoly. It has done so by converting itself into the vessel of Chinese nationalism that will recover China's lost territories and make her again the first nation on earth, and by bringing a better life to the Chinese people. The regime must deliver or the regime is at risk.

The danger is that Beijing must now constantly stoke the nationalist fires, and the most effective way is to confront rival powers, as with the constant threats to Taiwan and repeated challenges to U.S. planes and ships in the Exclusive Economic Zone.

Second, China's opening to the world, the education abroad of hundreds of thousands of her young, and the presence of hundreds of thousands of foreign businessmen, students, and tourists in China have introduced her people to ideas subversive of their own authoritarian regimes.

Third, industrialization is creating a middle class and making

China's people aware of what others have that they do not. Millions of young annually leave rural areas to come to the cities in search of a better life. If they do not find it, they will make trouble for the regime.

As China's middle class expands, it will demand more freedom and a greater voice in China's destiny. As factory hands attain job security, they will begin to demand wages, benefits, and rights commensurate with those of workers in other Asian nations. In coming decades, China is likely to experience the labor strife America experienced in plants and factories from the 1890s through the 1930s. Is the system sufficiently flexible and responsive to prevent a social explosion?

Fourth, China is not only preoccupied with consolidating control over the Tibetans and Muslim Uighurs in Xinjiang, who detest their Han Chinese overlords, and suppressing Christians and the Falun Gong, she has suspicious and even hostile neighbors in Russia, in the Muslim lands to the west, in an India still bitter over China's attack in 1962, in Vietnam, in the littoral states of the South China Sea, on Taiwan, and in Japan.

Anywhere China shifts her weight, she rubs up against a nation or people with reason to fear her. China is contained in the Taiwan Strait by U.S. naval power. Elsewhere on her frontiers, she is contained by Asian and Islamic nationalists who are her nervous neighbors.

Finally, China's prosperity depends on us. In 2002 and 2003, the United States purchased 10 percent of China's GDP. U.S. consumers are now responsible for 100 percent of China's growth. The dollars she earns from sales to America undergird her economy. Access to the U.S. market and the income she earns here has made China the world's premier market for foreign investment. Were Chinese goods to be excluded from America, China's factories would shut down, millions would be thrown out of work, foreign investment would dry up, and China's boom would become China's bust.

As America buys 30 percent of all of China's exports, any confrontation with the United States would be ruinous to China. And if Beijing believes time is on her side in the struggle for hegemony in Asia, why would she press a collision while she is still far the weaker of the two powers? The answer is Taiwan.

THE TAIWAN NETTLE

The United States has made clear in the Shanghai Communique and subsequent documents that it does not dispute China's claim to Taiwan. But the island is not to be brought back by force. When, whether, and how Taiwan and the mainland are reunited must be resolved peacefully. So the Taiwan Relations Act declares. And this is what President Bush meant when he said he would do "whatever it took" to defend Taiwan.

However, first, last, and always, the United States must consider its own vital interests. We cannot give any nation a blank check to drag us into war. That was the blunder of Chamberlain in handing an unsolicited war guarantee to Poland, then giving the dissolute Polish Colonel Beck a free hand to negotiate, or to resist, the return of Danzig to Nazi Germany.

If Taiwan agrees to reunite peacefully with the mainland, to accept the status of Hong Kong, a "One China, Two Systems" policy, the United States could not object. Indeed, Taiwan, looking out for her own interests first, is deeply engaged in China. Some fifty thousand Taiwanese companies have $60 billion in investments on the mainland. Over 1 million Taiwanese visit there each year. Hundreds of thousands of Taiwanese live in Shanghai.

As Taiwan is looking out for her interests, so must we. If Taiwan declares independence, she must win it herself. "Who would be free," wrote Byron, "themselves must strike the blow."

Our mutual security treaty has been dead for a quarter century. It cannot be revived. Yet, our national interest and honor dictate that we not permit an old friend to be brutalized and bound off into captivity. Beijing must understand that. Any attempt by China to bring Taiwan back by force would be a manifestation of contempt for the United States, dictating a suspension of economic and trade ties.

If the people of Taiwan wish to declare independence, it is asked, do they not have the same right as Lithuanians, Latvians, and Estonians, who broke free of Moscow, or the Slovenians, Croatians, and Macedonians who broke free of Belgrade? In population and wealth, Taiwan ranks above 85 percent of the nations of the UN. Why would the United States or any free nation refuse to recognize an independent Taiwan? Simple. Fear of Beijing's wrath. That is reality.

In deciding on when and how to reunite Taiwan with the mainland, the Chinese leadership also faces a dilemma. The longer Beijing waits, the greater the spirit of independence on the island grows and the more the Taiwanese come to see themselves as a unique and separate people, entitled to stand in equality with the other nations of the world.

But should China resort to force to bring Taiwan under her wing, she would rupture her trade ties with America and risk a clash with the U.S. Navy. Nor is there any guarantee Taiwan would capitulate, but a high probability Taiwan would declare independence. Beijing's Olympic Games in 2008 would be boycotted by the United States as were the Moscow games after the invasion of Afghanistan.

In brief, a resort by China to intimidation by threatening missile strikes or blockade, or any attack on the island, carry great risks and could return the mainland to the isolation out of which China broke free only after the death of Mao Tse-tung.

A NEW POLICY TOWARD CHINA

Though U.S. purchases of Chinese-made goods are responsible for its prosperity, Beijing refuses to use her leverage to help us disarm North Korea of nuclear weapons and allows Pyongyang to use Chinese bases to transfer missile and nuclear technology to Iran and the Middle East. U.S. policy has been rooted in hope, not realism.

For President Bush to have called Beijing a "partner in diplomacy working to meet the dangers of the twenty-first century" was naive. The history of China since 1949—indeed, since 1989—teaches that, unlike Russia, which is a changed nation, China is not a strategic partner. But China need not be an enemy.

U.S. policy toward China should become one of strict reciprocity. As America holds the high cards in this table-stakes poker game, we should inform the Chinese that:

1. While we do not dispute China's sovereignty over Taiwan, any attack on the island would mean a rupture in trade ties and risk a naval clash.

2. To remove China's fears of encirclement, we should declare our intent to dismantle U.S. bases in South Korea, Japan, and in the old Soviet republics of Central Asia. Such a declaration would awaken Tokyo and Seoul to the necessity to end their "free-riding" on U.S. defense and to buy or build the weapons to ensure their own security.

3. We should tell China the United States sees no threat to its own vital interests in the natural growth of Chinese economic and military power and influence in Asia. We have no desire to surround and contain China or deny her a place in the sun.

4. However, if China will not assist the United States in effecting the nuclear disarmament of North Korea, we will cease placing restrictions on Japan and South Korea, should they seek their own nuclear deterrents.

5. Failure of China to cooperate in restricting sales of ballistic missile and nuclear technology to nations hostile to the United States will be taken as a sign China is indifferent to U.S. interests.

6. While we take no sides in the territorial disputes in the South China Sea, the U.S. Navy will continue to treat that sea as inter-

national waters. As for the settlement of China's border disputes, that is for China and her neighbors to negotiate. We are not the title office or the sheriff of the South China Sea.

7. The one-sided trade relationship must be renegotiated. With an exchange rate of 8.28 renminbi to the dollar, China is sucking factories, technology, and jobs out of the United States, amassing huge trade surpluses at our expense, treating us like a colonial source of raw materials.

We must manage trade with Beijing and make it reciprocal. If America is to buy 30 percent of China's exports, Beijing must give preference in its purchases to goods made in the USA. In 2002, China imported $250 billion worth of goods and services, but only $22 billion, or 9 percent, from the United States. The share of China's imports that come from America should begin to rise to match the share of China's exports that go to America.

Should China refuse, we should shift U.S. purchases to Free Asia by imposing a tariff on goods made in China. Should Beijing impose a reciprocal tariff, fine. As we buy forty times as great a share of China's GDP as she buys of ours, there is no doubt who loses that trade war.

America must open her eyes. Rulers who brutalize Christians and dissidents, conduct cultural genocide in Tibet, and forcibly perform abortions on and sterilize married women for becoming pregnant with a second child, speak with forked tongue when they tell us they share our values. What they do to their own, given the power, they will do to us.

Given the character of the Chinese regime, we are not fated to be friends. Yet we need not be enemies. The world is big enough for both of us. And it is in the interests of both to do as America and Russia did in the second half of the twentieth century, and Britain and Germany failed to do in the first half. Avoid the apocalypse that could destroy us both.

SIX

ECONOMIC TREASON

When the necessaries of life have been taxed in any country, it becomes proper to tax not only the necessaries of life imported from other countries, but all sorts of foreign goods which can come into competition with anything that is the produce of domestic industry.

—Adam Smith

Are the good times really over for good?
—Merle Haggard, 1974

In the title of a 1921 biography by Arthur Vandenberg, he was the Greatest American.

Born illegitimate, "the bastard son of a Scotch peddler" in Adams's insult, he came to America from the West Indies as a boy and began to agitate for independence. When war came, he enlisted and fought at Trenton. Pleading for his own command, he was given the honor of leading the bayonet charge at Yorktown. After victory, when the thirteen independent states went their separate and quarrelsome ways, he plotted with Madison and Washington to hold a constitutional convention. He coauthored the Federalist Papers to explain the new nation he helped create. Washington named him secretary of the treasury. In that capacity, he wrote *The Report on Manufactures*, laying out the blueprints by which the American economy would be constructed and operate.

He was Alexander Hamilton, master architect of the United States. His vision had been forged in the fire of revolution and the furnace of war. The deprivations of the British blockade and winters at Valley Forge and Morristown had taught him the price of dependency. Without French muskets and French ships, the revolution would not have survived. Reflecting on how close his country had come to losing its liberty, Hamilton wrote:

> Not only the wealth, but the independence and security of a country, appear to be materially connected with the prosperity of manufactures. Every nation . . . ought to endeavor to possess within itself all the essentials of a national supply. These compromise the means of *subsistence, habitation, clothing and defense.*

America's political independence, Hamilton was saying, could not survive without economic independence. The guidelines he laid down, and nationalists from Washington to Madison to Lincoln to Theodore Roosevelt followed, were these:

• America must not be thirteen separate markets but a single free market. All state tariffs that impede domestic commerce are to be abolished. Free trade among the thirteen states is embedded in the Constitution.

• To ensure free trade among the states, a new national government has been created. How is it to be financed? With tariffs on imports from abroad, imposed at customs houses at the port of entry. All exports and all income of U.S. citizens are to be exempt from taxation. This prohibition was to be written into the Constitution.

• The tariff revenue extracted from foreign merchants will be used to build a new capital, create an army and navy to defend us from imperial predators, and construct the roads, harbors, and canals that will bind us together as a people.

From Hamilton's mind and pen had come the greatest free market in history. But as Hamilton was, like Washington, an American nationalist, it was a *national* free-trade zone he had created. All Americans participated in that free market as their birthright, but British merchants, who had held life-and-death power over the colonies, would pay a price of admission—a tariff. That tariff would finance a small but strong central government. And by raising the price of foreign goods, tariffs would stimulate our own people into building factories here in the United States. Strategic goal: Cut the ties of dependency to Europe and create bonds of commerce among Americans. The U.S. economy was designed to weld us into one nation and one people, dependent upon one another. What was best for America, and for our people as a whole, was the basis of Hamilton's great idea.

Washington and Hamilton wanted to wean the republic off a reliance on foreign trade so Americans would never again be drawn into the wars of the old continent. They wanted to cut the umbilical cord to Europe and set out over the mountains for the West. They were statesmen, visionaries, and patriots.

PROTECTIONIST AMERICA

From the ratification of the Constitution to World War I, Hamilton's vision guided the nation.

On July 4, 1789, Washington signed the first legislation sent down by Congress, the Tariff Act of 1789. In 1816, confronted with British dumping to kill the infant industries that had sprouted up during the War of 1812 and British blockade, Madison, relying on congressional allies Henry Clay and John C. Calhoun, signed the Tariff Act of 1816, America's first protective tariff.

In 1828, Congress enacted the "Tariff of Abominations," a 62 percent tax on 92 percent of all goods entering the United States, import duties that make the Smoot-Hawley tariff of a century later look like an excise tax.

By now the tariff issue divided Americans as bitterly as slavery. Southerners seethed with indignation. Dixie traded cotton for British manufactures. Tariffs raised the price of her imported goods. And while the South was paying the tariff, the revenue was going north to Washington. The tariff wall also protected Yankee industries. Thus, the South was coming to look upon high tariffs as a system for enriching the industrializing North at the expense of an agricultural South.

By 1832, Calhoun, now vice president under Jackson, had become antiprotectionist, and, under his leadership, South Carolina threatened secession if the tariffs were not reduced.

"Our Federal Union! It must be preserved!" thundered Jackson. He warned the state in which he had been born that if it made good on its threat to secede, he would lead an invasion and hang the traitors to a man. Henry Clay stepped in with a compromise. The nation backed away from civil war.

By the 1830s the economic nationalism of Clay, architect of the American System, as it came to be called, had been embraced by young Abe Lincoln. Like Clay, a fellow Whig he called his "beau ideal of a statesman," Lincoln was a high-tariff man. "Give us a protective tariff," he declaimed during the Clay-Polk election of 1844, "and we shall have the greatest country on earth."

In 1860, Lincoln carried Pennsylvania and the nation on a high-tariff platform, and the Morrill tariffs were raised a dozen times during the Civil War. From 1865 to the Great Depression, protectionism would be biblical truth for the Grand Old Party. How did America fare?

From 1869 to 1900, real wages rose 53 percent, commodity prices fell 58 percent, America's GNP quadrupled, and our national debt fell by two-thirds. Customs duties provided 58 percent of all federal revenues.

From 1870 to 1913, the U.S. economy grew more than 4 percent a year. Industrial production grew at 5 percent. The Protectionist Era was among the most productive in history. When it began, America was dependent on imports for 8 percent of its GNP. When it ended, America's dependency had fallen to 4 percent. The nation began the era with an economy half the size of Britain's and ended it with an economy more than twice as large as Britain's.

Tariffs alone cannot explain the economic success of the era. There was also sound money, the energy and ingenuity of our people, soaring population growth, and boundless resources in the land we inherited. But high tariffs, nevertheless, went hand in hand with the rise of the most awesome industrial power the world had ever seen. And the Republican Party, which preached protectionism as the key to prosperity, controlled the White House for all but eight years of the half century from the Civil War to the inauguration of Woodrow Wilson.

THE DECLINE OF GREAT BRITAIN

What happened to Great Britain in this era?

She abandoned the economic nationalism that had built the nation to embrace the free-trade dogma of nineteenth century classical liberals, none of whom had gone through the searing experience of revolution and war as had Washington and Hamilton.

While Jackson, Lincoln, McKinley, TR, and the empire builders derided as robber barons—Rockefeller, Carnegie, Vanderbilt, Morgan, Harriman, Hill—were laying the foundations for the American Century, British statesmen were heeding scribblers like David Ricardo, James and John Stuart Mill, and Richard Cobden, the great evangelist of free trade who called it "God's diplomacy" and "the international law of the Almighty."

America was using tariffs to price British goods out of U.S. markets and protect and strengthen U.S. manufacturers. Britain, faithful to free-trade dogma, refused to retaliate, though even Adam Smith had urged this.

Bismarck, as he observed the steady shift of industrial power and preeminence from Britain to America, adopted the American

System for the new Germany. He abolished internal tariffs, shel-
tered the German home market, and began to target the markets
of the British Empire. Like Hamilton, Bismarck believed in national free trade, not global free trade, for Bismarck believed in
Germany first.

Having seen his country lose its manufacturing primacy to
America, and fearing it would fall behind the kaiser's Germany as
well, British statesman Joseph Chamberlain led a brave campaign
on behalf of the Tariff League, but was felled by a stroke in 1906.
Free-trade Liberals, with the young Churchill defecting from his
party to join their ranks on the issue, took and held power up to
World War I. A German submarine blockade finally awakened the
British from their dogmatic slumber. But only an endless line of
merchant ships hauling cargo from protectionist America enabled
Britain to survive the U-boat menace until General Pershing and
the Yanks came over.

In *The Collapse of British Power,* historian Corelli Barnett as-
cribes the fall of his nation to "a political doctrine; a doctrine
blindly believed in long after it had ceased to correspond with reality." The doctrine was

> . . . liberalism, which criticized and finally demolished the
> traditional conception of the nation-state as a collective or-
> ganism, a community, and asserted instead the primacy of
> the individual. According to liberal thinking a nation was no
> more than so many human atoms who happened to live un-
> der the same set of laws. . . .
>
> Central to liberalism was the belief that human progress
> and human happiness alike were best assumed by elevating
> individuals to compete freely with each other: *laissez-faire;*
> let them get on with it. What was socially necessary should
> be entrusted to spontaneous creation by private initiative. As
> Adam Smith, the founder of liberal economics, put it in
> 1776: "By pursuing his own interest [an individual] fre-
> quently promotes that of society, the more effectually than

when he really intends to promote it." It was Adam Smith who formulated the doctrine of Free Trade, keystone of liberalism, which was to exercise as long-lived and as baneful effect on British power as Wesley and Whitfield's preaching.

Barnett savages the dogmatists he believes brought Britain down. By 1914, Britons still believed theirs was the most powerful, productive, and self-sufficient country on earth. But already the rot was deep as the free-trade cancer had eaten away the vitals of the nation. Again, Barnett:

> British industry had . . . changed its character from an army of conquest, mobile, flexible and bold, into a defensive army pegged out in fixed positions, passively trying to defend what it had won in the past. The fire of creative purpose flickered low in the blackened grate of the British industrial regions.
>
> Nor was British agriculture less decrepit. It was the German submarine which reminded the British Government after 1914 that the price of cheap food from overseas under the policy of Free Trade had been the ruin of British farms and the terrifying vulnerability of the British population to starvation by blockade.

Britain never recovered from its fifty-year addiction to free trade. Now we follow in her footsteps. The Republican Party whose Lincolnian protectionism helped to build the greatest manufacturing power the world had ever seen is now enthralled by the same fatal dogma: What is best for America is what is cheapest now for the consumer.

After World War II, the Republican Party gradually converted to the Democratic doctrine of free trade. Where Republicans had once followed the principles and policies laid down by conservatives like Hamilton, Lincoln, McKinley, and Coolidge, now they read Milton Friedman on free trade, and believed. With merchandise trade deficits now surging past $600 billion a year, factories shutting down across America, and our dependence on nations like China growing yearly, Bush Republicans now echo Clinton Democrats and celebrate the tenth anniversary of NAFTA, as they hurry to change U.S. laws to conform to WTO commands.

THE FRUITS OF GLOBALISM

At the end of World War II, with most of Europe and East Asia devastated, the United States undertook to open her markets to goods made in the countries that had suffered in the war. It was a necessary and selfless sacrifice of domestic industry to enable allies to get back on their feet to be able to contribute to the defense of the West.

This Eisenhower policy of opening America's markets to the world was continued by Kennedy, Johnson, and Nixon, despite a rising clamor at home that Europe and Japan had recovered and America should look again to the protection of her home industries and manufacturing base.

But Republican presidents of the postwar era had abandoned tradition. They were now all converts to the free-trade faith preached by the party of Wilson and FDR. Eisenhower and Nixon openly embraced what Theodore Roosevelt called the "pernicious" doctrine. "I thank God I am not a free trader," TR had once written to Henry Cabot Lodge.

Ronald Reagan championed free trade with Canada, a nation with first-world wages and environmental and labor standards. But it was the son and the grandson of Prescott Bush—who, with Barry Goldwater and Strom Thurmond, was among only eight U.S. senators to oppose JFK's Trade Expansion Act—who finally and forever renounced the America First economic patriotism of the Grand Old Party.

A third of a century has elapsed since completion of the Kennedy round of trade negotiations that inaugurated our free-trade era. Time to measure the promise against the performance.

In one generation, the house Hamilton built has collapsed. The most awesome industrial machine the world had ever seen has been gutted. The U.S. manufacturing base has been hollowed out. For seven decades, until 1970, Americans produced 96 percent of all they consumed. Now, a fourth of our steel is foreign-made, a third of our cars, half our machine tools, two-thirds of the clothes we wear, and almost all our shoes, radios, telephones, TVs, cameras, VCRs, and bicycles.

We have witnessed the fall of the American dollar, the end of our economic independence, the deindustrialization of our country, and the abandonment of our working men and women to Darwinian competition with foreign labor forced to work for a fifth or a tenth of U.S. wages.

In 2002, the United States ran a merchandise trade deficit of $484 billion. In 2003, it hit $550 billion. Every month of the first thirty-eight of George W. Bush's presidency, manufacturing jobs disappeared. One in six have vanished since he took his oath, 2.6 million in all.

In 1950, a third of our labor force was in manufacturing, and ours was the most self-sufficient republic the world had ever seen. Now only 11 percent of U.S. workers are in manufacturing, which is in a death spiral, and it is not a natural death. It is premeditated murder. Globalists and corporatists plotted the evisceration of American manufacturing with the collusion of free-trade fundamentalists who cannot see that the theories they were fed by economics professors in college are killing the country they profess to love. Or they do not care.

IN SPRING 2004, after mass at St. Mary's, a retired FBI agent who had worked as a boy in the giant steel plant in Weirton, West Virginia, and whose father had died in an accident at the mill, handed me the *Weirton Daily Times*. "Where Do We Go From

Here?" read the May 20 banner. The front page was devoted to the bankruptcy filing of Weirton Steel, which had once employed fourteen thousand workers in a town of twenty-three thousand.

Mark Glyptis, president of the Independent Steelworkers Union, said it didn't have to happen. It was a poignant story. When I had begun my campaign of 2000 at the Weirton mill, Mark and his ISU had endorsed me.

That same week, a friend e-mailed me. Timco lumber, where we spent the last day of the New Hampshire campaign of 1996, had shut down. As Weirton Steel had been hammered by subsidized steel dumped into the U.S. market from overseas, Timco had to compete with subsidized lumber from Canada.

Across America, the story is the same. Steel and lumber mills going bankrupt, textile plants moving out to the Caribbean, Mexico, Central America, the Far East. Auto plants closing and opening overseas, mines being sealed in the Southwest, farms being sold off.

Michael Boskin, chairman of the Council of Economic Advisers under Bush I, flippantly remarked, "It does not make any difference whether a country makes computer chips or potato chips." Former Bush budget director Richard Darman said of U.S. makers of computer chips: "If our guys can't hack it, let 'em go."

Why does it matter where our goods are produced? As I wrote six years ago in *The Great Betrayal: How American Sovereignty and Social Justice Are Being Sacrificed to the Gods of the Global Economy,*

> Manufacturing is the key to national power. Not only does it pay more than service industries, the rates of productivity growth are higher and the potential of new industry arising is far greater. From radio came television, VCRs and flat-panel screens. From adding machines came calculators and computers. From the electric typewriter came the word processor. Research and development follows manufacturing.

Manufacturing is the muscle of a modern nation. In the eternal struggle of nations, the industrial powers have always risen to the top. When the Industrial Revolution began in England, Britain vaulted to the forefront. The Acts of Navigation kept her there. British statesmen knew it. Pitt, architect of victory in the Seven Years' War that drove France out of North America, knew it. He supported the American colonies in their demand—"No taxation without representation!" But Pitt warned that if ever he caught Americans engaged in manufacturing—exclusive province of the Mother Country—he would send his ships into their harbors and blow their factories off the map.

Manufacturing power and the economic independence it gave Great Britain enabled her to adopt a policy of "splendid isolation" from the quarrels and wars of the continent, as she ruled her empire. But when Germany, united in 1871, began to eclipse Britain as first industrial power in Europe, Britain felt forced to enter the alliances that dragged her into the greatest war in history. Only U.S. industrial power, greater than that of Britain, France, and Germany combined, turned the tide in that war. And America, self-sufficient as she was by World War I, did not need allies and could stay out of the war as long as she wished. No more.

Since 1971, the trade deficits run by the United States add up to $4 trillion. The annual trade deficit in goods is now running at $600 billion. These dollars, shipped abroad to buy the products of foreign factories, are now being used by foreigners to buy up our stocks, bonds, companies, and real estate. By 2002, foreigners owned U.S. assets equal to 78 percent of our GDP. They owned 13 percent of our equity market, 22 percent of our corporations, 24 percent of our corporate bonds, 48 percent of the U.S. treasury market. Like Esau, we are selling our birthright. As Lou Dobbs declaims nightly on CNN, we are "exporting America."

"[F]oreigners are using our $1 billion per day trade deficit to buy up American firms," writes columnist Paul Craig Roberts, who helped craft the Reagan fiscal policy. "In 2000," he reports, "97%

of direct investment by foreigners went for the purchase of existing U.S. assets. We are not only losing industrial jobs, we are losing ownership of our companies."

Year by year, the deindustrialization of America proceeds, step by step, with the de-Americanization of our greatest companies, as we become an ever more dependent nation and people. We work for others. We depend on others for the necessities of our national life. And when others tire of taking our dollars for their goods, the value of those dollars will fall. The decline of the dollar has already begun. One day, all those "cheap foreign goods" will not be cheap anymore.

AMERICA'S NEW DEPENDENCY

Consider the depth of our dependency. Imports, 4 percent of GNP from 1900 to 1970, are now 14 percent, and a third of all manufactures we consume. From 1900 to 1970, America ran trade surpluses every year. We have now run thirty-three straight trade deficits, with the merchandise trade deficit now at $600 billion, or almost 6 percent of GDP. No great power has sustained trade deficits like these for decades without a collapse of its currency and the end of its supremacy.

Pat Choate, author of *Agents of Influence,* gives the following levels of U.S. dependency on foreign suppliers for critical goods.

Medicines and pharmaceuticals	72%
Metalworking machinery	51%
Engines and power equipment	56%
Computer equipment	70%
Communications equipment	67%
Semiconductors and electronics	64%

Dell computers of Austin has 4,500 suppliers. It has an inventory of four days and a just-in-time supply line that stretches across the

Atlantic and Pacific. A dock strike on either coast, writes Choate, and Dell begins to close down after ninety-six hours.

In 2003, Pentagon officials who buy for the U.S. armed forces and U.S. defense industries spoke out in opposition to a law that would require a 65 percent American content in U.S. weapons. Our missile defense system and Joint Strike Fighter would be imperiled, the Pentagon said, if two-thirds of their components had to be made in the USA.

NAFTA: THE BIG STING

In 1993, the NAFTA debate gripped the country and Congress. In promoting his trade pact with Mexico, President Clinton had the backing of the Council on Foreign Relations and U.S. Chamber of Commerce, the *Wall Street Journal* and *Washington Post*, Heritage Foundation and the Brookings Institution, the *New Republic* and *National Review*. Ross Perot, Ralph Nader, this writer, and the AFL-CIO opposed it, as did the American people. It did not matter. Before the vote, the bazaar opened, and members of Congress began selling their votes to the White House. NAFTA won. Ten years later, the returns are in.

A year after NAFTA passed, Mexico devalued the peso, and the United States began running an unbroken string of rising trade deficits with Mexico that now runs over $40 billion a year. Drug cartels shifted operations from South America to the U.S. border. Mexico has became the primary source of the marijuana and heroin pouring in and poisoning the minds and souls of American children.

As the narcotics came north, U.S. companies began laying off $10- and $20-an-hour U.S workers and moving south in search of labor willing to work for $2 an hour. By 2000, more than a million Mexicans were at work in *maquiladora* plants at jobs once held by Americans. In 2002, over 21 percent of the entire GDP of Mexico was shipped north. This is not trade in the traditional sense. It represents the transfer from the United States to Mexico of a large slice of U.S. production in pursuit of cheaper wages and tax avoidance. The "creative destruction" of globalization has now hit Mexico. Factories there are shutting down and moving to China, where wages are even lower.

Americans were told during the NAFTA debate that the only jobs we would lose were the "dead-end" jobs our high-tech labor force should no longer be doing. We would be creating the jobs at which Americans excel, like building commercial jetliners.

Since 1994, America has lost 689,000 jobs in apparel and textiles, "dead-end jobs" to pundits and think tank scribblers but the best jobs they ever had to the folks who lost them. For those apparel jobs paid 23 percent more, and the textile jobs 59 percent more, than the retail sales jobs they and their wives now probably have.

After the textile industry went, the auto industry followed, though the jobs of U.S. autoworkers are among the highest-paid factory jobs on earth. Mexico now exports 90 percent more cars to the United States than we do to the world. In 2003, the United States had a trade deficit in automobiles, trucks, and auto parts of $122 billion.

Now comes the turn of aerospace, the crown jewel of American manufacturing. It, too, is heading south. "Like the automakers that turned the cities of Tolucca, Hermosillo, and Sautillo into Little Detroit in the 1990s," writes Joel Millman of the *Wall Street Journal,* "Boeing Corp., General Dynamics Co., Honeywell International Inc., and General Electric Co.'s GE Aircraft Engines are beginning to make Mexico a base for both parts manufacture and assembly."

What is the attraction?

"You can only cut costs so much with new machinery," says John Monarch, president of GE supplier Smith West. "Pretty soon you need to lower labor costs, too." Driessen Aircraft Interior Systems pays Mexican workers $20 a day, which breaks down to $2.50 an hour, less than half the U.S. minimum wage.

If aircraft parts can be made by Mexican workers for $20 a day and computers can be made by Chinese workers for $10 a day, what is there left that cannot be manufactured more cheaply abroad? Almost nothing.

And the Mexican people? Half of the 100 million are still mired in poverty. Tens of millions are unemployed or underemployed. Because of devaluations, real wages are below what they were in 1993. Thus the great migration north continues. Some 1.5 million are apprehended every year on our southern border breaking into the United States. Of the perhaps 500,000 who make it, one-third head for Mexifornia where their claims on Medicaid, schools, courts, prisons, and welfare have tipped the Golden State toward bankruptcy and induced millions of native-born Americans to flee in the great exodus to Nevada, Idaho, Arizona, and Colorado.

Ten years after NAFTA, Mexico's leading export to America is still—Mexicans. America is becoming Mexamerica.

CHINA: FACTORY FLOOR TO THE WORLD

The abolition of tariffs between the United States and Mexico sent hundreds of thousands of jobs south in search of lower wages and weaker health, safety, and environmental laws. But the annual granting of Most Favored Nation trade status to China, followed by President Bush's grant of Permanent Normal Trade Relations— and the admission of China to the World Trade Organization—has sent millions of jobs to China.

China's boom began after Beijing devalued in 1994 to give herself a competitive advantage over the "Asian Tigers"—South Korea, Taiwan, Singapore, and Malaysia. With unrestricted access to the U.S. market, Beijing began to invite Western companies into China to build factories there, to tap her inexhaustible pool of low-wage labor and to produce for export to America. As the price of access to her own market, Beijing demanded that the companies transfer technology to their Chinese partners. If the companies balked, the Chinese extorted or pirated the technology.

By offering workers at $2 a day, guaranteeing no unions, allowing levels of pollution no Western nation would tolerate, China has converted herself into the factory floor of the world. In 2003, China surpassed the United States as the world's largest recipient of direct foreign investment. Once home to tough "Yankee traders," America has supinely accepted what analyst Charles McMillion calls "The World's Most Unequal Trading Relationship."

In 2002, the U.S. trade deficit with China was $103 billion. In 2003, it hit $124 billion, the largest trade deficit between two nations in history. By mid-2004, that deficit was approaching $150 billion a year. It is false to say President Bush presided over a "jobless recovery." His trade deficits have created many millions of jobs in China.

The relationship between America and China cannot be called a true trade partnership. For what is taking place is the systematic transfer, factory by factory, of our manufacturing base to China. America is being looted of her manufacturing patrimony by her own corporate class in a way that calls to mind the looting of Germany by Red Army scavengers after World War II. Beijing understands what economic nationalist Friedrich List wrote: "The power of producing wealth is infinitely more important than the wealth itself." China sacrifices the present for the future, while America sacrifices her future to the present.

China has now amassed close to $500 billion in reserves from her trade surpluses. Much of that vast hoard is invested in U.S. Treasury bonds, earning Beijing billions in annual interest from U.S. taxpayers. America may be the most advanced nation on earth and China a developing country, but you cannot tell that by studying the trade statistics.

In 2002, Americans purchased 10 percent of China's entire GDP, while China purchased one-fifth of 1 percent of ours. We bought 40 percent of China's exports. China bought 3 percent of ours. China ran up her largest trade surpluses with us in computers, electrical machinery, toys, games, footwear, furniture, clothing, plastics, articles of iron and steel, vehicles, optical and photographic equipment, and other manufactures.

Among the twenty-three items in which America had a trade surplus with China were soybeans, corn, wheat, animal feeds, meat, cotton, metal ores, scrap, hides and skins, pulp, waste paper, cigarettes, gold, coal, mineral fuels, rice, tobacco, fertilizers, glass. "It comes as something of a shock," writes Paul Craig Roberts, "to discover that the U.S. . . . has the export profile of a 19th century third world colony."

One who has studied the behavior of capitalists courting China is columnist Terry Jeffrey. Inspecting the Web site of Motorola, Jeffrey found this description of how this American company sees its future:

> Motorola is moving toward . . . taking China as its home and development base. Motorola Chinese Electronics . . . has increased its investment several times in China without taking away a single dollar. The company reinvested all the profits in China. . . .
>
> Since the very beginning Motorola has brought forward the idea of trying to be a good citizen of China, taking China as its home and thriving with the Chinese people. . . . The development goal is to become a true Chinese company.

Motorola's kowtow reveals a hidden cost of globalization. When U.S. companies go global, they shed their loyalty to America. Boeing, last surviving U.S. manufacturer of commercial aircraft, threatened now by the European cartel Airbus, has apparently gone beyond making vertical fins and horizontal stabilizers for its fleet in China. On January 1, 2003, this item ran in the *New York Times*:

> The State Department has accused two leading American companies of 123 violations of export laws in connection

with the transfer of rocket and satellite data to China during the 1990s. The Boeing company and Hughes Electronics Corporation, a unit of General Motors, were notified of the accusations last week.

The economic nationalists who directed America's destiny in the nineteenth century would instantly recognize China's policy for what it is and act to counter it. But America's free traders are clueless, or do not care.

The most puzzling are the neoconservatives who talk of an American empire of "pith helmets and jodhpurs." Do they not understand that trade is a means to, and a measure of, national power? Free trade is not free. There are costs, both visible and hidden, in those mammoth trade deficits we are running. What are they? What has a third of a century of free trade wrought?

• *The deindustrialization of America.* Factories and plants everywhere are closing as America becomes a service economy.

• *An end to national self-sufficiency* and growing dependence upon foreign sources for the necessities of our national life and the weapons of our national defense.

• *A loss of national sovereignty* as WTO bureaucrats force U.S. laws to be rewritten to conform to global trade rules.

• A *falling dollar* that robs Americans of their wealth.

• *Shattered lives* as company towns become ghost towns in the "creative destruction" that deracinated economists celebrate from the security of tenured chairs.

• *A crisis in Social Security and Medicare* as Americans move out of high-paying manufacturing jobs into lower-paying service jobs, and thus contribute less in payroll taxes.

• *Growing public pressure for federalized health insurance* as manufacturing jobs are replaced by service ones that carry no health insurance.

• *A deepening farm crisis* as traditional U.S. markets here and abroad are captured by countries like Brazil and Argentina, whose lower labor costs have attracted Western capital. The scores of billions of dollars in subsidies taxpayers will give farmers in future years is to make up for what the farmers lost from globalization.

Why did the Republican Party convert to an ideology that produced this? First, in the colleges and universities of the postwar, protectionism became a dirty word, as it is today. The conservative Republicans of the pre–New Deal era—Presidents Harding and Coolidge and Treasury Secretary Mellon, who raised tariffs and cut income taxes—were demonized. Hoover and Smoot-Hawley were damned for the Great Depression. New Deal spending, not the war, was credited with its cure.

As important, the Fortune 500 concluded that protection of the home market was less critical to the bottom line than being able to move production out of the United States, thereby cutting the cost of taxes and regulations, and ridding their payrolls of highly compensated American workers, their own countrymen.

Finally, in the 1980s and 1990s, China abandoned Maoist isolation, India opened up, and the Soviet bloc overthrew Communism and broke free. These historic events, in a few short years, put literally hundreds of millions of workers into the world labor market, where they were willing and soon able to compete with American workers, whose wages were five, ten, and twenty times their own. For global corporations seeking lower taxes, lax regulation, and low-wage, high-productivity labor, it has become a buyer's market unlike any they have ever known.

CONSERVATIVES, SAID RONALD Reagan, believe in the values of "work, family, faith, community, and country." But free trade puts the demands of consumers ahead of the duties of citizens, the unbridled freedom of the individual in the marketplace ahead of all claims of family, community, and country. Free trade says what is best for me, now, at the cheapest price, is what is best for America. That is not conservatism.

Free trade does to a nation what alcohol does to a man. Saps him first of his vitality and energy, then of his independence, then of his life. America today exhibits the symptoms of a nation passing into late middle age. We spend more than we earn. We consume more than we produce. The evangelists of globalism who once promised us our trade deficits would disappear now assure us that trade deficits do not matter.

The truth: Free trade is the serial killer of American manufacturing and the Trojan Horse of world government. It is the primrose path to the loss of economic independence and national sovereignty. Free trade is a bright, shining lie.

WHY EXPORTS ARE BETTER

According to former GM executive Gus Stelzer, 50 percent of the sticker price of a new Cadillac goes to pay taxes—Social Security, Medicare, state and federal income taxes withheld from the wages and salaries of GM workers and executives, GM's corporate tax, the property taxes on factories, offices, and dealerships, and state sales taxes.

When we buy cars made in the USA, we contribute to Social Security, Medicare, and the national defense. When we buy an American-made car, we help pay for our roads, schools, teachers, and cops. When foreigners buy goods made in the USA, they, too, underwrite the cost of government in America. But when we buy foreign goods, we pay taxes to the governments of the nations where those goods are produced. When we buy goods made in China, we subsidize the regime in Beijing.

Free trade, adds Stelzer, "is the only competitive activity in which the rules are not the same for every competitor. . . . No other competitive activity would tolerate such immoral and unconstitutional double-dealing."

Under WTO rules, 14th Amendment protections no longer apply. U.S. manufacturers in America must obey minimum-wage laws, health-and-safety laws, environmental laws, civil rights laws, and tax laws, from which U.S. manufacturers in China are exempt. Equal protection of the law is made a mockery of in a free-trade world.

But tariffs are taxes, comes the retort of Libertarians. Tariffs raise the prices of goods. True. But all taxes—tariffs, income taxes, sales taxes, property taxes—are factored into the final price of the goods we buy. When a nation puts a tariff on foreign goods coming into the country, it is able to cut taxes on goods produced inside the country. This is the way to give U.S. manufacturers and workers a "home-field advantage." This was Hamilton's way and we have now abandoned it. And for what?

THE MYTH OF THE "LEVEL PLAYING FIELD"

What is President Bush's answer to the hemorrhaging of U.S. factory jobs? At a rally in Ohio, which had lost 160,000 manufacturing jobs since mid-2000, the president declared:

> We've lost thousands of manufacturing jobs because production moved overseas. . . . America must send a message overseas—say, look, we expect there to be a fair playing field when it comes to trade. . . . See, we in America believe we can compete with anybody, just so long as the rules are fair, and we intend to keep the rules fair.

But how do we maintain a level playing field when the United States imposes minimum-wage laws, environmental laws, health and safety laws, and antidiscrimination laws on manufacturers in America, from which U.S. manufacturers in China are exempt? When a U.S. factory worker earns $53,000 a year, while a Chinese worker can be hired for $2,000 a year, how does one keep the playing field level?

When President Bush speaks of keeping "the rules fair," does he mean China must start paying skilled workers $25 an hour and subject Chinese factories to the same wage-and-hour laws, OSHA inspections, and environmental rules as U.S. factories? That is impossible. Cheap labor in China and the lack of protections for Chinese workers are the "comparative advantage" that enables Beijing to lure away America's industrial base. Why should China, which is winning its trade war against America, adopt the policy of the United States, which is losing that war?

President Bush and trade czar Robert Zoellick celebrated their free-trade agreement with Chile as a triumph. But Chile has a GDP of $70 billion, not even 1 percent of ours. Her per capita GDP of $4,400 is one-eighth of ours. With a free-trade deal with Chile we gain access to a tiny market whose consumers cannot afford high-quality U.S. goods, while manufacturers who move production to Chile get free access to an $11 trillion U.S. market where consumers have a per capita GDP of $37,000. Bush and Zoellick traded Seabiscuit for a rabbit.

Democrats like Richard Gephardt argue that other nations should have to adopt U.S. standards in how they treat and reward workers. But the Third World will never have the same standards we do, and Democrats only delude themselves or deceive us when they threaten to cut off trade with these nations. It will not happen. Why? Because the hidden agenda of the global economy is global socialism, the steady transfer of the wealth of the West to the less fortunate of the earth. Equality is the end of socialism. For it to be attained on a global scale, the pay of Third World workers must rise and that of First World workers must be arrested or fall. That is what globalization is doing and is intended to do to U.S. workers—and that is the economic treason that dare not speak its name.

IS OUR CONDITION irreversible? Is the death of manufacturing an inevitability? The answer is no. There is nothing irretrievable about the loss of America's industrial base. It is a consequence of failed policies rooted in quasi-religious faith in a free-trade ideology that has failed every great nation that ever indulged: Holland, Spain and Great Britain. It is the result of a bipartisan betrayal of our citizens by their political elites. But if we are to restore America's self-sufficiency, we must act soon.

Restoration of American independence requires only that we put the national interest ahead of any globalist agenda, that we have the courage to throw over a failed policy of free trade and walk out of the WTO, that we revisit the wisdom of Hamilton and the Founding Fathers, that we be willing to accept temporary sacrifice for long-term security, that we put America and Americans first again. It can be done.

SEVEN

CONSERVATIVE IMPERSONATORS

The era of Big Government is over.

—Bill Clinton
State of the Union, 1996

We have a responsibility that when somebody hurts,
government has got to move.

—George W. Bush
Labor Day, 2002

As custodian of the national economy and decisive actor in the management of the Budget of the United States, George W. Bush has compiled a fiscal record of startling recklessness.

• By 2004, the last Clinton surplus of $236 billion had disappeared into a projected $521 billion deficit, and Bush had not vetoed a single bill.
• The federal government is borrowing almost 5 percent of our national economy just to pay its bills.
• From 2002 to 2004, Bush added $1.3 trillion to the national debt.
• In 2003, federal spending reached $20,300 per household, the first time it exceeded $20,000 since the height of World War II.
• By 2004, U.S. deficits had grown so large the IMF, monitor of Third World wastrels, was warning the United States that its enormous appetite for foreign borrowing was imperiling the world economy.

Critics blame the deficits on the Bush tax cuts, noting that federal revenues in 2003 fell to 16.5 percent of GDP, the lowest level since 1959.

President Bush blames the flood tide of red ink on the recession he inherited, the impact on the markets of the Enron-Worldcom scandals and revelations that CEOs cooked the books, and on vital spending for defense and homeland security after 9/11. But Brian Riedl of Heritage Foundation, a conservative think tank, reviewed the numbers. He found that the $296 billion leap in federal spending between 2001 and 2003 broke down thus:

- $100 billion for added defense
- $32 billion for 9/11 and homeland security
- $164 billion, or 55 percent, for programs unrelated to defense and 9/11

Something more serious, then, than a one-time burst in spending or fall-off in revenue has infected the American body politic, which makes permanent rescue from our fiscal crisis improbable. The Grand Old Party has become a big-government party. Tax cuts are no longer accompanied by spending cuts. Fiscal conservatism is dead. The Beltway Right has entered into a civil union with Big Brother.

Scholar Clinton Rossiter once derided conservatism as "the thankless persuasion." The professor had a point. Conservatives once accepted the unenviable role of Dutch Uncle. They had the character and courage to say no. They campaigned on credible pledges of fiscal prudence. They were trusted to raise the revenue to pay the bills for the social programs the liberals had enacted. And they regarded as heretics those Rockefeller Republicans who aped New Deal Democrats in their wastrel ways.

Those conservatives preached a politics of sacrifice for the common good and an economics of "a dollar good as gold," balanced budgets, and the prudent management of the nation's affairs. "Mr.

Conservative," Robert A. Taft, was the embodiment of that philosophy, and John F. Kennedy placed Taft among a handful of Profiles
in Courage in the history of the Senate.

But Robert Taft Republicanism is dead. "The conservatism that
defined itself in reaction against the New Deal—minimal government conservatism—is dead," writes George F. Will. There is no
conservative party in Washington. There is a Democratic Party of
tax-and-spend, and a Republican Party of guns and butter and tax
cuts, too. Washington is all accelerator, the brakes are gone.

In World War II, FDR cut nonwar spending by 54 percent. During Korea, Truman cut nonwar spending by 19 percent. But in the
first two years of the War on Terror, Bush, like his fellow Texan
Lyndon Johnson during Vietnam, increased domestic spending, by
11 percent. As America was fighting in Iraq, Afghanistan, and in
the War on Terror, George Bush assumed the role of Great Society
Republican.

"At 18.6%, the increase in non-defense discretionary spending
under the 107th Congress (2002–2003) is far and away the
biggest in decades," wrote the *Wall Street Journal* on January 20,
2004, the third anniversary of Bush's inauguration. The *Journal*
called the Bush administration "the most profligate . . . since the
1960s." Republicans now eagerly embrace federal programs they
once deplored.

IN *CONSCIENCE OF a Conservative*, Barry Goldwater, paragon
of postwar conservatism, declared federal aid to education unconstitutional, and warned of its inherent "evils and dangers." Federal
aid, he wrote, "invariably means federal control." Reagan and the
1990s Republicans pledged in their platforms to shut down Jimmy
Carter's Department of Education.

But George W. Bush, working in harness with Teddy Kennedy,
enacted No Child Left Behind. Columnist James Pinkerton summarizes the result: "When Bush took office, the Education Depart-

ment's budget was $35.7 billion; next fiscal year [2005], if he has his way, it will be $64.3 billion—an 80 percent increase." Newt Gingrich's Republican Revolution was empowered by voters to fulfill a "Contract with America" that promised deep cuts in federal spending. What happened?

"Elected in 1994 as the party of limited government, Republicans seem to have abandoned any effort to limit spending," said the *Journal*.

In the chapter "Freedom for the Farmer," Goldwater declared,

> The teaching of the Constitution on this matter is perfectly clear. *No power over agriculture was given to any branch of the national government.* . . . The problem of surpluses will not be solved until we recognize that technological progress and other factors have made it possible for the needs of America, and those of accessible world markets, to be satisfied by far fewer number of farmers than now till the soil.

Goldwater demanded "no equivocation here" but "*a prompt and final termination of the farm subsidy plan.*"

Forty years later, Bush signed a farm bill, the projected cost of which was $180 billion, for the benefit of half the number of farmers as were around when Barry Goldwater wrote his manifesto. While the number of farms and farmers has fallen by two-thirds since 1900, the Department of Agriculture workforce has increased thirty-three times over, from 2,900 employees to 96,400.

Candidate Bush was skeptical of nation-building. He promised a more "humble" foreign policy and a hard look at strategic commitments abroad. President Bush has plunged us into nation-building in Iraq and Afghanistan at a cost of $200 billion, and is erecting permanent bases in Eastern Europe, the Gulf, and the former Soviet republics of Central Asia.

To conservatives, foreign aid has always been the ugly duckling of federal programs. As Lord Peter Bauer pointed out, it is an inherently absurd program. A nation that adopts sound economic policies will not need foreign aid. It will attract foreign investment. A nation that does not adopt sound economic policies cannot truly be helped by foreign aid.

History has borne Bauer out. Indeed, if conservatives believe that sending tax dollars to the national government in Washington is the wrong way to promote prosperity in the United States, how can sending our tax dollars to the governments in capitals abroad be the right way to promote prosperity in the Third World? Americans have always been first to help people in crises with food, shelter, and medicine, and no president would discontinue that policy, but regular cash transfers to failed foreign regimes is a failed policy. Like welfare, it creates permanent dependency. One recalls that it was only when Taiwan and South Korea and the nations of Southeast Asia were taken off foreign aid that their economies began to take off. But this is unpersuasive to a White House that committed to increase foreign aid by 65 percent between 2002 and 2006. President Bush appears now to agree with the Left—that one measures true compassion solely by the amount of tax dollars one is willing to expend.

The twin altarpieces of Bush's foreign aid approach are a five-year, $15 billion program to fight AIDS in Africa and a Millennial Challenge Account to reward regimes that pursue sound policies. Virtue is no longer its own reward. But where in the Constitution is the president empowered to take tax dollars from U.S. citizens to reward foreign regimes for good behavior? As Joe Sobran writes, it appears that "The U.S. Constitution poses no serious threat to our form of government."

George W. Bush has also fathered the first new cabinet department of the twenty-first century and passed the largest entitlement program since LBJ: a $400 billion prescription drug benefit program under Medicare. Within months of passage, the cost of the new entitlement was refigured and raised to $540 billion. "Yet even this bait-and-switch tactic is deceptive," writes Congressman Ron Paul of Texas, "because independent groups estimate the true cost of the Medicare bill will be one trillion dollars over ten years."

Within weeks of his signing the prescription drug bill, the president promised to take us back to the moon and from there on to Mars with a new manned space program. Even Howard Dean had heard enough: "He's promising a trillion-dollar tax cut, a trip to Mars, and he has a half-trillion dollar deficit. Where do these Washington people think this money comes from?"

War is the health of the state, Randolph Bourne famously said in Wilson's war. Under Bush, America has fought two wars at a cost of $200 billion and rising, and created an immense new cabinet department. But if the purpose of the Department of Homeland Security is the defense of the homeland, what is the purpose of the Department of Defense? If we are to be secure, the president has stated, it will also be necessary to launch and prosecute a "world democratic revolution." But if democratic imperialism is to be our foreign policy in perpetuity, there will be no end of wars for America, but an early end to our democratic republic.

By the summer of 2004, George W. Bush had cut federal taxes twice, and dramatically, in the Reagan tradition. But he had not abolished a single significant federal program, agency, or department, or vetoed a single spending bill. Even the First Lady has gotten into the spirit of the times, announcing a 15 percent increase in the National Endowment for the Arts, an agency conservatives once swore on their family Bibles they would shut down. Even the mohair subsidies are back. Reagan was right. A federal program is "the closest thing to immortality on this earth."

What has happened to the Republican Party?

Ed Crane, longtime president of Cato Institute, the libertarian free-market think tank, traces the "philosophical collapse of the GOP" to the "2000 campaign of George W. Bush, who ran without calling for a single spending cut, much less the elimination of programs, agencies, or departments." Wrote Crane in despair of what had become of the party of so much hope:

> . . . neoconservatives moved to fill the philosophical vacuum
> created by the supply-siders. The neocons openly support

big government, and consider FDR to have been a great president. . . . the neocons are the ones who pushed Bush to call for greater federal government involvement in K-12 education than any president in American history.

And now the neocons are calling for American Empire. We have, indeed, come a long way from Reagan and Goldwater.

Early in the Bush administration, Marshall Wittman saw it coming: "Big Government Conservatism is the animating principle of the Bush presidency." A new species has evolved, he said, a new breed. Who are these heretics, these "big-government conservatives"? Fred Barnes of the neoconservative *Weekly Standard*, who coined the phrase, says they "tend to be realistic and programmatic." Jack Kemp as secretary of housing and urban development and Bill Bennett as secretary of education were Barnes's prototypes. He defined them thus:

> They take a relatively benign view of government and aggressively seek to expand the programs they believe in. A sense of realism means big government conservatives, Bush included, recognize Americans like big government. . . . Programmatic? That involves staying on offense politically by proposing new programs, often of small size and limited reach, for whatever national problems come up. For big problems . . . there are big solutions.

Republicans have come to believe that "the road to reelection is through government spending," writes Brian Riedl, a budget analyst at the Heritage Foundation. Republicans believe they have found the Rosetta Stone of American politics, the key to the permanent retention of power: Cut taxes consistently, and don't let Democrats outspend you. As Dick Cheney told a stunned Treasury Secretary Paul O'Neill, "Deficits don't matter."

The president's father, George H. W. Bush, raised taxes and lost his reelection bid. President Nixon funded the Great Society, ran huge deficits before his reelection year, named his friend Arthur

Burns to run-and-gun the money supply, imposed wage-and-price controls to prevent symptoms of inflation from appearing—and swept forty-nine states. George W. Bush has gone to school on Poppy's mistakes.

Though unconservative and unprincipled, the strategy has worked marvelously well. Bush the Younger has been paid in full at the ballot box by the devil to whom he and Rove have bartered their souls.

A conservative battle cry of a generation ago was "Defund the Left!"—eliminate federal grants to liberal activists and shut down their federal redoubts, such as the Legal Services Corporation. The new battle cry is "Fund us, too!" Conservative "causes" from global democracy to sexual abstinence now receive tax dollars. And neoconservatives, as ever, have provided the philosophical rationale for the betrayal of principle. Again, columnist James Pinkerton:

> Irving Kristol, defining "The Neoconservative Persuasion" in . . . *The Weekly Standard,* writes that his ideological fellow travelers are "impatient with the Hayekian notion that we are on 'the road to serfdom.'" Neocons, he says, see the growth of the state as "natural, indeed inevitable. They have no interest in a minimalist Goldwaterian state; it's 'National Greatness' they crave."

On the eve of the 2004 State of the Union, the *New York Times* ran this headline: "Bush Plans $1.5 Billion Drive for Promotion of Marriage." The story reported on how Bush aides were secretly "planning an extensive election-year initiative to promote marriage" and debating whether to float the scheme in the State of the Union. "For months," reported the *Times,* "administration officials have worked with conservative groups on the proposal, which would provide at least $1.5 billion for training to help couples develop interpersonal skills that sustain 'healthy marriages.'"

Why would a Republican White House, coping with a $500 billion deficit, fund such a scheme? "This is a way for the president to address the concerns of conservatives and to solidify his conservative base," one Bush adviser said. Former White House adviser Ron Haskins added, "A lot of conservatives are very pleased with the healthy marriage initiative."

Barry Goldwater, thou shouldst be living at this hour.

Where in the Constitution is the federal government empowered to take money from U.S. citizens to teach other citizens how to have "healthy marriages"? Or has that document become a meaningless artifact? What is a conservative White House doing dreaming up new social programs when we are running a deficit near 5 percent of GDP? What is the difference between the compassionate conservatism of George W. Bush and the Great Society liberalism of Lyndon Johnson? What do Beltway conservatives stand for anymore—besides tax cuts.

This was $1.5 billion of faith-based pork cooked up in the kitchen of Karl Rove to bribe the Religious Right not to howl too loudly should the White House decide not to support a constitutional amendment restricting marriage to a man and woman. Where LBJ funded poverty groups to build a power base in the cities independent of mayors, George W. Bush plans to fund God's Pork for "faith-based" groups to enable Republicans to get a foot in the church door by making the pastor dependent on federal dollars.

The contrast between the conservatism of Ronald Reagan and the neoconservatism of Bush is captured in their words. "Government isn't the solution, government is the problem," Reagan said again and again. Bush's retort: "Too often, my party has confused the need for limited government with a disdain for government itself."

Where Reagan challenged liberalism as a failed philosophy, Bush told Republicans the only thing wrong with the house liberalism built was that liberals were managing the estate. If we are in power, we can make it work, Bush seemed to be saying. The old temptation: Whig measures, but Tory means.

In his essay "The Neoconservative Persuasion," Irving Kristol openly argues for Republican cohabitation with Big Government and admits that in choosing heroes neoconservatives gravitate to the Roosevelts, while "such Republican and conservative worthies as Calvin Coolidge, Herbert Hoover, Dwight Eisenhower and Barry Goldwater are politely overlooked." Traditional conservatives may disagree, Kristol adds with fine conceit, but "it is the neoconservative public policies, not the traditional Republican ones, that result in Republican presidencies."

Examine the results of the presidential elections of the last three decades of the twentieth century when Republicans won by large margins. Richard M. Nixon won forty-nine states before neoconservatism was invented, and Ronald Reagan, who put Coolidge's picture in the cabinet room and considered himself the disciple and heir of Barry Goldwater, swept forty-four and forty-nine states in 1980 and 1984. Is Kristol suggesting that it was the neoconservatives who went out and won one for the Gipper?

Political history, since the Great Society, demonstrates that Republicans run strongest when the contrast with the Democratic opponent—McGovern, Mondale, Dukakis—is sharpest.

Why have traditional conservatives in the 1990s gone along with Big Government? Because they were tired of losing the White House to Bill Clinton, and being out of power. They were willing to make compromises at the expense of principle to get back in. And Bush seemed to offer the way back. Post 9/11, he had the country behind him. And so the party fell in line. George Bush now defines conservatism for this generation, though any resemblance to what Bob Taft taught and Barry Goldwater preached and Ronald Reagan practiced, and what we all once fought for, is purely coincidental.

Lobbying groups, manned by conservative activists, have now been set up in Washington to steer clients to the right GOP congressman to get their pet projects funded by taxpayers. Right, left, and center are all in on the scam. Everybody gets his or her slice of pork, so long as everyone votes for everyone else's slice. Earmarked projects in the federal budget now number over ten thousand, and the annual price tag by the end of 2003 had hit $23 billion. Among the entries:

- $50,000 for a tattoo-removal project in San Luis Obispo
- $2 million for the Center on Obesity at West Virginia University
- $270,000 to combat "goth culture" in Blue Springs, Missouri
- $150,000 for therapeutic horseback riding in Apple Valley, California
- $4 million for a dolphin-replacement project in Washington State

According to Adam B. Summers, a policy analyst at Reason Foundation, John McCain ran down the following pet pork projects among thousands stuffed into the $375 billion omnibus appropriations bill he called "The Incumbent's Protection Act of 2004":

- $1.8 million for exotic pet disease research in California
- $50 million for an indoor rain forest in Coralville, Iowa
- $200,000 for the West Oahu campus of the University of Hawaii for the making of a documentary film called "Primal Quest"
- $225,000 for the Wheels Museum in New Mexico
- $7.3 million for Hawaiian sea turtles
- $6 million for sea lions in Alaska
- $450,000 for the Johnny Appleseed Heritage Center in Ohio
- $100,000 for the State Historical Society of Iowa for developing the World Food Prize
- $200,000 for the Rock and Roll Hall of Fame in Cleveland, Ohio, for the Rockin' the Schools education program
- $450,000 for an Alaska statehood celebration
- $225,000 for a Hawaii statehood celebration
- $175,000 for the painting of a mural on a flood wall in a Missouri city

- $90,000 for fruit fly research in Montpellier, France
- $225,000 for the restoration of an opera house in Traverse City, Michigan
- $250,000 for the Alaska Aviation Heritage Museum
- $200,000 for the construction and renovation of a shopping center in Guadalupe, Arkansas
- $325,000 for the construction of a swimming pool in Salinas, California
- $100,000 for the renovation of the Coca-Cola building in Macon, Georgia
- $100,000 for the renovation of Paschal's restaurant and motel in Atlanta, Georgia
- $900,000 for the Lewis and Clark Bicentennial commemoration plan in Idaho
- $175,000 for the construction of a zoo in Detroit, Michigan
- $238,000 for the National Wild Turkey Federation
- $200,000 for recreational improvements in North Pole, Alaska
- $100,000 for the restoration of the Jefferson County Courthouse clock tower in Washington State
- $220,000 for the Blueberry Hill Farm in Maine
- $2 million for the First Tee Program, which teaches young people to play golf
- $40 million for the construction of a cargo terminal in the port of Philadelphia to support "high-speed military sealift and other military purposes" vessels which, as McCain notes, "do not even exist, nor are they being championed by the military"

"I've never known a sailor, drunk or sober, with the imagination this Congress has," said John McCain. In the "Pig Book" of Citizens Against Government Waste, the number of projects that never went through the appropriations process in 2004 but were funded for the benefit of senators and congressmen hit 10,656, at a cost just under $23 billion.

Moreover, the march of time has almost guaranteed that the era of balanced budgets in America is over, forever. The 1990s will prove to have been the Indian summer of fiscal responsibility. For, in 2008, the first wave of Baby Boomers, born in 1946, reaches sixty-two and becomes eligible for early retirement. In 2011, the first wave of that generation begins to reach sixty-five. For eighteen years thereafter, 77 million Baby Boomers, the largest population cohort in our history, will cease to be primary contributors to Medicare and Social Security—and become the principal con-sumers of Medicare and social security. By 2030, according to Heritage, spending for the two programs alone will drive up federal spending by 5 percent of GDP, and by 13 percent by 2050. Like Thelma and Louise, Medicare and Social Security are headed for the cliff. And we are in the back seat.

By the end of this decade we are halfway through comes the perfect storm. The Social Security and Medicare surpluses that have disguised the depth of our fiscal crisis will start to vanish. The true deficit, like an enormous undersea volcano, will rise through the surface and explode. U.S. budget demands on private savings will crowd out private borrowers. Baby Boomer contributions to IRAs, 401(k)s, and pension plans that fueled the bull markets of the 1980s and 1990s will taper off and end, and huge withdrawals from these flush funds will begin, depressing markets.

As manufacturing jobs depart for China, and white-collar jobs are outsourced to India, the displaced U.S. workers who move into lower-paying jobs in service industries will contribute less in Social Security, Medicare, and federal and state income taxes. As high-earning Baby Boomers are replaced in the labor force by immi-grants who lack their abilities, skills, education, and earning power, taxes on working America will have to be raised to compen-sate for the lost revenue from the retiring seniors.

What is happening to California where tax consumers are pour-ing in from Mexico as taxpayers head out for Nevada, Arizona, and Colorado will happen to America. Only there will be no place to run, no place to hide. The government will have to raise taxes or run mammoth deficits that will destroy the value of the dollar. As California is headed for Third World status, America is only two or three decades behind. In every way, we are becoming a Third World country.

In any free market, wages for the same work tend to find equilibrium. Over time, steelworkers in Birmingham, Alabama, begin to earn the same wages as the steelworkers in Pittsburgh, Pennsylvania. Inside the global economy, into which the Masters of the Universe are embedding us, the wages of U.S. workers will cease to rise and begin to fall as high-paying jobs are outsourced to Third World workers, and Third World workers are brought in, or break in, to take the jobs of Americans at lower pay. A Wal-Mart salesman does not take home the same pay as an autoworker. Nor does he pay the same taxes.

As the wages of First World workers are arrested or fall, and their tax contributions diminish, cutbacks in social spending will be mandated, as is happening already in California and Old Europe. In 2003, mandatory spending on entitlements such as Social Security, Medicare, welfare, and unemployment hit 11 percent of GDP. After 2008, we will look back on these as the good old days.

Another factor certain to increase the deficit is interest on our $7 trillion national debt. As the Fed cut interest rates to 1 percent, the cost of federal borrowing has been at its lowest in forty years. But when interest rates rise again, as they must, given our budget and trade deficits, the cost to the Treasury of raising money to finance our consumption will rise by the scores of billions. And an ever-increasing slice of that interest will be sent overseas to foreigners who hold an ever-increasing share of the U.S. national debt.

There is one other unstoppable engine of spending. In advocating increased funding for health, education, and welfare, Bush officials cite problems that need attention:

> 25 million children don't live with their fathers; 1.5 million have a parent in prison; half a million are in foster care; 1 million babies a year are born to unwed mothers; one of six families with children earns $17,000 a year or less.

But who and what destroyed the American family?

Was it not the social, moral, and cultural revolution that celebrated sex, drugs, rock 'n' roll, and women's liberation from the burdens of childbearing and child-rearing, and gave us condoms in junior high, no-fault divorce, abortion on demand, and daycare for the survivors?

Among the nearly 2 million American males in jails and prisons, the most common attribute is that almost all are from broken homes.

Liberals preached liberation from the duties of marriage and the moral norms of Christianity. Now conservatives tax and borrow to deal with the crisis created by that liberation. Having deconstructed our society, the revolutionaries demand we provide more and pay more to deal with the consequences of what they did to America.

Eisenhower spoke of a military-industrial complex that was a mighty engine driving federal spending. But it has been superseded in our television age by media-driven politics. Every local crisis that great newspapers uncover is instantly nationalized by network and cable TV. The White House and Congress are then forced to explain what they will do to resolve it. The response is always a new federal program to alleviate the suffering, or a new federal law to deal with such outrages as school shootings.

GOVERNMENT IN THE United States, state, local, and federal, today consumes 34 percent of GDP. In the absence of an unanticipated epidemic of fiscal courage, that figure will rise toward the 48 percent that is the norm in the EU. And because Europe's welfare states are so vast, West Europeans pay 50 percent of their income in taxes, have incomes that are 40 percent lower than ours, and unemployment rates twice as high. That is where America's glide path is taking this generation.

The U.S. budget at $2.4 trillion is so out of control U.S. officials can no longer give a reasonable accounting of what is being spent and lost. In 2003, Comptroller General David M. Walker told a National Press Club audience, for the sixth straight year, that the General Accounting Office "was unable to express an opinion as to whether the U.S. Government's consolidated financial statements were fairly stated."

Under the Sarbanes-Oxley Act, passed in the wake of the Enron and Worldcom scandals, CEOs who file financial statements that are off the mark may be sent to prison for criminal negligence. A U.S. Government that commits accounting blunders of scores of billions of dollars has criminalized accounting blunders in the corporate world. Where a CEO can be sent to prison for dipping into pension funds to pay operating expenses, the U.S. Government has been doing that for decades.

But perhaps Bush better understands the new America run by his own Boomer generation. The spirit of true conservatism appears to be dead. America's response to any social crisis or perceived injustice is now reflexive: What is the president doing about this? Why has the government not rectified this? In his 2004 State of the Union, the president demanded that the NFL and NBA do more about athletes using steroids. This had not previously been considered a federal responsibility.

When did fiscal discipline disappear? When was the idea of principled conservatism abandoned? The collapse can be traced to the rout of the Republican Revolution of 1994, when, in 1995, Newt Gingrich shut down the government but backed down in his showdown with Clinton.

Clinton, at the nadir of his presidency, refused to accept Gingrich-Dole cuts in the growth of Medicare, which they had embedded in a budget resolution and sent to the White House. Clinton vetoed the budget, shut down the government, and blamed the Republicans' insistence on "cutting Medicare." Polls showed the nation backing Clinton and backing away from Congress. Gingrich and the GOP capitulated and did as Clinton demanded, restoring the Medicare funds. Even at his weakest, Clinton had read the country right and bested the GOP when it thought the country was behind it. Like Lee at Gettysburg, the party had chosen to fight on the wrong battlefield.

Republican morale was broken then and there as effectively as the morale of the liberal establishment was broken on the wheel of Vietnam, when its children rose up to denounce the "dirty, immoral war" into which it had led the nation, and which it could not end, or would not win. By 2000, many of the Republican Class of 1994, elected on term-limits pledges to serve six years and go home, had decided to stay and vote for the programs they had been sent to Washington to cut. For that was the only way to guarantee they would never have to go home again.

By the late 1990s, Cato Institute budget watchdog Stephen Moore was reporting that the Republican Congress was voting to spend more than Clinton requested on foreign aid, home heating assistance, land acquisition, Export-Import Bank subsidies, federal aid to education, libraries, AIDS research, refugee assistance, subsidized housing, Head Start, and even the Food and Drug Administration. Alongside the Gingrich Republicans, Bill Clinton was Bob Taft.

Consider the change in the Grand Old Party. Between the end of the Civil War and World War I, Grover Cleveland was the only Democrat to be elected president. Except for a Civil War income tax, phased out in 1872, the government was financed almost entirely on tariff revenue. There was no Federal Reserve. The dollar was as good as gold.

Under McKinley, America's economy grew at 7 percent a year and federal spending was 2.6 percent of GDP. Under Bush, spending has risen above 20 percent of GDP and growth has averaged half of what William McKinley achieved.

Across the spectrum, there is concern that under the Patriot Act, terrorism suspects may, if the Justice Department can make a case to a special court, have their library records inspected. But there is instant obedience when citizens are told to produce records for the IRS of any charitable contributions and all income earned, be it in wages, salaries, dividends, interest, rents, royalties, gambling winnings, or yard sales. And there appears little objection to government seizure of half a man's income in taxes. Remarkable, when one considers that our forefathers almost rose in rebellion over a stamp tax.

During his campaign for a Senate seat from South Carolina in 2004, Congressman Jim DeMint, speaking of an "eleventh-hour crisis in democracy," asked a penetrating question: "How can a nation survive when a majority of its citizens, now dependent on government services, no longer have the incentive to restrain the growth of government?"

Does he not have a point? Today, 18 million Americans work in government—in health, education, the military, and local, state, and federal bureaucracies. The number of Americans receiving Social Security and Medicare is now in the scores of millions, with 77 million Baby Boomers not far back in line now.

There are millions receiving veterans benefits, tens of millions on food stamps, Medicaid, and welfare, and millions more who receive the Earned Income Credit, i.e., they pay no income taxes but get an annual income supplement from the U.S. Government.

The lower half of the U.S. labor force carries roughly 4 percent of a federal income tax burden that is largely borne now by the top ten percent of earners. Then, there is corporate welfare, which Beltway lobbyists fight to preserve and expand, and the pork barrel projects congressmen simply must take home to the district. We may have reached the tipping point. Even Ronald Reagan, who succeeded in so much, conceded to friends that he failed to cut back the growth and size of government as he had hoped.

Before the thirteen colonies were independent, Professor Alexander Tyler of Scotland, writing of the fall of the Athenian republic, came to a somber conclusion:

> A democracy cannot exist as a permanent form of government. It can only exist until the voters discover that they can

vote themselves money from the public treasure. From that moment on the majority always votes for the candidates promising the most money from the public treasury, with the result that a democracy always collapses over loose fiscal policy followed by a dictatorship.

Is that the inevitable fate of America? We're going to find out.

EIGHT

FALLING DOLLAR, FAILING NATION

> There is no subtler, no surer means of overturning the existing basis of society than to debauch the currency. The process engages all the hidden forces of economic law on the side of destruction, and does it in a manner which not one man in a million is able to diagnose.
>
> —Lord Keynes

> In the absence of a gold standard, there is no way to protect savings from confiscation through inflation. There is no safe store of value.
>
> —Alan Greenspan
> *The Objectivist,* 1966

In July 1944, at the Mount Washington Hotel in the resort town of Bretton Woods in the White Mountains of New Hampshire, John Maynard Keynes and Harry Dexter White created the new world order.

Both were exotic birds. The most famous economist of the age, Lord Keynes was a cultural icon of the Bloomsbury Group, a closet homosexual married to a Russian ballerina. He had been famous for a generation as the author of *The Economic Consequences of the Peace.*

A member of the British delegation at Versailles, Keynes had left that fateful conference in righteous rage over the Carthaginian peace imposed by Clemenceau, Wilson, and Lloyd George. The imposition of draconian war reparations the Germans could never pay, Keynes believed, must lead to a default, rearmament, and a new war. World War II had made Keynes a prophet in his own time.

During the Depression, Keynes wrote the most influential economic treatise since Adam Smith's *Wealth of Nations*. *The General Theory of Employment, Interest and Money* rejected laissez-faire and championed government intervention and deficit spending to restore prosperity to nations in economic depression. Keynes's book did not appear until 1936. Yet, his were said to have been the ideas behind the New Deal. Since the 1930s, the Keynesian gospel has divided academics. Indeed, the economic history of the twentieth century can be divided into Before Keynes and After Keynes. In 1971, President Nixon would startle conservatives and liberals alike by declaring, "We are all Keynesians now."

Harry White had a different pedigree. A closet Communist and spy, White was part of an underground espionage cell whose liaison with his Soviet handlers was the courier Whittaker Chambers.

In the 1941 diplomatic confrontation with Japan, White was activated by Moscow as an agent of influence. When Hitler scrapped his pact with Stalin with the blitzkrieg on the Soviet Union in June of 1941, Moscow feared Japan would join its Axis partner and attack Siberia. White was instructed to press his superior, Treasury Secretary Morgenthau, to urge Secretary of State Hull to reject all Japanese peace feelers and hand Tokyo an ultimatum. That ultimatum of November 26, 1941, ordering Japan out of Indochina and China, led straight to Pearl Harbor.

White was also the secret author of the infamous Morgenthau Plan that called for the destruction of the factories of the Ruhr, the flooding of German mines, and the pastoralization of that defeated nation with the consequent starvation of millions. If Morgenthau had had his way, there would have been a peace of retribution and revenge that would have prevented the German nation and people from ever rising again.

Though secretly adopted by FDR and Churchill at the 1944 Quebec Conference, the Morgenthau Plan was hastily repudiated by both Allied statesmen after it was unearthed by the press. But its revelation was seized upon by Nazi propaganda minister Goebbels to convince Germans that the Allied demand for "unconditional surrender" meant starvation and death for Germany.

White would also hold up a $500 million loan voted by Congress to aid the Chinese Nationalists in halting postwar inflation. This act of treachery was a critical factor in the loss of the most populous nation on earth to the Stalinists of Mao Tse-tung.

White would later be charged with giving Stalin's agents the plates, paper, and ink for Germany's postwar currency, enabling Moscow to firm up its grip on the Soviet sector of Germany and to loot the U.S. Treasury, which backed the German currency, of hundreds of millions of dollars.

The "Venona transcripts"—decrypted messages from Soviet agents in the United States back to Moscow during World War II—identified White by three code names: "Lawyer," "Richard," and "Reed." Though Harry Dexter White never achieved the notoriety of Alger Hiss, he was a more vital asset of Soviet intelligence and Stalin. So valuable was he that Moscow offered to pay the college tuition of his daughters if White would stay at his Treasury post.

In 1953, White's name would surface when Eisenhower's attorney general charged ex-President Truman with having known he was a spy as early as 1946. By then it did not matter to White. For in August 1948, just days after his questioning by the House Committee on Un-American Activities, whose rising star was Richard Nixon, Harry Dexter White died of a heart attack. Senator Pat Moynihan said there was no doubt "Harry Dexter White was a Soviet agent."

IN THE SUMMER of 1944, however, White was unknown and Keynes a legend. Yet it was the White scheme for a new world financial system that prevailed at Bretton Woods. For while Keynes could speak for Great Britain, Assistant Secretary of the Treasury White spoke for the power that alone had the resources to underwrite the rebuilding of a devastated Europe. At Bretton Woods, Harry White held the trumps and he played them masterfully.

Fearful of U.S. economic domination, Keynes had arrived at Bretton Woods with a plan to check American power: a world central bank that would print the world's money and control the supply and distribution of international credit. Keynes wanted no return to a gold standard. The discipline of a gold standard, he believed, would restrict creation of the money and credit vital to the recovery of Europe. He wanted the dollar as the world's reserve currency, but severed from gold and backed only by the full faith and credit of the United States. In Keynes's vision, Uncle Sam would meet the demand for the new world currency, but Keynes and colleagues would decide upon the supply. They, in effect, would be the mandarins of the new world order, the first Masters of the Universe.

UNDER THE WHITE plan, however, the dollar was to be the coin of the realm in global commerce. It was to be pegged to gold at $35 an ounce. Any nation that came to Treasury's door with dollars could exchange them, at $35 an ounce, for America's gold bullion. The dollar-gold link would be the hitching post of the new world monetary system.

Other nations were to link their currencies to the dollar at fixed rates of exchange. Purpose of the gold exchange standard: Establish monetary stability to facilitate trade and the free flow of capital— and to prevent the beggar-thy-neighbor devaluations that had occurred in the decade before World War II.

To monitor the system and provide bridge loans to nations facing a run on their currencies, an International Monetary Fund was created. The United States transferred 104 million ounces of gold to the new IMF and billions in cash. Other nations contributed in their own currencies. Each nation received voting strength in the IMF consistent with its contribution.

Harry Dexter White, traitor and spy, was thus the founding father of the International Monetary Fund and, on appointment by Truman in 1946, became its first U.S. executive director.

A sister institution, the International Bank for Reconstruction and Development, was created to provide loans to war-ravaged Europe. It would come to be known as the World Bank. Mission: Borrow from rich nations and lend to ruined nations at low rates of interest with long repayment schedules.

Through the creation of the IMF and World Bank, the United States assumed the lead role Britain had played up until World War I when the pound was the international reserve currency and the City of London was banker to the world. British primacy in global finance had been forever destroyed in the Great War when Britain, to purchase the necessities of national survival, fell deeply in debt to the United States.

Like the British statesmen of the Victorian era, the Bretton Woods Americans were free traders. They had come to New Hampshire with a sense of guilt and duty. They believed the United States—by rejecting the Versailles treaty, refusing to join the League of Nations, and returning to protectionism under Harding, Coolidge, and Hoover, culminating in the Smoot-Hawley tariff of 1930—bore major responsibility for World War II.

As an article of faith, they believed that "Republican isolationism" had smoothed the path to power of Hitler and come close to losing the world to Fascism. Though a cocktail of myths and mendacities, this was a potent brew. American elites have ever since imbibed that sense of guilt and served it up to each generation of American schoolchildren.

Keynes, who had been at Versailles, was resolved not to repeat the blunders of that disastrous conference. He wanted a magnanimous peace where the vanquished Axis powers as well as the victorious Allies would be helped to rebuild. This view was not shared by the secret author of the Morgenthau Plan to turn Germany into pastureland. But both Keynes and White wanted Stalin's Russia invited in to their new world order.

There were, however, inherent flaws in the system White had created. The United States was responsible for providing the dollars, the liquidity, to oil the wheels of international trade. However, America, the most self-sufficient nation in history, had been running surpluses in her trade and financial accounts for decades. Peacetime America sold the world twice as much in dollar volume as she bought.

Money was pouring into the United States, not out. Ways had to be found to shovel out dollars to revive the economies of Europe and Japan. So it was that U.S. troops would be stationed overseas in the hundreds of thousands, spending their paychecks supporting local economies. U.S. banks began to lend abroad and U.S. companies to invest in overseas subsidiaries. Marshall Plan assistance began to flow. Foreign aid followed.

America's domestic market was thrown open to goods made in the factories of countries where wages were a fraction of those in the United States. Our new allies had to sell to us to earn the hard currency to rebuild their shattered countries and pay back their loans from America. Soon, U.S. mills in the Mahoning Valley of Ohio and Mon Valley of Pennsylvania that had made the iron and steel for the weapons that won World War II were being driven into bankruptcy by imports from German and Japanese mills newly constructed with U.S. capital and the latest technology. Veterans came home to see the company towns they grew up in gutted by cheap imports from the nations they had fought to defeat.

Nations free-riding off the U.S. defense budget began to target U.S. industries for destruction. Japan attacked and destroyed America's TV manufacturing. The U.S. auto industry was sent reeling by German, then by Japanese imports, even as U.S. armies stood on the Elbe, and American soldiers fought Free Asia's wars in Korea and Vietnam.

But the fatal flaw in White's international system was this: Once

U.S. dollars began to flow out of America in mighty streams, the dollar-gold link was certain to come under strain, and snap. And that is what finally happened in 1971.

A quarter century after Bretton Woods, with Great Society spending and the cost of Vietnam soaring, America had begun to run budget deficits near 5 percent of GDP. Seven decades of trade surpluses were coming to an end. A third of a century of rising trade deficits was about to begin. U.S. dollars were pouring out to Europe, and Europeans had begun to cash them in for U.S. gold. Fort Knox was about to be cleaned out. But Nixon and Treasury Secretary John Connally refused to let it happen.

In August of 1971, Nixon slammed shut the gold window, canceled the U.S. commitment to redeem dollars for gold, let the dollar float, and imposed a 10 percent across-the-board tariff. "Nixon shock!" said the stunned Japanese.

The dam broke. After the dollar was cut loose from gold, the price of gold shot to as high as $800 an ounce in a decade. Bretton Woods was dead. Speculators who had bet against the dollar and against American credibility in defending its currency were hugely rewarded.

With the dollar no longer pegged to gold, and all currencies floating free, there was no longer any need for an IMF to maintain exchange rates. For the exchange rates no longer existed. But just as the March of Dimes did not close up shop when Drs. Sabin and Salk found the cures for polio, the IMF found a new mission to stay in business: Banker of last resort to the world. Henceforth, any nation about to default on its debts would find the IMF at its door, with billions to lend, in exchange for that nation's surrender of its economic independence and a pledge to follow a strict IMF regimen for a return to economic health.

WHEN NIXON LET the dollar float, a dollar was worth 360 Japanese yen. The yen was so undervalued Japan was able to flood the U.S. market with high-quality cars that sold far below the price at which the Big Three could afford to build, sell, and survive.

In 1985, the dollar, at 220 to the yen, was still too high to arrest the rising U.S. trade deficit. In the Plaza Accord of 1985, Secretary of the Treasury James Baker and Undersecretary Richard Darman agreed to act jointly with the allies to bring the dollar down. For the Big Three were at death's door. Refusing to let any of them go under, Reagan intervened to save the industry by imposing import quotas on Japanese cars. Free traders denounced Reagan as a heretic. The death of Ford and Chrysler were of far less concern to them than fidelity to the free-trade gospel of David Ricardo and Adam Smith.

But Reagan's intervention succeeded. The U.S. auto industry was saved. By now, the boom of the 1980s was underway, propelled by the tax cuts of Reagan and the sound money policy of the Fed. With the collapse of the Soviet Union in 1991 came deep cuts in defense spending, balanced budgets, and surpluses in the late 1990s.

This new prosperity enabled the United States to rescue Mexico, Thailand, Indonesia, South Korea, Russia, Argentina, and Brazil in the financial crises of 1995–98. Hundreds of billions of dollars poured out in loans from the United States, the IMF, and the World Bank to enable these countries to continue servicing their mounting foreign debts.

In return, however, the IMF insisted that these countries devalue their currencies, slashing the dollar price of their exports. The idea was to have the defaulting countries export their way out of their economic crises by flooding the American market with goods to earn the dollars to pay back the IMF and international banks. It worked. Clinton threw open America's markets to imports at fire-sale prices. Thus did Clinton and Robert Rubin sacrifice American labor on the altar of global capital to a thunderous ovation from the Davos elite.

Now, the U.S. merchandise trade deficit fairly exploded. Today it is $600 billion, nearly ten times as large as it was under George

H. W. Bush. And there appears no end in sight to these mammoth trade deficits despite three years of a falling dollar.

Early in George W. Bush's term, the euro was worth 83 cents. Since then it has risen 50 percent, to $1.27. The price of gold has gone from $260 an ounce to $390. To America's globalists this is welcome news. A falling dollar makes U.S. exports cheaper and imports more expensive, easing the pressure for protectionism. This is like celebrating the loss of an arm, as one can now buy one's shirts more cheaply.

A falling currency is the mark of a failing country, and our fading dollar mirrors fading confidence in the Bush administration's ability to manage America's affairs. And there are solid grounds for alarm. In 2005, the trade deficit in goods and the budget deficit may together reach 10 percent of GDP. We are borrowing over $1 trillion a year to finance our new empire, our welfare-warfare state, and our binge-buying at the malls.

A sinking currency represents the silent theft of a people's wealth by their rulers. And when the currency of an imperial power sinks, there are strategic consequences. Citizens lose faith in government. Aid dollars do not go as far as they once did. U.S. troops abroad and their families find their lives harsher. It becomes more difficult to maintain forces overseas. You begin to rely on mercenaries. You cannot run a world empire on a collapsing currency. Just ask the Brits.

Oil is priced in dollars. When the euro fell to 83 cents, it took 36 euros to buy a barrel of oil at $30 a barrel. With the euro at $1.27, that barrel of oil can be bought for 24 euros, a price cut of 33 percent for Europeans. OPEC, feeling itself cheated, cut back production, forcing up the price of oil as high as $42 a barrel, sending gasoline prices here to record highs, and dealing a body blow to the recovering U.S. economy.

A greater danger is that foreign central banks that now hold $1 trillion in Treasury bonds will begin to shed them. Such dumping would force the Federal Reserve to raise interest rates to finance our trade and budget deficits, aborting recovery. It is hard to see an early or painless end to the downward spiral. As the cancer of devaluation eats up America's wealth, the world, seeing us unable to stop printing dollars, grows increasingly reluctant to hold them.

In the long run, a cheaper dollar will cut the trade deficit by making imports intolerably expensive and exports cheaper. But in the short run, a falling dollar can send a trade deficit soaring. For we have now come to depend on foreigners for one-seventh of all the goods and services we buy each year and a far higher share of the manufactures we consume. If we do not produce VCRs, TVs, cell phones, and radios, we have no alternative but to buy abroad. As with narcotics, such dependencies are not easily ended.

CONSIDER THE NEW world we have entered.

When the Asian crisis broke in the 1990s, the U.S. economy was booming. With the IMF, we were able to pour $200 billion in loans into Thailand, Indonesia, the Philippines, South Korea, Russia, Argentina, and Brazil. To enable them to earn the dollars to pay down those debts, we promised to keep the U.S. market wide open to foreign goods. But conditions have changed.

The U.S. merchandise trade deficit is now over $600 billion, the largest annual wealth transfer in history. Some 2.6 million manufacturing jobs in America, one in every six, were lost in Bush's first term. White-collar jobs are being outsourced. The dollar is sinking. With the money we are pumping out for imports, foreigners are buying up America.

The three pillars upon which the global economy rests are now all weaker than they were in the 1990s.

First, there is a reduced willingness on the part of the United States to bail out deadbeat nations on the brink of default on their foreign loans. Second, U.S. willingness to take in all the goods foreigners are able to sell here is diminishing. As of 2002, according to the U.S. Business and Industry Council, America was importing 3 percent of Japan's total production, 10 percent of China's, 16 percent of Singapore's, 21 percent of Mexico's, 25 percent of

Malaysia's, and 29 percent of the GDP of Canada. Finally, the willingness of Congress to accept continued job losses, due to trade deficits, and to continue financing the IMF, is dissipating.

And foreigners will not forever finance our consumption binge. As historian Niall Ferguson wrote in the *New Republic* in June 2004, Asian nations have been willing "to buy mind-boggling quantities of dollars to sustain the system" of international trade.

Between January 2002 and December of last year, the Bank of Japan's foreign exchange reserves grew by $266 billion. Those of China, Hong Kong, and Malaysia grew by $224 billion. Taiwan acquired more than $80 billion. Nearly all of these increases took the form of purchases of U.S. dollars and dollar-denominated bonds. In the first three months of 2004 alone, the Japanese bought another $142 billion.

Asian nations continue to accept and hold depreciating dollars in return for their goods for two reasons: To maintain and increase their share of the U.S. market and to continue to suck production out of the United States. This cannot go on indefinitely. We are approaching a precipice, and the only question is when we reach it. Writes Ferguson:

> Should Asian central banks even temporarily lose their appetite for dollars, interest rates could spike immediately, creating a self-reinforcing cycle of a falling dollar exchange rate and rising U.S. interest rates. The United States, then, could face a crisis not unlike the ones that afflicted the Mexican peso in 1994 or the Thai baht in 1997.

Then there is the issue of national defaults. In 2002, Argentina threw in its hand and said it would no longer service its $100 billion foreign debt. Rising to the challenge, America and the IMF defiantly refused to lend Buenos Aires any new money. Argentina defaulted. Now Buenos Aires is refusing to pay more than 25 cents on the dollar on her foreign loans. Message: Unless Third World countries receive fresh cash in new loans, they will stop paying off the old loans. Call it extortion.

A spirit of economic nationalism is afoot. In October of 2003, legendary investor Warren Buffett revealed that, for the first time, he was speculating against the dollar by buying foreign currencies. This son of a Middle American congressman was betting the capital placed in his custody by American citizens against the ability of their government to put its house in order:

> our country has been behaving like an extraordinarily rich family that possesses an immense farm. In order to consume 4% more than we produce—that's the trade deficit—we have, day by day, been both selling pieces of the farm and increasing the mortgage on what we still own.

That farm is now markedly diminished in size, the mortgage payments are rising, and the possibility exists that we may lose our home.

How did it happen?

The gathering crisis of the global economy was traceable to 1964 and the rout of the Goldwater Republicans who believed in small government and balanced budgets. Reduced to 38 seats in the Senate and 140 in the House, the GOP could no longer serve as a blocking force against the advance of Big Government. Exhilarated by a triumph that rivaled FDR's over Landon, LBJ and his Democrats felt that this was their hour of power, their heaven-sent opportunity to exceed FDR's New Deal with a Great Society that would ensure the party's near permanence in power.

There followed the Vietnam-era guns-and-butter budgets, which, by 1968, had ignited inflation and inspired a belief abroad that the Americans had lost control of their affairs. They began cashing in dollars for gold.

Elected with only 43 percent of the vote in 1968, Nixon completed the Great Society, running up the largest deficits since World War II. Nixon also maintained the free-trade policies of JFK and LBJ, as U.S. trade surpluses continued to shrink and disappear. Believing the recession of 1958 and tight-money policy of the Fed had cost him the election of 1960, Nixon appointed his old friend from Ike's inner circle, Arthur Burns, to chair the Federal Reserve. Burns would ensure that money was cheap and plentiful in 1972. Nixon then cut the dollar loose from the discipline of gold and, to keep inflation invisible, imposed wage and price controls.

The result was an unemployment rate under 4 percent when voters went to the polls, and a forty-nine-state landslide. The bill came due as Nixon was being driven from office in the Watergate scandal. As Andrew Jackson's economic policies would cost his heir and successor Martin Van Buren a second term, so the economic consequences of the Johnson-Nixon era cost Ford and Carter a second term.

The appointment of Paul Volcker to the Fed, however, and the 1980 election of Reagan rescued the nation. Volcker brutally tightened money until he squeezed double-digit inflation out of the economy, while Reagan unleashed the private sector with the boldest tax cuts since the 1920s. And the eagle soared for two decades, despite the tax hikes of Bush and Clinton. The federal budget, flush with revenue, not only came into balance, but began to generate surpluses.

The free-trade fundamentalism of Bush I and Clinton, however, accelerated the export of America's industrial base. To produce for the U.S. market at higher profits, U.S. companies transferred factories to countries where the cost of domestic labor was a fraction of that of American labor.

Under Bush II, the chickens have come home to roost: A sinking dollar, the deindustrialization of America, and a current-account and fiscal deficit that combined have hit 10 percent of GDP. Like the great commercial and trade empires that preceded us—Holland, Spain, and England—the United States has now entered upon its time of decline. Only heroic action and painful decisions can reverse it. And success will require the better part of a decade.

NINE

THE ABDICATION OF CONGRESS AND THE RISE OF JUDICIAL DICTATORSHIP

The power, which has the right of passing, without
appeal, on the validity of your laws is your sovereign.
—John Randolph

Thirty years ago, in *Conservative Votes, Liberal Victories: Why the Right Has Failed*, this author wrote:

> Much has been written about how the Imperial President
> has usurped the powers of the Congress of the United
> States. But it is to the judiciary and the bureaucracy that
> Congress has truly surrendered power and authority. These
> are the institutions which interpret and administer the laws
> with increasing indifference to congressional intent.

That this remains true today, despite the Reagan Revolution and the Bush Restoration of 2000, despite the fact that seven of nine justices on the Supreme Court were put there by Republican presidents, underscores the point. Here, too, the Right has failed. What went wrong?

That Congress was meant to be the first branch of government seems indisputable. The Continental Congress that declared independence, named Washington commander in chief, fought the Revolution, sent abroad such envoys as Benjamin Franklin, John Adams, Thomas Jefferson, and John Jay, negotiated the alliance with France, and concluded the peace with Britain, was a legislative body.

As James Burnham writes in *Congress and the American Tradition,* the "primacy of the legislature in the intent of the Constitution is plain on the face of that document, as it is in the deliberations of the Philadelphia Convention."

> It is the Constitution's first Article that defines the structure and powers of the legislature. The legislative Congress is to be the sole source of all laws (except the clauses of the Constitution itself). . . . Congress alone can authorize the getting or spending of money. It is for Congress to support, regulate and govern the Army and Navy, and to declare war. Save for the bare existence of a Supreme Court, it is for Congress to establish and regulate the judicial system. All officers of both executive and judiciary are subject to congressional impeachment; but for their own official conduct the members of Congress are answerable only to themselves.

Before World War II, Congress seemed a truly coequal branch, dominating weak presidents and struggling with strong ones in the disputed borderlands where powers collide. Not so long ago, schoolchildren were more familiar with Webster, Clay, and Calhoun than any president between Jackson and Lincoln. In his 1884 *Congressional Government*, Woodrow Wilson wrote that, no matter what the Constitution ordained, "the actual form of our present government is . . . a scheme of Congressional supremacy."

When Wilson brought home the Treaty of Versailles with the League of Nations charter embedded in the text, a Senate led by Henry Cabot Lodge rejected it. Between 1844 and 1920, Congress gave us three presidents: Polk, Garfield, and Harding. In the eighty years since, only one has come directly out of Congress: John F. Kennedy.

In postwar America, the Congress has fallen into eclipse and shown itself incapable of resisting encroachments upon its constitutional powers. Worse, it has colluded in its own dispossession and seems not really to care greatly that it is an object of derision and contempt.

Consider the lost or forfeited powers of the first branch.

In the Constitution, Congress is given sole power to declare war, to raise and spend revenue, to coin money, to regulate foreign trade. Yet, all these primordial powers Congress has surrendered.

Harry Truman took us to war in Korea and called a conflict in which thirty-three thousand Americans died a "police action." He did not ask for, and Congress did not demand that he ask for, a declaration of war, though Congress was in session when North Korea invaded. Vietnam was a second presidential war. Congress transferred its war power to Lyndon Johnson in a Tonkin Gulf Resolution passed in the House by a unanimous vote. Only two senators dissented on a war resolution that was based on sketchy evidence of a second North Vietnamese attack on a U.S. destroyer.

George H. W. Bush barely won Senate approval to order U.S. troops to eject Iraq from Kuwait, but signaled that, had the Senate voted down his war resolution, he would have gone ahead and invaded.

Serbia did not threaten us, had not attacked us, did not want war with us, and had agreed to permit twelve hundred UN inspectors in Kosovo. And the House refused to authorize Clinton to wage war. Yet, Clinton ordered the bombing of Serbia for seventy-eight days, waging an illegal war against that small nation for rejecting an ultimatum that it allow NATO troops to transit its territory and occupy a province. What did Congress do about the seizure of its war power? It impeached Clinton for high crimes and misdemeanors—in the Monica Lewinsky affair.

In 2002, leaders of the Democratic Party, including Hillary Clinton and John Kerry, voted to give George W. Bush a blank check to wage war on Iraq at a time of his choosing. Yet, Iraq, too, had not attacked us, did not threaten us, did not want war with us, had permitted UN inspectors in, and was prepared to admit CIA inspectors to search for the weapons of mass destruction no one has been able to find.

What was the principal complaint of congressional Democrats about that vote? That President Bush had forced members to vote on war in the middle of an off-year election. How inconsiderate of the president.

As for the neoconservatives, they are presidential supremacists and compulsive interventionists, impatient with any restrictions or restraints, constitutional or otherwise, on the commander in chief's authority to take us into war.

CONGRESS'S SURRENDER OF its constitutional authority over trade has been total. In 1994, Congress was allowed only a yes or no vote on a twenty-three thousand-page GATT treaty. No amendments were permitted. With its yes vote, Congress put the United States under the jurisdiction of an institution of world government, the World Trade Organization, whose dispute panels operate in secret and where America now has one vote to twenty-five for the EU. The WTO was also granted power to authorize fines on the United States and to demand the repeal of American laws. This it has repeatedly done.

With "fast track," Congress voted to surrender its right to amend trade treaties negotiated by the executive, a right that Hamilton and the Founding Fathers expressly wanted Congress to have and keep.

In 1995, over congressional opposition, President Clinton bailed out Mexico City with scores of billions of tax dollars directly out of the U.S. Treasury. The World Bank and IMF routinely put U.S. taxpayers at risk for loans running into scores of billions of dollars without even consulting Congress.

In 1997, Congress attempted to dilute its power of the purse by giving Clinton a line-item veto of appropriations bills. The Supreme Court had to rescue Capitol Hill from its own Munich. Congress cannot surrender its constitutional power through law, said the court. But Congress had tried. Why? Because granting the president a line-item veto would enable members to lard up appropriation bills to gratify constituents and lobbyists while leaving the onus and duty of cutting spending to the White House.

The Constitution gives Congress the power to coin money. But in 1913, this power was transferred to a new Federal Reserve, whose present chairman, Alan Greenspan, barely contains his boredom when called on to explain why he has decided to raise or lower interest rates, to expand or contract the money supply, to slow or speed up the growth of an economy upon which 290 million Americans depend.

When the economy is growing, Greenspan is a miracle worker. When the economy slows and jobs are not being created, calls go out for his resignation. But no one in Congress suggests that the first branch of government abolish the Fed and give America back a dollar as good as gold.

On the issues or religion, race, morality, and culture that define us as a people, Congress has, for half a century, been surrendering its law-making power to judges and justices. The Supreme Court first seized these powers in a bloodless coup. It marched in and occupied the terrain because Congress did not defend it and would not fight for it.

Why does Congress refuse to challenge court aggressions? Because Congress is an institutional coward. Many members are men and women of character and courage, but the institution of Congress prefers to let the cup pass away and let the courts make the decisions on issues that divide us deeply and emotionally.

For, should a congressman vote "wrong" on abortion, affirmative action, or flag burning, his career could be over. Truth be told, in the culture war, many Republicans are summer soldiers and sunshine patriots, while neoconservatives are, all too often, appeasers. In 1992, when I called on the party in Houston to engage Clinton & Clinton in the struggle for the soul of America, Irving Kristol wrote in the *Wall Street Journal*, "I regret to inform Pat Buchanan that those [culture] wars are over and the left has won."

To Congress, discretion is the better part of valor. Let the judges decide. Let them take the heat. So, while court encroachments are angrily protested and "activist judges" loudly denounced, Congresses do nothing. Unlike Esau, Congress does not want its birthright back.

Congress has also yielded power to unelected bureaucrats. When Congress passed the Endangered Species Act in 1973, it sought to protect the bald eagle, timber wolf, and grizzly bear. It did not intend that all logging end in 7 million acres of forest in California and Oregon and thousands of logging jobs be abolished so the habitat of the northern spotted owl might be undisturbed. Or that the Tellico Dam in Tennessee be held up for years lest the local snail darters be endangered. Or that middle-class homes in Riverside not be built until accommodations could be found for the Stephens kangaroo rats residing there. Threatened with prosecution if they cleared fire breaks for their homes, twenty-nine families lost homes, and the k-rat habitat burned to the ground. While Congress sits idly by, bureaucrats and judges, in league with environmental extremists, imperil the livelihoods of workers, families, and towns to protect the vital interests of rats, bugs, and weeds.

"We had envisioned trying to protect pigeons and things like that. We never thought about mussels and ferns and all those subspecies of squirrels," said Representative Don Young of Alaska. But what Congress intended is of no consequence when bureaucrats and judges take custody of the laws they enacted. Why does Congress capitulate? Why does Congress take it? Because the legislators fear that if they stand up to extremism, they may be painted as enemies of the environment, a potentially fatal charge at election time.

Why has Congress yielded power to presidents, judges, bureaucrats? The dirty little secret is that Congress no longer wants the accountability that goes with the exercise of power. It does not want to govern. Both parties prefer to make only those decisions that will be applauded by constituents and rewarded at the ballot box, and to pass on to others decisions that deeply divide or roil the public.

Among the reasons a Democratic Senate gave President Bush a blank check to go to war was the felt belief that senators, like the esteemed Sam Nunn, who had voted to deny George H. W. Bush authority to go to war in 1991, were never again seriously considered as presidential contenders.

Members prefer the perception of power to the reality. They would rather remain in office than risk defeat by governing America. And there is this benefit to their surrender of authority: A seat in Congress is now almost as secure as a federal judgeship. Absent indictment or scandal, it is almost impossible to unseat a congressman.

So it is that the vast estate of congressional powers granted in the Constitution has been seized and subdivided between presidents and a Supreme Court that is now the final and binding authority on what new laws Congress may enact and what Congress meant when it enacted the old laws. When great controversies arise—how to resolve a crisis in Social Security, whether to build an MX missile, how to allocate blame for 9/11—Congress creates a commission. So doing, it gives itself cover for the final decision and an alibi: "We have no control over what the commission did."

"What kind of government do we have?" a lady asked Dr. Franklin when he emerged from the constitutional convention in Philadelphia. "A republic—if you can keep it," said the wise old man. We did not keep it. This generation lost it. America has ceased to be the republic of the Founding Fathers.

Five years after FDR's New Deal was launched, journalist Garet Garrett, citing Aristotle, wrote of a "revolution within the form," when "one thing takes the place of another, so that the ancient laws will remain, while the power will be in the hands of those who have brought about revolution in the state."

> There are those who think they are holding the pass against a revolution that may be coming up the road. But they are gazing in the wrong direction. The revolution is behind them. It went by in the Night . . . singing songs to freedom. . . . You do not defend what is already lost.

"A revolution within the form" is what happened to our republic in the twentieth century. The Constitution remains clear. Congress is the first branch. But that is no longer the reality. Congress has been eclipsed by the president, Supreme Court, Federal Reserve, the media, the regulatory agencies, even the bureaucracy. Congress now ranks below them all in power and influence over the lives of our people. Could it recapture its birthright, if we elected congressional leaders of the kidney and courage that America once knew? That is the only question still open.

THE IMPERIAL JUDICIARY

In November 2003, Chief Justice Margaret Marshall of the State Supreme Judicial Court gave the Massachusetts legislature six months to enact a law granting homosexuals the right to marry. In July, the U.S. Supreme Court had prepared the ground for Marshall's decision when it struck down the laws of seventeen states and declared homosexual sodomy to be a constitutionally protected right. Following that *Lawrence* decision, Justice Antonin Scalia fairly exploded:

> . . . state laws against bigamy, same-sex marriage, adult incest, prostitution, masturbation, adultery, fornication, bestiality, and obscenity [are now] called into question. . . . The court has largely signed on to the homosexual agenda . . . The court has taken sides in the culture war.

Indeed, it had. Nevertheless, on May 17, 2004, Governor Mitt Romney bowed to the order of the court and began handing out the marriage licenses, though he and the state legislature believed that nothing in the constitution of the commonwealth mandated gay marriages. Few better examples exist of how unelected judges have usurped the law-making power, and how elected officials have abdicated.

When did this revolution begin?

Sixty years to the day before Romney's surrender, May 17, 1954, the U.S. Supreme Court handed down its 9–0 decision in *Brown v. the Board of Education.* In the name of equal rights, the Warren Court had effected an historic coup d'état. It had usurped power over state schools never granted to courts either in federal law or the Constitution.

That the 14th Amendment did not outlaw segregation was obvious. That amendment was approved by a Congress that presided over the segregated schools of Washington, D.C. But the Warren Court, fed up with the torpor of the democratic process, decided to desegregate America—by court order.

The coup succeeded. Though Eisenhower was stunned by *Brown,* he and the Republican Congress accepted the court ruling as federal law to be enforced by federal troops, as it would be at Central High in Little Rock in 1957. And because we agreed with the goal—an end to segregation—we accepted, without questioning the implications, the means adopted: judicial dictate. Having written its views of segregation into the Constitution and imposed its will on the nation, a confident Warren Court now began to impose a social, cultural, and moral revolution upon America.

Under this secularist and egalitarian revolution, America's schools were as de-Christianized as in the Soviet Union. Voluntary prayer and Bible readings were abolished. All replicas of the Ten Commandments were removed. Easter pageants and Christmas carols were forbidden. Teachers were ordered to stop wearing replicas of crosses and crucifixes to class. This remorseless campaign to de-Christianize the public life of the nation was only the beginning. In the half century after Brown, the Supreme Court and its subordinate courts:

• Declared pornography and naked dancing in beer halls to be constitutionally protected freedom of expression.
• Created new rights for criminals.
• Imposed broad new restrictions on state and local prosecutors.

• Outlawed the death penalty across America for a generation.

• Declared abortion a constitutional right and ruled that states cannot protect babies from a grisly procedure that involves stabbing the child in the head with scissors when halfway out of the womb.

• Ordered both houses of all state legislatures reapportioned on the basis of population alone.

• Ordered VMI and the Citadel to end their 150-year-old all-male cadet corps traditions and stop saying grace before meals.

• Abolished terms limits on members of Congress enacted in popular referenda.

• Forbade Arizona to make English the official language for state business.

• Ordered California—60 percent of whose people had voted to end welfare to illegal aliens—to restore welfare benefits to illegals.

• Approved of discrimination against white students to advance the "compelling state interest" of "diversity" in college.

• Declared homosexual sodomy a constitutional right.

• Declared that the First Amendment protects the right of adults to burn the American flag—but prohibits school children from reciting the pledge of allegiance to that flag.

In each case, courts overthrew laws supported by majorities, to replace them with policies demanded by minorities. "The judiciary, led by the Supreme Court, is in the vanguard of the elite imposing nonmajority values and policies on the country," write legal scholars William Quirk and R. Randall Bridwell in *Judicial Dictatorship*. "They are, as Jefferson said, the 'miners and sappers' of democracy."

Today, America meekly awaits the Supreme Court's judgment on whether all fifty states must legalize gay marriage. Were George III to return to life, he would erupt with laughter at what a flock of sheep the descendants of the American rebels have become.

No congress, no president could have survived the issuance of such radical dictates. Yet the Supreme Court has prospered to become the first branch of government. Why do we submit?

"Here, sir, the people rule!" was the proud boast of nineteenth-century Americans. But the people no longer rule in America. Though our society is democratic, our government is not. Like ancient Israel, the republic has fallen under a rule of judges. How serious is our situation? Robert Bork answers:

> [I]t is extremely serious . . . the court is steadily shrinking the area of self-government without any legitimate authority to do so, in the constitution or elsewhere. In the process it is revising the moral and cultural life of the nation. The constitutional law it is producing might as well be written by the ACLU.

How did it happen that a republic born of a rebellion against a king and parliament we did not elect has fallen under a tyranny of judges we did not elect? How did we come to live under what Jefferson warned us would be "the despotism of an oligarchy"?

THE COURT'S ASCENT TO POWER

In Federalist #78, Hamilton famously described the judiciary as the "least dangerous" and "weakest" of the three branches.

> The judiciary . . . has no influence over either the sword or the purse; no direction either of the strength or the wealth of the society, and can take no active resolution whatever. It may truly be said to have neither FORCE nor WILL but merely judgment; and must ultimately depend upon the aid of the executive arm for the efficacy of its judgments.

Rarely was Hamilton more wrong.

The great leap forward came with John Marshall. In *Marbury v. Madison* (1803), that chief justice asserted a right of review of all laws enacted by Congress to ensure they conformed to the Constitution. "It is emphatically the province and duty of the judicial department to say what the law is," said Marshall. The court's interpretation of the Constitution, Marshall was saying, was final and binding. Though universally accepted today, Marshall's claim of judicial supremacy was rejected by Jefferson, Madison, Jackson, Lincoln, Theodore Roosevelt, FDR, and many historians and legal scholars.

"Nothing in the Constitution confers superiority upon the Supreme Court," wrote conservative scholar and author Robert Nisbet. "Mr. Justice Holmes put it this way, 'I do not think the United States would come to an end if we lost our power to declare an Act of Congress void.'" Said Judge Learned Hand: "One cannot find among the powers granted to the Court any authority to pass upon validity of the decisions of another Department," and "there is nothing in the United States Constitution that gave to the Court authority to review the decisions of Congress."

THE DRED SCOTT DECISION

Not for fifty-four years after *Marbury v. Madison* did the Supreme Court use the authority claimed by Marshall to strike down a federal law. But in 1857, Chief Justice Roger Taney handed down his decision in the case of Dred Scott.

A slave in Missouri, Scott had been brought across the Mississippi to Illinois, and then to Minnesota, and, as a resident of those free states, had petitioned the court to declare him a free man.

Taney's ruling stunned the country. As Dred Scott was a descendant of Africans brought in bondage to America, Taney ruled, Scott was a slave for life and had no right to sue in a federal court or become a U.S. citizen. Under the Constitution, slaves are property, said the chief justice, and slave owners do not lose the right to their property when they move into free states.

Taney had torpedoed the Missouri Compromise, which Congress had reached in 1820, on whether new states carved out of the

Louisiana Territory would be admitted to the Union as slave or free, thereby affecting the balance of power in an evenly divided Senate. At the time of that compromise, the aging Jefferson had heard "a fire bell in the night" and feared his country was headed for dissolution or civil war. Under the compromise, states formed out of the territories above a certain latitude would enter the Union as free states, while those formed from territory below the line would enter as slave states.

But with Taney declaring the entire Union safe for slavery, the Missouri Compromise was dead. Horace Greeley said of Taney's ruling that it was "entitled to just so much moral weight as would be the judgment of a majority of those congregated in any Washington bar-room." Said Lincoln: "I have expressed my opposition to the Dred Scott decision. All I am doing is refusing to obey it as a political rule."

In his first inaugural, Lincoln challenged John Marshall's doctrine of judicial supremacy as a mortal threat to democracy itself:

> . . . if the policy of the Government upon vital questions
> affecting the whole people is to be irrevocably fixed by the
> decision of the Supreme Court, the instant they are made
> in ordinary litigation between parties in personal actions,
> the people will have ceased to be their own rulers, having to
> that extent practically resigned their Government into the
> hands of that eminent tribunal.

When Taney denounced Lincoln's dispatch of troops to Maryland to prevent the election of secessionists and rejected his suspension of habeas corpus, an enraged president had had enough. He ordered Taney arrested. Cooler heads prevailed upon Lincoln to pull back from sending soldiers to lay hands on the chief justice of the United States.

THE REVOLUTION BEGINS

Yet, the full flowering of judicial supremacy did not begin until FDR. Enraged at "the nine old men," the conservative activists who had thrown out his New Deal laws, Roosevelt packed the Supreme Court with liberal jurists who shared his political philosophy.

Gradually, however, these jurists went beyond allowing New Deal laws to stand, and began to explore and to exploit their latent power to impose their ideology on society. No issue is more central to this debate than the one that has divided us more than any other—race—and no decision is more central to the social revolution than Ike's nomination of California governor Earl Warren to be chief justice.

Warren, who backed Ike over Taft at the 1952 convention, was promised the first opening on the court. It occurred when Chief Justice Fred Vinson died in 1953. On May 17, 1954, the new chief justice read the court's opinion in *Brown v. the Board of Education*. "With *Brown,* the Warren Court spit out the bit of judicial restraint," wrote Robert Bartley of the *Wall Street Journal*.

In his decision, Warren had cited the 14th Amendment prohibition: "Nor shall any state deny to any person the equal protection of the laws . . ." Speaking for a unanimous court, he declared: "We conclude that in the field of public education the doctrine of 'separate but equal' has no place. Separate educational facilities are inherently unequal."

The decision overturned a fifty-eight-year-old precedent and was rooted in sociology, not the Constitution. Wrote *New York Times* columnist James Reston: "The Court's opinion reads more like an expert opinion on sociology." Ike was said to be furious. But unlike Andrew Jackson, who roared, "John Marshall has made his decision. Now let him enforce it!" Ike fumed and did nothing. Later, he would say of Warren's nomination that it was the "biggest damfool mistake I ever made."

Historian William Manchester wrote of Ike that, "as an old soldier he knew that orders must be obeyed. The Court had interpreted the Constitution; the chief executive had to carry out its instructions." Manchester reveals how deeply the idea of judicial supremacy had embedded itself in the consciousness of the country. When the Supreme Court gives an order, Manchester was saying, presidents must salute and obey.

Seeing the Warren court seize such powers, lower courts began to push the envelope. In 1967, U.S. District Judge J. Skelly Wright declared that D.C. public schools, though desegregated, were still denying equal opportunity by operating a "track system" that permitted brighter students to proceed at a faster pace. Wright ordered the track system abolished. Superintendent Carl Hansen resigned. By 1970, most white students were gone. Today, minority children make up 96 percent of the student body and test scores are the lowest in the nation, though per-pupil spending is near the nation's highest.

In 1968, the Warren Court itself moved beyond desegregation. In *Green v. New Kent County*, it declared unconstitutional a "freedom of choice" plan in Virginia, where students were allowed to choose which of two high schools they wished to attend. Where *Brown* had prohibited the assignment of students by race, *Green* commanded it. Integration was now deemed more important than freedom.

Green was followed three years later by *Swann v. Charlotte-Mecklenburg Board of Education,* which ordered the busing of students out of their neighborhoods to achieve racial balance. For millions of families, it was the end of life in the city. They moved out to the suburbs. Forced busing to integrate urban schools, "an experiment noble in purpose," like Prohibition, had brought about the resegregation and the ruin of countless urban schools.

Had the Constitution been followed and the divisive issue left to legislators, it might have been better for us all. Citizens in a democracy will accept the decisions of elected officials they can remove far more readily than the dictates of judges who serve for life. Governor George Wallace told this writer he stood in the schoolhouse door to protest the integration of the University of Alabama because the order had been handed down by a federal judge. Congress had never legislated the integration of the public schools.

EQUALITY AS A RESULT

By the time of the Civil Rights Act of 1964, almost all of America had been converted to the idea of equality of opportunity, guaranteed by law. But for the federal judiciary, this was no longer enough. In 1978, in *California Regents v. Bakke,* the Supreme Court upheld an admissions policy at the Medical School at the University of California at Davis that set aside sixteen out of one hundred slots for minorities, and declared them off-limits to white applicants.

Twice, Allan Bakke had been denied admission to Davis, though his test scores were well above the average of the sixteen minority applicants admitted. Bakke's complaint: Had he not been white, he would have been admitted. He was a victim of racial discrimination.

Ruling against Bakke, Justice Harry Blackmun gave a high court benediction to discrimination, if done to benefit minorities, in almost Orwellian language. "In order to get beyond racism we must first take account of race," wrote Blackmun. "[I]n order to treat some people equally, we must treat them differently."

A year after *Bakke* came *United Steelworker v. Weber.*

When the United Steelworkers in Louisiana set up a program to bring production workers into craft training at the Kaiser Aluminum plant, they set aside 50 percent of the slots for minorities. Brian Weber filed suit, alleging he had been denied entry into the training program though he had greater seniority at the plant than the black workers being admitted. Weber argued that this violated the Civil Rights Act of 1964. The trial and appellate courts decided for him. The Supreme Court came down against.

Justice William Brennan argued that the "spirit" of the 1964 law permitted a 50 percent set-aside for African-Americans. What the court was saying was that a Civil Rights Act that outlawed discrimination permitted discrimination if the beneficiary was black and the victim white. Hubert Humphrey had said in 1964 that if his bill contained any such provision for quotas, he would eat it page by page.

In 2003, the Supreme Court struck down an admissions policy at the University of Michigan, where twenty points were automatically added to test scores of all minority applicants. But, by 5–4, the court upheld an affirmative action program at Michigan law school, since the purpose of the discrimination in favor of minority applicants and against whites was the "compelling state interest" of "diversity." "We expect," said Justice O'Connor, "that twenty-five years from now the use of racial preferences will no longer be necessary."

The next generation of American students of European descent will thus, because of their race, endure discrimination in admissions to college and graduate schools until some future court determines that "diversity" has been achieved. And President Bush's reaction?

> I applaud the Supreme Court for recognizing the value of diversity on our Nation's campuses. Diversity is one of America's greatest strengths. Today's decisions seek a careful balance between the goal of campus diversity and the fundamental principle of equal treatment under law.

With George W. Bush declaring neutrality in the struggle for a colorblind society, Middle America is leaderless.

The Left has found the Ho Chi Minh Trail around democracy. It has found the way—through filing court cases with collaborator-judges—to impose its views and values upon our society without having to win elections or persuade legislators. And the Republican Party has begun to accept the new racial preferences that have re-

placed the old. We have let the Jeffersonian idea of a "natural aristocracy" of virtue and talent, where men and women are rewarded
on the basis of merit, character, excellence, and ability, slip away, to
be replaced by an ethnic spoils system that is un-American.

Had the issues that divide us so deeply—prayer in school, the
Ten Commandments, busing, flag burning, abortion, gay rights, the
death penalty, pornography, limits on lewd behavior, welfare benefits
to illegal aliens—been left to legislators, they would have been dealt
with in fifty states in fifty ways. Congress could have found compromises in the legislative process. The nation would have accepted
the decisions of men and women they had voted into office and
could vote out. But by taking up the most explosive social issues,
as the Warren Court did in *Brown,* and its successor did in *Roe
v. Wade,* and dictating all-or-nothing solutions, against which a
majority had no recourse, the Supreme Court ignited America's
culture wars as surely as General Beauregard ignited our Civil War
when he ordered the Confederate guns to fire on Fort Sumter.

A REPUBLICAN FAILURE

Traditional conservatives continue to fight on these fronts, but
neoconservatives have begun openly to counsel surrender.

"I, for one," declares Max Boot, "am not eager to ban abortion or
cloning." In a *Financial Times* piece titled "Another Lost Cause for
the Social Conservatives," Boot says the Right "would be better off
caving in on gay marriage." Neoconservative David Brooks of the
New York Times goes Boot one better: "We shouldn't just allow gay
marriage. We should insist on gay marriage."

In a National Review Online column titled "Time to Face Facts:
Gays Gain Victory," Jonah Goldberg declares the battle over but
urges the gay rights lobby to show "magnanimity in victory." Andrew
Sullivan, former editor of the *New Republic,* who appears often in
conservative publications, is the leading champion of homosexual
marriage in the United States.

To neoconservatives obsessed with Iraq, such matters as abortion, gay marriage, stem cell research, cloning, are but distractions. But to traditionalists, they go to the most fundamental questions of right and wrong and whether we shall remain one nation and one people. For, as the columnist Arnold Beichman quotes the famed British jurist Lord Devlin,

> [I]f men and women try to create a society in which there is no fundamental agreement about good and evil, they will fail; if having based it upon a common set of core values, they surrender those values, it will disintegrate. For society is not something that can be kept together physically; it is held by the invisible but fragile bonds of common beliefs and values. . . . A common morality is part of the bondage of a good society. . . .

Let it then be said again. If the faith that gave birth to the culture and civilization is pulled up by its roots and dies, as Christianity is dying in Europe and post-modern America, the culture and civilization born of that faith will also soon die. What, then, will keep us together? For democracy is not enough.

Since the Nixon administration, conservatives and Republicans have failed in a primary mission: To stop the Supreme Court from imposing a social revolution on America. President Nixon named four justices to the Supreme Court. Three voted for *Roe v. Wade,* with Nixon nominee Harry Blackmun writing the decision. President Ford's sole appointee, John Paul Stevens, is the most reflexive liberal on the bench. Ronald Reagan named Antonin Scalia and elevated Justice William Rehnquist to be Chief Justice—the two strongest constitutionalists—but also Sandra Day O'Connor and Anthony Kennedy, the unpredictables. As for George H. W. Bush, his choice of Clarence Thomas strengthened the court minority in battling activism, but his earlier nomination of David Souter cancels Thomas out.

Today, there are four solid Supreme Court votes—Stevens,

Souter, Stephen Breyer, and Ruth Bader Ginsburg—for the social revolution. The Left needs but one more vote to continue prosecuting their culture war on America. Usually, that fifth vote is O'Connor's, which gives her more power over the character of our country than Congress, a strange situation for a self-governing people.

In court-nomination battles, Republicans have proven to be diffident warriors. Democrats are not. Judge Robert Bork, nominated by Reagan, was rejected 58–42 by a Democratic Senate after being savagely slandered. But liberal activists Stephen Breyer and Ruth Bader Ginsburg, an ACLU feminist nominated by Bill Clinton, sailed through with bipartisan support, 87–9 and 96–3.

If Republicans wish to do battle, President Bush has shown the way. His judicial appointments have been equal in quality or even superior to those of President Reagan. And he has shown a disposition to fight for his judges. When Democrats denied him a floor vote on four nominees to the U.S. appellate courts, the president waited until Congress was out of session and, by recess appointment, put two on the bench. Should a filibuster prevent a Senate vote on a future Supreme Court nominee, that road lies open. The precedent exists. After Chief Justice John Jay resigned in 1795, President Washington named John Rutledge of South Carolina to replace him while the Senate was out of session.

No issue is more important to conservatives than the character and judicial philosophy of the men and women on the Supreme Court. In the next presidential term, which will run to 2009, there is a good possibility—given age, illnesses, and talk of retirements—that the president chosen in 2004 could name a new chief justice and three or more associate justices, as Nixon did in his first term. For conservatives, there is no more compelling argument for a Republican president—and a Republican Senate to confirm his nominees—than who will shape the Supreme Court for the next quarter of a century.

"CHAINS OF THE CONSTITUTION"

Each time the Supreme Court hands down a decision without precedent in the law or the Constitution—outlawing school prayer or declaring abortion a right—conservatives demand that the Constitution be amended to overturn it. This is the amendment trap, a fool's errand. Any amendment must be approved by two-thirds of both houses of Congress and three-fourths of the state legislatures in seven years. No truly controversial amendment has been enacted in our lifetime. Invariably, the amendment is buried in committee as passions cool and the court decision is grudgingly accepted as the law of the land. Amendments on busing, flag-burning, school prayer, abortion, and a balanced budget all perished this way. Is there any recourse? Bork is pessimistic: "There is no obvious cure for the situation. . . . there appears to be no way to contain the imperial judiciary."

This is defeatist. There is a way. That is for Congress to use its constitutional power to limit the jurisdiction of the Supreme Court and restore to the states the right to decide these matters.

In Article III, Section I, the Supreme Court is established and the Congress given power to "ordain and establish" inferior courts. All U.S. courts, save the Supreme Court, are thus creations of Congress and can be abolished by Congress. And if Congress can abolish a court, it surely has the power to restrict the issues those courts may decide. And that power is explicitly granted in Section II of Article III.

> In all cases affecting Ambassadors, other public Ministers and Consuls, and those in which a State shall be a party, the supreme court shall have original jurisdiction. In all the other cases before mentioned, the supreme Court shall have appellate jurisdiction, both as to Law and Fact, *with such Exceptions, and under such Regulations as the Congress shall make*. (emphasis added)

From this passage, it is clear that Congress can restrict the Supreme Court to decisions "affecting Ambassadors, other public Ministers and Consuls, and those in which a state shall be a party."

What does this mean?

Under Article III, Congress could reenact the Defense of Marriage Act (DOMA)—by which marriage licenses issued to homosexuals in Massachusetts need not be recognized by any other state—and add a single line asserting that no federal court, including the Supreme Court, has authority to review this legislation. Stated succinctly, Congress and the president could tell the Supreme Court to keep "hands off!" the issue of marriage. As Professor Quirk writes,

> Congress could . . . reenact the Defense of Marriage Act restricting marriage to men and women adding one sentence, "This law is not subject to review by the lower Federal Courts or the U.S. Supreme Court." Then the issue would return to the States which is where President Bush and John Kerry . . . have said it should be.

Governors and legislatures can rein in renegade judges in several ways. First, by defiance, like Jefferson and Jackson. When the Massachusetts Judicial Supreme Court ordered Governor Romney and the legislature to rewrite state law to give homosexuals the same right to matrimony and its benefits, Romney could have told the court:

"My response to your order is no. I, too, have taken an oath to defend the Constitution of the Commonwealth, and there is nothing in that constitution to support your decision. No judicial authority can order the governor or the legislature to enact laws with which we deeply disagree. Therefore, I conclude your order is null and void."

What would Margaret Marshall and the Supreme Judicial Court do? Order Romney's arrest? Declare him in contempt?

The nation would have roared its approval of Romney as loudly as Castro Street cheered Mayor Gavin Newsom when he began handing out marriage licenses to homosexuals. With this basic difference: Romney would not be defying a validly enacted law. He would be refusing to obey a court order that had no basis in law, morality, common sense, or the Constitution of Massachusetts. As Martin Luther King argued in *Letter from a Birmingham Jail,*

> A just law is a man-made code that squares with the moral law or the law of God. An unjust law is a code that is out of Harmony with the moral law. To put it in the terms of St. Thomas Aquinas: An unjust law is a law that is not rooted in eternal law and natural law.

Homosexual marriages do not square with the "law of God," are not "rooted in eternal law or natural law," and are "out of harmony" with the moral law. By Dr. King's reading, the Massachusetts court need not be obeyed. Indeed, its immoral order ought to be defied.

Romney and the legislature could then have submitted to the voters an amendment to the state constitution declaring that marriage is between a man and a woman, no matter what Justice Marshall rules. "On issues of power," said Jefferson, "let us hear no more of trust in men, but bind them down from mischief with the chains of the constitution."

BUT WHAT IF the Supreme Court defied Congress and the president, declared DOMA unconstitutional, and ordered all states to recognize all marriage licenses issued by any state? Congress and the president could respond by declaring that no U.S. Government jurisdiction will recognize nontraditional marriage and no U.S. officers will enforce the decision.

A precedent exists. Jefferson became president after the Alien and Sedition Laws had been enacted and enforced by Adams's administration. While the Alien Laws gave the president the power to deport threatening aliens, under the more ominous Sedition Laws, the Adams administration had been empowered to imprison writers and editors who libeled federal officers. "The Sedition Laws," wrote the biographer of the Constitution Burton Hendrick, "seemed to strike at the freedom of the press and thus to violate the recently adopted, and much cherished First Amendment."

On taking office, Jefferson ordered all editors or writers convicted under the Sedition Laws freed from prison, and ordered an end to all prosecutions. As he wrote Abigail Adams in 1804, the Alien and Sedition Laws were a

> . . . nullity, as absolute and palpable as if Congress had ordered us to fall down and worship a golden image: and that it was as much my duty to arrest its execution in every stage, as it would have been to have rescued from the fiery furnace those who should have been cast into it for refusing to worship the image.

Jefferson had asserted a presidential right not to enforce laws that did not conform to the Constitution, as he read it. Jefferson, as Quirk and Bridwell write, "held that the Constitution does not assign to any branch the authority to interpret its meaning . . . No branch has absolute or final authority to control the others, especially an unelected judiciary."

To Jefferson, judicial supremacy violated "the mother principle, that 'governments are republican only in proportion as they embody the will of the people, and execute it.'"

On this, Hamilton and Jefferson seemed to agree. For, as Hamilton wrote in Federalist #78, the Supreme Court "must ultimately depend upon the aid of the executive arm even for the efficacy of its judgments." Were a president to direct the executive branch to ignore an order, the Supreme Court claim to be the final and deciding authority on what the Constitution commands would be exposed as hollow. Marshall's doctrine of judicial supremacy would be history.

Invoking Article III, six senators have cosponsored a Constitution Restoration Act to strip all federal courts of all authority to hear cases brought against any government or government officer for acknowledging God. This would return the nation to where it stood when Justice Douglas declared in 1952, "We are a religious people whose institutions presuppose a Supreme Being." All future decisions on the pledge of allegiance and classroom prayer and courthouse displays of the Ten Commandments would be returned to the states for decision, which is where they belong.

There are other judicial reforms Congress, if it had conviction and courage, could enact. As all federal courts below the Supreme Court are creations of Congress, Congress could:

A). Impose term limits on federal judges. Legal scholar Michael Mazzo writes that political figures as well known and diverse as Thomas Jefferson, John F. Kennedy, Lyndon Johnson, George H. W. Bush, and Justice Byron White have all advocated the termination of life tenure.

B) Require reconfirmation of all federal judges after eight years, giving Congress the power to remove incompetents and ideologues without having to go through impeachment.

C) If it is found that putting term limits on judges would require a constitutional amendment, Congress could enact a law whereby nominees to the U.S. Court of Appeals revert automatically, after six years, to the U.S. district courts. Federal judges would still have life tenure, just not life tenure on the second highest court in the land.

Finally, the impeachment road remains open. "[F]or the safety of society," Jefferson wrote, "we commit honest maniacs to Bedlam, so judges should be withdrawn from their bench, whose erroneous biases are leading us to dissolution. It may indeed injure them in fame or in fortune; but it saves the Republic, which is the first and supreme law."

TEN

THE WAY BACK HOME

This is the established Order of Things, when a
Nation has grown to such an height of Power as to
become dangerous to Mankind, she never fails to lose
her Wisdom, her Justice, and her Moderation, and
with these she never fails to lose her Power; which
however returns again, if those Virtues return.
—John Adams, *Autobiography*

There is no security at the top of the world
—Garet Garrett

"Back to the catacombs!"

So Richard J. Whalen, a friend from the Nixon campaign of '68,
who, like this writer, began his political life in the movement first
led into battle by Barry Goldwater, said to me last year.

President Bush had just signed the largest entitlement program
since the Great Society, proposed amnesty for a million illegal
aliens, and declared his intention to wage a "world democratic revolution."

Was it for this we had rolled the rock up the hill?

Columnist Sam Francis, biographer of the intellectual life of
James Burnham, calls the conservative movement a "colossal failure." Excepting the Cold War victory won under Ronald Reagan—
and a great exception it was—it is difficult to fault his assessment.

Republicans have been winning elections, but conservatives are losing the culture wars. The "Era of Big Government" Clinton declared over is back. America is becoming an empire. Despite ten successful Republican nominees to the Supreme Court since 1969—and only two by Democratic presidents—the courts continue to impose an unwanted social revolution on the nation. And Republican resistance is slackening.

What went wrong?

First, neoconservatives captured the foundations, think tanks, and opinion journals of the Right and were allowed to redefine conservatism. Their agenda—open borders, amnesty for illegal aliens, free trade, an orderly retreat in the culture wars, "Big Government Conservatism," and Wilsonian interventions to reshape the world in America's image—was embraced by Republican leaders as the new conservative agenda.

Second, the character of corporate America, the exchequer of the GOP, has changed. Once, Fortune 500 companies believed in economic nationalism and protecting the home market. These companies have now gone global. In return for their continued support of the Republican Party, its foundations, PACs, and think tanks, they want not just tax breaks, but corporate welfare, open borders and mass immigration to keep wages down. They want the right to import workers to take American jobs at lower wages, and the freedom to export jobs and factories abroad—and bring their finished goods back, free of charge, into the American marketplace.

Third, the social and cultural revolution of the 1960s has put down roots and captured a far larger share of the nation than it had in the 1960s. Traditional conservative stands on issues like abortion, affirmative action, and gay rights are now opposed by a growing minority within the GOP.

Fourth, as Old America—those of European stock—shrinks as a share of our population, Republicans feel they must attract minorities or the party is doomed. The GOP has set its sights on the exploding Hispanic population, now approaching 40 million. But, while Hispanics may accept the GOP's social conservatism, they are believers in expanded government programs for health care, education, employment, and the social safety net. To compete for the Hispanic vote, the GOP is giving up its traditional role as a party of small government, and alienating its base.

Under the rubric of conservatism, the Republican party of Bush I and II has been reinventing itself into what conservatives would have once recognized as a Rockefeller Republicans reciting Reaganite pieties. The problem for the GOP hierarchy is that its policies—save for the tax cuts—are not working, and a rebellion is brewing among principled and populist conservatives about the direction of the party and country.

IF THERE IS a word for the present situation of the nation, it is "unsustainable." America cannot sustain annual $600 billion merchandise trade deficits without seeing the dollar slide to peso status. We cannot sustain present levels of spending with a Social Security–Medicare crisis looming, without reaching national bankruptcy. We cannot sustain this mass immigration, legal and illegal, without America becoming a Tower of Babel of people of all colors, creeds, cultures, and languages, with little in common. We cannot sustain a Bush Doctrine of preemptive war to deny rogue nations weapons of mass destruction, and preventive war to keep rival powers from rising, with an active-duty army of fewer than 500,000. We cannot sustain an empire abroad with $500 billion deficits at home.

A crunch is coming, and a civil war is going to break out inside the Republican Party along the old trench lines of the Goldwater-Rockefeller wars of the 1960s, a war for the heart and soul and future of the party for the new century. The issues are these:

Immigration

The great majority of Americans now want illegal immigration halted, illegal aliens sent home, no amnesty, a moratorium on legal immigration, and our borders protected by U.S. troops, if necessary, to stop the invasion of the United States.

President Bush, the neoconservatives, and the *Wall Street Journal* (which has for twenty years, championed a constitutional amendment—"There shall be open borders"), want unrestricted immigration and amnesty for illegal aliens. On this issue, the neoconservatives are intolerant of dissent, branding it "nativist," "xenophobic," and "racist." When Samuel Huntington, the distinguished Harvard professor, wrote in his new book *Who Are We?* that limitless immigration from the Third World now imperils the "Anglo-Protestant" cultural core of the nation, a line of thought that tracks Dr. Kirk, he was set upon by the *New York Times* house neoconservative David Brooks. In a scathing review in *Foreign Affairs* by Alan Wolfe, Dr. Huntington was accused of exhibiting a "moralistic passion . . . bordering on hysteria" and "contemptuous disdain" for American elites. Wolfe denounced *Who Are We?* as "Patrick Buchanan with footnotes."

This issue is reaching critical mass. Huntington warns that failure to address the immigration issue will invite "white nativist movements" as "a possible and plausible response." And Wolfe concedes: "There is a rising opposition to immigration among ordinary Americans and, if Huntington is any indication, among academic observers as well."

In 2004, three GOP congressmen—Arizona's Jeff Flake and Jim Kolbe and Utah's Chris Cannon—faced primary challenges for supporting amnesty. By 2006, this issue will be at the top of the national agenda and will separate Bush Republicans and neoconservatives from traditionalists and populists alike.

Intervention and Empire

With casualties still coming in from Iraq and the cost of war rising, support for the Bush policy of democratizing the Islamic world with American blood and U.S. tax dollars is dissipating.

We are not an imperial people. Americans will go abroad to destroy enemies who attack them. But they will not stay long where they are not wanted. And after eighteen months of guerrilla war and the pictures from Abu Ghraib, we are no longer seen as liberators in Iraq, but as occupiers. President Bush seems to recognize this and seems determined to transfer not only sovereignty but responsibility for their own defense and their own democracy to the Iraqis themselves.

Failure is now an option. And if Iraq collapses in chaos and civil war, there will be a ferocious fight in this country over who misled us and who may have lied us into war. An accounting will be made, and into the dock will go the neoconservatives whose class project this was and had been, long before George W. Bush even thought of running for president.

The rising costs of Iraq and Afghanistan, our mounting trade and fiscal deficits, and our overstretched army are certain to ignite an even broader debate on U.S. foreign policy. Proposition: Is America overextended? Have we reached imperial overstretch? Can the United States afford to keep troops in one hundred countries on five continents? Can we still remain committed to fight new wars on behalf of some fifty nations to which we have given solemn treaty commitments?

With Iraq giving interventionism a bad name, and with America reviled across the Arab world and beyond, even in countries we support with aid and defend with troops, a demand is arising— long overdue—for America to bring the troops home, husband our strength for threats to our own vital interests, and let foreign governments start paying their own bills, defending their own frontiers, and fighting their own wars.

As conservative Congressman John Duncan Jr. of Tennessee writes in *Chronicles,* such a policy represents the wisdom of Robert Taft who wrote, "No foreign policy can be justified except a policy devoted . . . to the protection of the liberty of the American people, with war only as the last resort and only to preserve that liberty." And of John F. Kennedy, who said in the year of the missile crisis:

> [W]e must face [the] fact that the United States is neither omnipotent nor omniscient—that we are only six percent of the world's population—that we cannot impose our will upon the other 94 percent of mankind—that we cannot right every wrong or reverse each adversity—and that therefore there cannot be an American solution to every world problem.

Congressman Duncan concluded his essay with this simple statement: "There is nothing conservative about the U.S. policy in Iraq." Indeed. How other countries govern themselves is not a vital interest of the United States. It is not our business, so long as these nations do not threaten our vital interests. As Benjamin Harrison said over a century ago, "We Americans have no commission from God to police the world."

Terrorism and Islam

Neoconservatives believe America is at war with militant Islam and there is no substitute for victory in that war. And victory requires, as Charles Krauthammer asserted in his lecture at the AEI dinner in 2004, that we "commit blood and treasure" and "come ashore . . . where it really counts. And where it counts today is that Islamic crescent from North Africa to Afghanistan."

We must, declared Krauthammer, seize Arab and Islamic territory and establish "civilized, decent, non-belligerent pro-Western polities in Afghanistan and Iraq and ultimately their key neighbors"—Iran, Syria, and Saudi Arabia. This is the "World War IV" scenario of Podhoretz, Cohen, and James Woolsey. Why must we wage this war? Because, Krauthammer insists, there is "not a single remotely plausible alternative strategy for attacking the monster behind 9/11."

This is the rhetoric of yesterday, of the hours after 9/11, of the days before Iraq. But, as we—and the neoconservatives—have discovered, an American army can capture a capital but it cannot kill a virus of malign hatred. It is more likely to spread that virus, as it has in Iraq.

Thus, after months of guerrilla war, with the cost in blood and treasure and national unity rising, President Bush seems to have changed his mind. We are not going deeper in. We are coming out.

There is a better way to fight Islamic extremism. We must recognize truths forgotten. U.S. dominance of the Middle East is not the corrective to terror. It is a cause of terror. Were we not over there, the 9/11 terrorists would not have been over here. And while their acts were murderous and despicable, behind their atrocities lay a political motive. We were attacked because of our imperial presence on the sacred soil of the land of Mecca and Medina, because of our enemies' perception that we were strangling the Iraqi people with sanctions and preparing to attack a second time, and because of our uncritical support of the Likud regime of Ariel Sharon.

Again, terrorism is a symptom, terrorism is not the disease. Behind almost every act of revolutionary terror lies a political purpose. What is it the Islamic militants seek? They want us out of Saudi Arabia and Iraq, and they want to bring down all pro-Western regimes in the Middle East. That is what 9/11 was all about.

Initially we responded wisely, overthrowing the hated Taliban and canalizing our attack on Osama and Al Qaeda. In the Afghan phase of this war, we had the support of the world and the acquiescence of Arab and Islamic governments. But when we invaded

Iraq, we played into bin Laden's hand. The Arab and Islamic world turned hostile, for they could not see the link between the Saudis who attacked us and the Iraqis we were attacking. And just as the appearance of Suleiman at the gates of Vienna united the quarrelsome Christian kings against the Turk, so the appearance of Bush in Baghdad united Islam against America.

The enemy here is Al Qaeda and its allies. How do we defeat them?

First, by working with any nation that will help us run these killers down. And almost every nation will support us in counterterrorism, for almost every government, even in the Islamic world, is a target of Al Qaeda.

Second, by removing the recruiting issue of Islamic extremists, America's imperial presence in the Islamic world. The United States should withdraw its forces from any nation in the Gulf or Central Asia where we are not wanted, from every nation where vital U.S. interests are not at risk, from every base not essential to our one strategic interest in that region: a steady flow of oil to the free Asia and the West. Who rules the former Soviet republics of the Caucasus and Central Asia has never been of vital interest to us. What are U.S. troops doing in those countries where ex-Communist despots rule the roost in a region certain to become the locus of a great-power struggle between China, Russia, and Islam?

Terrorism is the price of empire. If we do not wish to pay it, we must give up the empire. Strategic disengagement is not a strategy of defeat but a recognition of reality. The Islamic world, roiled by its own tribal, religious, and national struggles, must work out its own destiny. U.S. intervention to dictate the outcome is no more welcome there than was the intervention of Ottoman Turks when the Catholic and Protestant nations of Europe were working out their destiny in those wars of centuries ago.

Strategic withdrawal does not mean strategic surrender. In the quarter century in which the United States has been isolated from Iran, a generation has grown up that knew nothing of the shah,

Savak, or the Great Satan, but came to loathe the mullahs who misruled them, and to vote by 70 percent twice to throw them out. Time is on our side in this struggle, for Islamic radicals cannot build great nations nor solve the problems of modernity. The only problem of Islamic peoples these extremists can help them solve is the problem of America's massive presence. Remove that root cause of this war, and Arab and Islamic peoples will see no longer through a glass darkly, but face to face, who their true enemies are.

The Middle East

The nation of Israel is a "thunderously failed reality" that "rests on a scaffolding of corruption, and on foundations of oppression and injustice." Were these words spoken by an American leader, he would be denounced by the ADL as an anti-Semite.

But these are the words of a former speaker of the Knesset who cries for his country. "The countdown to the end of Israeli society has begun," writes Avraham Burg, "the end of the Zionist enterprise is already on our doorstep." He adds: "Israel, having ceased to care about the children of the Palestinians, should not be surprised when they come washed in hatred and blow themselves up in the centers of Israeli escapism."

Burg implores "Diaspora Jews" to "speak out." To little avail.

Why? Why, when a Knesset leader is unintimidated, are we all so silent? Army Chief of Staff Moshe Ya'alon has bluntly told Israel's press it was Sharon himself who undermined Palestinian leader Mahmoud Abbas. Twenty-seven Israeli Air Force pilots have refused to obey "immoral orders" for air strikes on "populated civilian centers." Israeli soldiers have refused to serve in the occupied territories.

Four ex-chiefs of Shin Beit—Ami Ayalon, Carmi Gillon, Yaakov Peri, Avraham Shalom—have charged Sharon with leading Israel to ruin. "We are heading downhill toward near-catastrophe," says Peri. "If we go on living by the sword, we will continue to wallow in the mud and destroy ourselves." Ayalon and Palestinian academic Sari Nusseibeh have issued a joint declaration of principles, calling for Israel's withdrawal to her 1967 borders. Ex-Justice Minister Yossi Beilin has negotiated a detailed accord with a former Palestinian minister on a two-state solution. Colin Powell wrote a letter of support. Where was President Bush? Why do we not tell these brave Israelis that they are not alone?

Sharon promised peace and security. Since his provocation on the Temple Mount in September of 2000, he has delivered war and hatred. Over 900 Israelis are dead. Some 3,300 Palestinians have died, including hundreds of children. Scores of thousands have been wounded. Homes and olive groves have been destroyed. Yet, when Howard Dean suggests that U.S. Mideast policy needs to be more "even-handed," he was warned by Democrats never to use that term again.

Israel is in an existential crisis. It can wall itself off and annex what it wants on the West Bank, and leave Palestinians in tiny, truncated, nonviable bantustans that will become the spawning pools of terror. Or it can give the Palestinians what Oslo, Camp David, Taba, and the "roadmap" promised: a homeland, a nation, and a state of their own.

Israel is free to choose. But America needs a Middle East policy made in the USA, not in Tel Aviv, or at AIPAC or AEI.

In the Middle East, we are reaping the fruits of neoconservatism. Almost a decade ago, in their paper "A Clean Break," Richard Perle and Douglas Feith urged Prime Minister Netanyahu to dump the Oslo peace accords and reoccupy the West Bank, though Feith conceded that "the price in blood would be high." Eventually, the Perle-Feith scenario played out. Yet, it is hard to see how the situation is better today than in the hopeful days of 1994, before Yitzhak Rabin was murdered by a Zionist enraged at his policy of trading land for peace.

Under the Sharon Plan, Israel will annex all five major settlements on the occupied West Bank. The Palestinian right of return is forfeit. Israel's security wall will snake in and out of the West Bank. Jerusalem will not be shared with a Palestinian state. In the spring of 2004, President Bush endorsed this Sharon Plan that had been worked out by his NSC aide Elliott Abrams, a prominent neoconservative. In June, the Sharon Plan was endorsed 407–9 by the U.S. House, which declared the United States will "do its utmost to prevent any attempt by anyone to impose any other plan."

America has given up its role as "honest broker." President Bush no longer sits at the head of the negotiating table, but directly behind Sharon. While this may serve the political interests of the president and his party, it does not serve the interests of America, or of those Israelis who have sacrificed so much to create a secure country, or of those Palestinians who have suffered so much for a nation of their own.

The Sharon Plan is not a peace plan. It is a unilateral solution to be imposed by Israel, that no Arab nation will accept. A Palestinian leader who signs on to this surrender of land and rights would be signing his death warrant. Like the Versailles peace imposed on Germany in 1919, the Sharon Plan ensures a new and wider war.

Might is on Israel's side in this conflict, but time and demography are not. The Arab population of Israel, the West Bank, and Gaza is 4.5 million. Its birth rate is among the highest in the world. Outside of Palestine, Arab populations are exploding, Islam is growing more militant, and pro-American regimes are under strain, if not under siege.

America has a vital stake in a just peace. For when pictures of the Palestinian dead and wounded resulting from U.S.-built helicopter gunships and F-16s go out to an Arab world of 300 million via Al Jazeera, it is not only hatred of Israel that flourishes, but hatred of an America that arms and sustains Israel. Americans, especially Jewish-Americans who dissent from the neoconservative party line, need to speak out in support of Israelis who are bravely speaking out for a just peace. As Burke said, "To sin by silence when they should protest makes cowards out of men." It applies to us all.

Trade, Outsourcing, and Lost Jobs

In May 2004, the U.S. trade deficit of $48.3 billion approached $600 billion annually, and the deficit in goods swept past that figure on the way to $700 billion. Free-trade fundamentalism is both a failed policy and a faltering faith. *USA Today* reported in February of 2004 that "High-income Americans have lost much of their enthusiasm for free trade as they perceive their own jobs threatened by white-collar workers in China, India and other countries." Citing a University of Maryland poll, the paper reported that, in five years, "among Americans making more than $100,000 a year, support for actively promoting more free trade fell from 57 percent to less than half, 28 percent."

The Democratic Party has begun to realize this. In the primaries of 2004, Senator John Edwards of North Carolina revived his campaign and won a place in Democratic hearts and on the Kerry ticket by attacking U.S. trade policy as a primary cause of the hemorrhaging of manufacturing jobs. That we are becoming "two Americas"—one privileged and rich, the other struggling and poor—proved a compelling theme to Democratic voters and the media in the final days of that campaign.

Edwards was soon being echoed by Senator Kerry who took to denouncing "Benedict Arnold CEOs" who move factories and jobs abroad. Kerry declared his opposition to CAFTA, the Central American free-trade agreement negotiated by President Bush and his neoconservative trade representative Robert Zoellick, modeled on NAFTA. It was the first time Kerry had broken with the free-trade phalanx in Congress.

In the White House and Republican Party, too, reality has begun to intrude. When the chairman of President Bush's Council of Economic Advisers, free trader N. Gregory Mankiw, hailed outsourcing as "just a new way of doing international trade," and "a good thing," Republicans on Capitol Hill suggested an early return to Harvard. In the Bush era, no two journalists have done better at documenting what is happening to America than Lou Dobbs of CNN and Paul Craig Roberts. As Roberts has reported repeatedly, the U.S. Bureau of Labor Statistics paints a bleak picture of America's future. In its job projection for the next ten years, the BLS

> . . . emphasizes that seven of the 10 occupations with the largest projected job growth are so menial they can be learned with short-term on-the-job training. They are not high-paying jobs, and they do not produce any export earnings: nursing aides, orderlies and attendants; waiters and waitresses; janitors and cleaners; cashiers, food preparation and serving including fast food; customer service representatives; and retail salespersons. As *Business Week* notes, "Most of the big growth areas will be low-skill and low-paying."

This issue is about the future of our young, and of our country. If present U.S. trade policy is not radically altered, virtually every factory in the United States that produces tradable goods will leave in search of lower taxes, less regulation, and cheaper labor abroad. China, whose trade surplus with us is nearing $150 billion, has become the new Sun Belt. India is emerging as the big winner in capturing the white-collar jobs being outsourced from the United States. And these jobs are no longer confined to call centers.

They are in accounting, architecture, computer programming, data processing, insurance, financial and legal analysis, tax preparation, and medicine. And if we do not care about American workers, most of the paperwork of federal and state governments, including that of the Social Security Administration, could easily be outsourced.

In 2004, Siemens announced it was moving most of its 15,000 software programming jobs out of the United States and Europe to India, China, and Eastern Europe. Of 10,000 new jobs recently announced by IBM, two-thirds will be overseas. According to an AP story in February 2004, professional accountants in India prepared 1,000 U.S. tax returns in 2002, 20,000 in 2003, and

150,000 to 200,000 in 2004. Reason: The average accountant in India makes $250 to $300 a month. In the United States, he or she makes $3,000 to $4,000 a month.

Engineering schools from Georgia Tech to MIT are reporting declines in enrollments as the brightest of the young see the hand-writing on the wall. As Roberts writes, even the million-plus jobs the Bush recovery began to create in 2004 are concentrated in construction, bars, restaurants, health care, and social services. We are not creating jobs in industries that produce for export, and that can turn this trade deficit around. If politicians fail to address the monstrous and mounting trade deficits, that problem will, as it has through history, solve itself.

The dollar will fall until all those cheap imports at the mall aren't all that cheap anymore and the U.S. standard of living falls toward the level of the nations where the necessities of our national life are now produced. What Washington and Hamilton sought and won for posterity, the Baby Boomers and their progeny are tossing away.

Even President Bush, by the spring of 2004, with outsourcing on the minds of millions, and with Ohio, West Virginia, Pennsylvania, and Michigan at risk because of lost manufacturing jobs, seemed to sense that toasting CAFTA, NAFTA, and free trade was a losing proposition.

Deficits and Big Government

On the issue of tax cuts, a unifying one for conservatives, George W. Bush has more than kept faith with the country that elected him. His Reaganite commitment to principle on this issue was rewarded in 2003, when, as he had predicted, recovery took hold when the tax cuts took hold. Values, judicial appointments, and retention of the Bush tax cuts remain a great divide between the national parties and, for many conservatives, the most compelling arguments for George W. Bush.

Inside the GOP, on Capitol Hill and in the country, however, a battle is shaping up between "deficit hawks," who hold to the old-time religion of balanced budgets, and "Big Government conservatives," who favor tax cuts forever and echo Dick Cheney's "deficits don't matter." As long as the economy is growing and the deficit shrinking from rising tax revenue, this front will remain quiet. But when the next recession hits and the Baby Boomers begin to queue up for Social Security and Medicare, we will be in the perfect storm, deficits will explode, and the submerged conflict inside the conservative movement and Republican Party will surface and perhaps sunder the party on economics as badly as it is already on social issues.

Ideological Fissures

If the success of the Bush presidency hinges on the outcome of the war in Iraq, that war is even more critical to the cabal that exploited 9/11 to maneuver us into it. That neoconservatives plotted and propagandized for war years before 9/11, that they "stove-piped" to the White House intelligence "cherry-picked" at the Pentagon, and that they demonized opponents as unpatriotic is now widely known. All the neocon eggs are now in the Baghdad basket.

Moreover, neoconservatives are today identified with positions—open borders, amnesty for illegal aliens, NAFTA, the WTO, outsourcing, Big Government, appeasement in the culture wars—that are the causes of the coming conflict in the GOP. Beyond this, neoconservatives, by their sheer vindictiveness, have made more enemies than they need to have made inside the broader conservative-Republican coalition.

When the late Russell Kirk quipped that neoconservatives often seemed to confuse the capital of the United States with Tel Aviv, Midge Decter charged the Sage of Mecosta with anti-Semitism. Former Centcom commander General Anthony Zinni received the same treatment when he openly broke with the neoconservatives at the Pentagon. Robert Novak, the famous reporter-commentator who has long taken issue with the U.S. bias toward Israel has repeatedly gotten the same treatment from Norman Podhoretz and *Commentary*. Playing the anti-Semite card has become the last refuge of the neoconservative.

In their *Foreign Affairs* piece, "Toward a Neo-Reaganite Foreign Policy," William Kristol and Robert Kagan, in advocating "benevolent global hegemony," even back-handed President Reagan for his lifelong theme of America as a "shining city on a hill."

Mocking this "charming old metaphor," Kristol and Kagan wrote: "A policy of sitting atop a hill and leading by example becomes in practice a policy of cowardice and dishonor." Nor has Podhoretz ceased to attack President Reagan for withdrawing U.S. Marines from Lebanon in 1983, charging him unto the final days of his life with having "cut and run."

In December 2002, when the liberal media drove Trent Lott from his post as Senate majority leader for a thoughtless compliment to Strom Thurmond at his one hundredth birthday party—Charles Krauthammer, David Frum, and Jonah Goldberg rejoiced and squabbled publicly over who had been first to stick in the knife.

Some neoconservatives seem to have an almost visceral hostility to working-class white Southerners. "Howard Dean wants the white trash vote," wrote Krauthammer, "that's clearly what [Dean] meant when he said he wanted the votes of 'guys with Confederate flags in their pickup trucks.'" When Dean was attacked by Al Sharpton, who called the Confederate battle flag an "American swastika," Krauthammer was ecstatic. His humiliation serves Dean right, Krauthammer chortled, Dean should never have pandered to these Southern "yahoos" and "rebel-yelling racist redneck[s]."

This seems gratuitous and foolish. In South Carolina and Georgia, governors have lost office for breaking faith with voters on the flag issue. Two-thirds of Mississippians voted in a referendum to retain a replica of the old battle flag in their state flag. And these Mississippians routinely vote Republican.

Krauthammer's disparagement of the South was anticipated by

Chris Caldwell of the *Weekly Standard* in the *Atlantic Monthly* in June of 1998.

"The most profound clash between the South and everyone else," Caldwell instructed us, "is, of course, a cultural one. It arises from the southern tradition of putting values—particularly Christian values—at the center of politics." Dismissing these "Christian values" as the "folkways of one regional subculture," Caldwell pronounced himself "put off to see that 'traditional' values are now defined by the majority party as the values of the U-Haul renting denizens of two-year-old churches and three-year-old shopping malls."

"Southerners now wag the Republican dog," wailed Caldwell. "How did the party let that happen?" So much for a Nixon-Reagan strategy that delivered to the GOP five victories in six presidential contests from 1968 to 1988, with two of them forty-nine-state landslides.

The Right was united on foreign policy until the fall of the Berlin Wall. Anti-Communism held the coalition together. But when the Cold War ended, traditional conservatives rediscovered their differences with our coalition partners. We really did not agree. Since then, dissent to the neocon line on Iraq or Israel has come to be equated with near treason. In the runup to war in Iraq, in a cover story titled "Unpatriotic Conservatives," *National Review* read a dozen free-market libertarians and conservatives out of the movement and out of the company of decent men, and cast them as haters of America and traitors to their country:

> There is . . . a fringe attached to the conservative world that cannot overcome its despair and alienation. . . . Only the boldest of them as yet explicitly acknowledge their wish to see the United States defeated in the War on Terror. But they are thinking about defeat, and wishing for it, and they will take pleasure in it if it should happen.
>
> They began by hating the neoconservatives. They came to

hate their party and this president. They have finished by hating their country. . . .

Specifically named as haters of America praying for her defeat were Novak, this writer, and five editors and writers for the *American Conservative*. Of the dozen traitors, virtually all had once appeared in the pages of *National Review*.

By mid-2004, the war in Iraq had proven not to be the "cakewalk" neoconservatives predicted. Conservatives like George Will began having second thoughts about the wisdom of invading and investing blood and treasure in a utopian scheme to build democracy in a region of the world that has never known it. William F. Buckley, whose *National Review* had branded antiwar conservatives as haters of America and traitors, was confessing to the *New York Times*: "If I knew then what I know now about what kind of situation we would be in, I would have opposed the war." President Bush and secretaries Powell and Rumsfeld appeared to be seeking an early exit.

To William Kristol, this was grounds for abandoning conservatism altogether. He called for the firing of Rumsfeld and Powell and threatened to bolt the party and convert to neoliberalism.

"If we have to make common cause with the more hawkish liberals and fight the conservatives," he told the *New York Times*, "that is fine with me, too." Alluding to his father's definition of a neoconservative as a liberal who had been mugged by reality, William Kristol described a neoliberal as a "neoconservative who has been mugged by reality in Iraq."

Ranking his political preferences, Kristol added, "I will take Bush over Kerry, but Kerry over Buchanan. . . . If you read the last few issues of the *Weekly Standard*, it has as much or more in common with the liberal hawks than with traditional conservatives."

Indeed it did. But as John Kerry supported partial-birth abortion, quotas, raising taxes, civil unions, liberals on the Supreme Court, and has a voting record to the left of Teddy Kennedy, how can Kristol prefer him to other conservatives? Answer: Iraq and Israel.

Like Kristol, Kerry wanted more U.S. troops sent to advance the neocon project of empire and hegemony. And at a fund-raiser in Juno Beach, Florida, Kerry had sworn fealty to Israel: "I have a 100 percent record—not a 99, a 100 percent record—of sustaining the special relationship and friendship that we have with Israel."

Kristol's warning that neoconservatives could go to Kerry was an admission of what many have long recognized. The neoconservatives are not really conservatives at all. They are impostors and opportunists. They were Leftists in the 1930s, New Deal and Great Society Democrats through the 1960s, and slid to the right and the Republicans after Nixon and Reagan began rolling up forty-nine state landslides. They defected from liberalism only when they saw conservatism in the ascendancy, and they rode the Reagan revolution into power. Their heroes—Wilson, FDR, Dr. King—are men of the Left. Their tracts denouncing rivals and critics as traitors, fascists, and anti-Semites come straight out of the hard Left. Their agenda—endless struggle and war if necessary to impose secular democracy and social revolution on the Islamic world—is neo-Jacobin, out of the French, not the American Revolution. In "Western Tradition, Our Tradition," in the fiftieth anniversary edition of *Intercollegiate Review,* James Kurth has it right:

> From their origins (be it as followers of Leon Trotsky or Leo Strauss), neoconservatives have seen the Christian tradition as an alien, even a threatening one. . . . The only Western tradition the neoconservatives actually want to defend is the Enlightenment. . . . [T]hey have wanted to advance it in the rest of the world with the establishment of a kind of American empire. . . . [This] is not a conservative project but a radical and revolutionary one. For the most part, it might be said that, with friends like the neoconservatives, Western civilization does not need enemies.

Neoconservatives, Kurth continues "may think that they will create a global and universal civilization, abroad and at home, but the evidence is accumulating that they instead opened the doors to the barbarians both without (e.g., Islamic terrorists) and within (pagan disregard for the dignity of human life)." He concludes that the West's last, best defense against the new barbarians is not empire at all, but the Christian faith and tradition that are indispensable to our Western civilization.

COMING HOME

Though millions of conservatives dissent from his policies on trade, immigration, amnesty for illegal aliens, Big Government, and invading Iraq, President Bush retains the support of 80–90 percent of Republicans. He had no challenger in the primaries and almost all conservatives will vote for him in November. Their case runs thus:

George W. Bush is a God-fearing and good man, and he and his First Lady restored dignity to the White House after the Clinton years. He kept his commitment to cut taxes, which means greater freedom and security for families. He has revived an economy sinking into recession when he took office. He has chosen fine judges. His willingness to accept international abuse by rejecting the Kyoto Protocol and the International Criminal Court show him to be a patriot who will not yield national sovereignty. After 9/11, he led America boldly and brilliantly in building an alliance to oust the Taliban and run Al Qaeda out of Afghanistan. Atop the rubble of the World Trade Center, George W. Bush bonded with the country in a way his father never had. From 9/11 to the summer of 2004, he defended the nation from new terror attacks. Through tough diplomacy, he disarmed Khadafi and has persuaded the Saudis to crack down on imams preaching jihad against our country. He speaks up and he speaks out for freedom.

And while their disappointments with him are many and serious, conservative differences with a party led by John Kerry are monumental and legion. There is simply nothing that party offers to the Right. And there is another reason they will stand by the president, a reason found in words Barry Goldwater used when he took the podium at the Chicago convention of 1960 and admonished my generation: "Let's grow up, Conservatives. We want to take this party back and I think, some day, we can."

Goldwater had refused to put Nixon's name in nomination because of the "Pact of Fifth Avenue" with Nelson Rockefeller. Goldwater was saying that a struggle for the soul of the party was coming. But not now. Now was Nixon's turn. Senator Goldwater began with these words: "We are conservatives. This great Republican house is our historical home. This is our home." For conservatives, it has ever been so.

Tip O'Neill famously said that all politics are local. But when the quadrennial struggle for national leadership comes around, all politics are tribal. Almost all of the disputatious sons and alienated daughters come home. Goldwater himself, abandoned by the Rockefeller Republicans in '64, carried a huge majority of Republicans and conservatives. And they will come home for George W. Bush.

Also, since Reagan came to Washington, the Republican Party has been the party of ideas. This is where the direction of the country will be debated and likely decided. Clinton, boasting of balanced budgets and a welfare reform that abolished a federal entitlement, was but a "ratifier" of Reaganism, as ex-aide Dick Morris testifies.

Lastly, no Supreme Court vacancy has occurred for ten years. The president chosen in November will probably pick the next chief justice and decide the composition of the court for the next generation. If Kerry is making those nominations, the justices will be in the tradition of Warren, Douglas, Brennan, Blackmun, Ginsburg, and Marshall. If George Bush is reelected and the Senate that confirms new justices remains Republican, there is the chance they will be in the tradition of Rehnquist, Scalia, and Thomas, and the curtain can be brought down on the court's fifty-year run as a battering ram of social revolution. And if one wishes to be a part of the fight for a new court, and for the soul of the Republican Party, one cannot be found AWOL in November.

What is to be done? As Barry Goldwater said at the beginning of *Conscience of a Conservative,* "The ancient and tested truths that guided our republic through its early days will do equally well for us." And as Ronald Reagan reminded us, there are simple answers, there are just no easy answers. What are the simple answers?

We must give up the empire, bring the troops home, let lapse the old treaty commitments dating to a Cold War ended fifteen years ago. As the greatest republic in history, America has never been and can never be an isolationist nation. But we must cease to be a compulsively interventionist one. We must stop volunteering to fight other nations' wars, defend other nations' borders, and pay other nations' bills, or we will go down as all the other empires of the twentieth century did before us. And for the same reason. It was once said of Kaiser Wilhelm that he could not stand the idea that there was a quarrel going on somewhere in the world and he was not part of it. Such leaders and their nations are ever on the road to ruin. Madison's warning bears repeating:

> Of all the enemies to public liberty war is, perhaps, the most to be dreaded, because it comprises and develops the germ of every other. War is the parent of armies; from these proceed debts and taxes; and armies, and debts, and taxes are the known instruments for bringing the many under the domination of the few. . . . No nation could preserve its freedom in the midst of continual warfare.

If America is about anything, she is about freedom. We have seen in the burgeoning Department of Homeland Security and at our airports and in the color-coded alerts the beginning of the erosion of that freedom. We need to revive the Jeffersonian idea of "Peace, commerce and honest friendship with all nations; entangling alliances with none."

To restore America's economic independence, we need to revisit the wisdom of Hamilton, whose genius first ensured the economic independence and sovereignty of the republic whose Constitution he helped to write.

To make us one nation and one people again, we need to stop the invasion from the south and seal the U.S. border with troops, send back home those who have broken into our country and have no right to be here, and declare a moratorium on new immigration as we did from Coolidge to JFK. They gave the melting pot time to do its work—and it did.

To rein in a federal budget being used by politicians of both parties to buy votes and bribe campaign contributors, we need to elect men and women of the virtue of Washington and Adams, who have the courage to say no and, if need be, cheerfully to give up their careers to rescue this republic from the disaster toward which it is careening.

To win the culture wars, we need new justices who will restore the Supreme Court to constitutionalism, but, most of all, we need a will to persevere in this struggle, for it is about who we are, what we believe, and what we stand for as Americans.

Asked to rid the army of General Grant, whose personal conduct was becoming an embarrassment, Lincoln responded: "I can't spare this man. He fights." America needs conservatives who will fight—like Bob Taft, and Barry Goldwater, and that good man and great president who has just left us for his "shining city on a hill."

THE IRREPRESSIBLE CONFLICT
IN BUSH'S HOUSE

In endorsing George Bush in late October, I wrote that while the president was wrong on trade, immigration, Big Government, and Iraq, he was right on taxes, judges, sovereignty, and values. For conservatives, John Kerry was right on nothing. The now-famous exit polls show that Americans gave President Bush roughly the same grades in the same subjects, as it reelected him to a second term.

Among Americans who voted with taxes on their minds, Bush won 57–43. Among those who put concerns about jobs first, Bush lost 80–18. Had sixty thousand more Ohioans voted out of anger at the loss of manufacturing jobs to Mexico and Asia, due to the Bush trade policies, Kerry would have been inaugurated on January 20.

Of the 12 percent of voters who gave education or health care as the most critical issue, Kerry won 3–1. Thus, No Child Left Behind, the expansion of the Department of Education, and Bush's creation of the first major entitlement since the Great Society, prescription drug benefits for seniors, availed him nothing.

What won for Bush? Twenty-two percent of voters went to the polls with moral values in mind and supported the president 80–18.

Credit for that earthslide among moral-values voters must go to two icons of progressivism: Chief Justice Margaret Marshall of the Supreme Judicial Court of Massachusetts and Mayor Gavin Newsom of San Francisco. Justice Marshall ordered the state legislature and Governor Mitt Romney, in the name of equality, to begin issuing marriage licenses to homosexuals, and Newsom began handing out marriage licenses to gays in violation of a law that had passed 2–1 in a statewide referendum.

In the spring of 2004 Americans were thus treated to nightly TV footage of homosexuals celebrating the bonds of matrimony by kissing on the steps of San Francisco's city hall. Initiatives to ban gay marriage were soon on the ballot in thirteen states, eleven of them to be voted upon in November, including in critical Ohio. Every antigay marriage initiative won in a landslide.

The Left had gone a bridge too far for Red State America.

Yet, whether Bush won or lost, I wrote in the closing chapter of this book, "a civil war is going to break out inside the Republican Party along the old trench lines of the Goldwater-Rockefeller wars of the 1960s, a war for the heart and soul and future of the party for the new century."

The first skirmish in that civil war occurred on the morning of November 3. Senator Arlen Specter, the social liberal Republican from Pennsylvania, fired a shot across the bow of the White House. He warned President Bush not to send to the judiciary committee any nominee who might even think of overturning *Roe v. Wade*, the 1973 decision that declared abortion a constitutional right. Within hours, social conservatives and Evangelical Christians—the latter, 23 percent of all voters, had gone for Bush 78–21—had sounded general quarters and gone to battle stations.

With Chief Justice William Rehnquist ailing and Specter about to ascend to the chairmanship of the judiciary committee where he could delay any court nominee, traditionalists and Christian conservatives demanded that the GOP caucus deny Specter the chair to which seniority and GOP rules entitled him. The White House went silent on Specter's fate.

Aware that unless he backed down from his challenge to President Bush, his dream of the judiciary chairmanship was dead, Specter opted for appeasement. He was soon ubiquitous on television talk shows, reminding conservatives how he had voted for all of Bush's judges, assuring them every Bush nominee would receive an expedited hearing and vote, and promising to oppose any Democratic filibuster of a Bush appointee to the Supreme Court.

De-clawed, housebroken, neutered, Arlen Specter was permitted to take his chair. With his capitulation, the first skirmish in the GOP civil war had gone decisively to the Christian Right.

But it was three weeks after his reelection, while Bush was at the Asia-Pacific economic summit in Santiago, that the first major insurgency broke out in his household.

Led by Duncan Hunter, chairman of armed services, and James Sensenbrenner, chairman of judiciary, Republican rebels told Speaker Dennis Hastert the party would reject the president's intelligence reform bill if it did not include a provision prohibiting the states from granting driver's licenses to illegal aliens. The nineteen hijackers of 9/11 had sixty-three driver's licenses among them, visas for admission onto airliners and trains. In a stunning setback for President Bush, Hastert pulled down the bill.

The House version had contained the driver's license provision, but it had been stripped out in conference with the Senate, igniting the rebellion. Republicans were also enraged that, only days after the election, Colin Powell and Tom Ridge had traveled to Mexico to assure Vicente Fox that the Bush guest-worker program, de facto amnesty for illegal aliens, was back on the table.

"(N)ational security . . . dictates that we get control of our borders," an angry Elton Gallegly admonished Powell and Ridge. We must not "reward Mexican nationals living and working illegally in the United States. . . . It is our hope that in future discussions with the Mexican government, you will encourage Mexico to do its part to address illegal immigration rather than encourage their citizens to illegally enter the U.S."

Only after promising that border security would be high on the agenda in 2005 did President Bush convince House Republicans to vote for reform and a new intelligence czar. But sixty-seven Republicans, defying the president, voted no. Sensenbrenner spoke to those who had urged him to stand firm for tighter and tougher border controls:

> How could we face grieving families in the future and tell them that while we might have done more, the legislative hurdles were just too high? I, for one, cannot, and I, therefore, oppose this bill . . . .
>
> I want to say to them and to everyone else that is listening: I will not rest until these provisions are enacted. . . . I will bring them up relentlessly, and the job will be completed. This bill was a chance to complete the job. That chance was missed, but it will come again.

In January, 2005, true to his word, Sensenbrenner reintroduced his bill. By mid-February, it had passed by a 100-vote margin. With Congressman Tom Tancredo's immigration caucus in the House now numbering seventy-five and growing and Arizona having voted 56–44 percent to require welfare applicants and voters to give proof of citizenship—despite the opposition of John McCain—the immigration issue has reached a boil on Capitol Hill and across America.

In November, the U.S. trade deficit hit $55.5 billion, or $666 billion a year, a record. The merchandise trade deficit was running at over $700 billion, and the U.S. dollar was in a free fall. Where a euro had been worth 83 cents early in Bush's first term, by Christmas 2004, it was at $1.35.

On November 19 in Berlin, Alan Greenspan admitted to global bankers that the dollar's slide could continue indefinitely. The man responsible for protecting the savings of the people was conceding he could not protect those savings. Even the pied piper of globalism, the *Wall Street Journal,* seemed alarmed: "Sorry to interrupt the current White House euphoria, but someone ought to mention that the great American middle class didn't reelect President Bush so he could debase the currency." By year's end, the sinking dollar had become the world's concern.

As the New Economics of JFK guttered out in LBJ's guns-and-butter budgets, free-trade-*über-alles* seems to have run its course. Yet, while there appears to be growing recognition of the gravity of our fiscal and monetary condition—the prospect of endless deficits, a dying dollar, the steady bleeding of manufacturing jobs to Asia, a growing dependency upon imports for the necessities of our national life—there seemed neither the vision nor the will in Washington to arrest the inexorable decline. But it is on the Iraq war and the Bush Doctrine that the decisive battle for the soul of the Republican party and destiny of the nation loomed by year's end.

Among the 19 percent of voters who gave terrorism as the issue most on their minds, President Bush won 84–16. But voters who considered Iraq separate from the war on terror and voted on the Iraq issue cast their ballots 3–1 against President Bush. He had won national approval for how he had dealt with Al Qaeda, but no mandate for a long war in Mesopotamia.

November also proved the cruelest month yet for Americans, with 135 soldiers and Marines dead, many lost recapturing Fallujah, which U.S. forces had abandoned in April. By New Year's Day, 2005, the Iraq war had lasted longer than World War I for Americans, and still with no end in sight, no light at the end of the tunnel.

Yet, those like Colin Powell who had warned the president of the risks of war on Iraq were gone, while those who had assured him it would be a cakewalk, that we would be welcomed with flowers, that democracy would take root and spread across the Middle East, that he would be the Churchill of his generation, had almost all been retained.

While this appears unjust, it is politically healthy. For, should Iraq turn out a triumph, the War Party can claim credit. But should America find herself in an endless war, or Iraq collapse in chaos or civil war, and U.S. intervention be judged by history to have been an act of hubristic folly, this time, unlike in Vietnam, we share accountability.

The neoconservatives who plotted and propagandized for this

war for years before 9/11 cannot now escape culpability. Nor do they have President Kerry to blame. And as they push for more troops in Iraq, for U.S. strikes on Iran, for invading Syria, for the nuclear castration of North Korea, either President Bush will restrain them, or this nation is headed into a series of wars that will destroy his presidency. Only George Bush can corral the neoconservatives now.

By the end of 2004, some had already begun to place new demands on his desk. Calling his reelection an endorsement of their agenda, Frank Gaffney issued a "checklist" of things to be done in a second Bush term. He called for "regime change—one way or the other" in Iran and North Korea, and for confronting "China's increasingly fascistic trade and military policies, Vladimir Putin's accelerating authoritarianism at home and aggressiveness toward the former Soviet republics, the worldwide spread of Islamofascism, and the emergence of a number of aggressively anti-American regimes in Latin America." Quite a spoonful.

To the neoconservatives, China, Russia, the Islamic world, and nations in Latin America are drifting toward fascism, and we must act against them all, and if need be, fight them all, as did the Greatest Generation in the "Good War." Their agenda for Bush's second term is perpetual war for Pax Americana.

With Colin Powell's departure and the purge at CIA, traditional conservatives and foreign policy realists seemed sunk in the Slough of Despond, assuming the neocons were now unleashed and empowered to advance their agenda of preventive wars on Iran, Syria, and North Korea.

In his second inaugural, President Bush seemed to confirm that he had been converted to their world view that only through "regime change" across the Islamic world, using U.S. military might as the *ultima ratio*, could we ever again be secure.

All presidents seek to alchemize wars, begun over lesser interests, into epochal struggles for universal principles. By late 1863, Lincoln's war to crush secession was now about whether "government of the people, by the people, for the people shall . . . perish from the earth." By 1917, a war whose causes Wilson professed not to discern in 1916 had become "the war to end all wars" and "make the world safe for democracy."

Bush in his inaugural had trumped Wilson. He was not only going to make the world safe for democracy, he was going to make the whole world democratic. Where Lincoln abolished slavery in the South, Bush was going to abolish tyranny from the earth: "So, it is the policy of the United States to seek and support the growth of democratic movements and institutions in every nation and culture, with the ultimate goal of ending tyranny in our world."

President Bush had asserted a right to interfere in the internal affairs of every nation because the "survival of liberty in our land increasingly depends on the success of liberty in other lands."

He further declared his intent to hector and badger all foreign leaders on the progress each was making toward attaining U.S. standards of freedom: "We will persistently clarify the choice before every ruler and nation: The moral choice between oppression, which is always wrong, and freedom, which is eternally right."

Here was a formula for collision with every autocrat on earth, virtually every African and Arab ruler, all the "outposts-of-tyranny" identified by Secretary Rice, most of the nations of Central Asia, and China and Russia. It is a prescription for permanent war, though, as Madison warned, "No nation can preserve its freedom in the midst of continual warfare."

Among those who had converted the president to the notion that without Arab democracy there can neither be a Middle East peace nor a secure America was Natan Sharansky, whose *Case for Democracy* Bush had encouraged his staff to read. "This is a book," the president told CNN, that "summarizes how I feel." Sharansky depicts a universe of moral clarity, a Manichaean world divided into "free societies," which promote peace, and "fear societies," which foster war.

Enraptured with Bush's inaugural, neoconservatives rushed to compare it to Lincoln's second. And though they had been wrong on every count about Iraq, Bush seemed willing to wager his presidency and U.S. interests in a vast Islamic world on their assurances that, once the autocrats fell, democracy would flourish among people who today appear to revile him and revere bin Laden.

Even traditional conservatives who had supported the war seemed shocked by the inaugural. "A God-drenched speech," said Peggy Noonan, a writer for Ronald Reagan and George H. W. Bush. It was "over the top," "somewhere between dreamy and disturbing."

That stunned reaction from Bush allies and hostile reaction abroad caused the president's father and the president himself to hold press briefings to assure the world there was nothing new or radical in it.

Perhaps a sense of realism had begun to intrude. After all, America was not going to stop buying Saudi oil, or cut off $2 billion in annual aid to Egypt, or sever relations with President Musharraf of Pakistan, or sanction a China that could sink the dollar, because those regimes refuse to reform themselves as the neocons demand.

America "goes not abroad, in search of monsters to destroy," said John Quincy Adams, "She is the well-wisher to the freedom and independence of all. She is the champion and vindicator only of her own."

Under the tutelage of neo-Jacobins, who call themselves idealists, Bush had formally repudiated this core doctrine of U.S. foreign policy—for a policy of intervention in the internal political affairs of every nation, to realize his vision of ending tyranny on earth. Yet, in his State of the Union, ten days after the inaugural, Bush, while resolute in his warnings to Damascus and Teheran, gave no sign he intended to enlarge the U.S. military presence in Iraq or expand the war to Syria or Iran. Neoconservatives, however, were still pressing the case for a bigger army and a wider war.

Senator McCain had told *Meet the Press* we may need forty to fifty thousand more combat troops in Iraq. In the *Weekly Standard*, American Enterprise Institute's Tom Donnelly had called for enlargement of the U.S. Army of 480,000 and pumping up of defense spending from 4 percent to 5 percent or 6 percent of the gross domestic product that Reagan spent in the decisive years of the Cold War.

Why did we need an enlarged army? Because, wrote Donnelly, this war is about "preserving Pax Americana." It is "a contest between liberalism and radical Islam to supplant the crumbling autocracies that have dominated the region since the fall of the Ottoman Empire."

Even with Iraq a hellish mess and casualties rising, the neocons were calling for new wars against hostile Middle East regimes and occupation of their nations with U.S. troops who would fight beside indigenous forces to crush any insurgents who dare resist our hegemony.

"(America) will continue to contribute the lion's share of the blood and treasure in the effort to transform the greater Middle East," Donnelly wrote. But it is "impossible to have a Bush Doctrine world with Clinton-era defense budgets. The problem for the United States is not imperial overstretch, it's trying to run the planet on the cheap."

Yet, what is crucial is not what the neocons say—but what the president does. And while he still rhapsodizes about ending tyranny on Earth, he has yet to will the actions. As of February 2005 there was no evidence of any large imminent increase in the U.S. Army or Marines, or of fifty thousand more troops embarking for the Sunni Triangle.

Consider Iran. Relying on reports from an exile group we once labeled terrorist, Colin Powell warned in November that Teheran may be at work on a nuclear warhead for its Shahab-3 missile, which can reach Israel. Neoconservatives and Sharonites began to demand "Action this day!" to effect the nuclear castration of Iran.

But, as President Bush had yet to warn the nation, or U.S. forces in Iraq, to brace for the consequences of a strike on Iran, it seemed his near-term agenda did not include preventive war on the mullahs' regime. And the same appeared true for North Korea.

In that same *Weekly Standard*, AEI's Nick Eberstadt called Bush's approach to Pyongyang "dangerously flawed" and urged the "readying [of] non-diplomatic instruments for North Korea threat reduction"—i.e., sanctions, blockade, air strikes, or invasion. But, again, there was no evidence President Bush was contemplating any preemptive strike that could ignite a Korean war this country was unprepared to fight. His only mention of axis-of-evil dictator Kim Jong-Il's hermit kingdom in the State of the Union was the single sentence, "We are working closely with governments in Asia to convince North Korea to abandon its nuclear ambitions."

As for the Iraq war, in the week before Christmas, Republican anger spilled out and splashed Defense Secretary Donald Rumsfeld. Senator McCain expressed "no confidence" in the secretary. Other GOP senators echoed McCain, and William Kristol of the *Weekly Standard* rushed into print in the *Washington Post* to call for Rumsfeld's firing.

Rumsfeld had been bleeding for days after a seemingly arrogant answer to Specialist Thomas Wilson of the Tennessee National Guard at a soldiers' meeting in Kuwait. Wilson had demanded to know why he and his men had to scrounge around junkyards for "hillbilly armor" to protect their trucks and humvees going into Iraq. "As you know, you have to go to war with the army you have, not the army you want," Rumsfeld had retorted.

But Rumsfeld's clumsy response was not the real reason neocons wanted him out. The motive: Rumsfeld no longer shared their agenda, if ever he did, of "World War IV" leading to a Pax Americana in the Middle East. As Kristol explained to the *Post*, Rumsfeld's

> fundamental error . . . is that his theory about the military is at odds with the president's geopolitical strategy. He wants this light, transformed military, but we've got to win a real war, which involves using a lot of troops and building a nation, and that's at the core of the president's strategy for rebuilding the Middle East.

To the neoconservatives the invasion of Iraq was never about any Saddam connection to 9/11 or threat of WMD. That was propaganda to agitate and mobilize the masses for war. The real reason for the invasion and occupation of Iraq was empire-building, and making the Middle East safe for Israel.

Kristol was echoed by Donnelly in the year's last issue of the *Weekly Standard*. The piece was titled "Rumsfeld's War," and the one-time hero of neoconservatives was disparaged therein as "an arrogant and isolated Beltway bigwig."

By Bush's second inaugural, the GOP was dividing over whether to escalate in Iraq, to stay the course, or to get out, and the coalition of neoconservatives and Pentagon hawks was cracking up.

Still, when one considers all Rumsfeld had done for them, the depth of the betrayal astounds. Ever since he signed on with their Committee on the Present Danger in the 1980s, Rumsfeld has been a neoconservative hero. In 1998, four years before 9/11, he had signed the Kristol open letter to Clinton calling for war on Iraq. Named defense secretary, he brought in Paul Wolfowitz and Douglas Feith as No. 2 and No. 3 and let them fill the building with friends from the American Enterprise Institute. Richard Perle was given the chairmanship of the Defense Review Board, which was converted into a neoconservative nest inside the Pentagon. In the hours after 9/11, Rumsfeld made the case to Bush for immediate war on Iraq.

By late December, what was happening was apparent to all in the capital. The Iraq war was going badly and Rumsfeld was being set up by the neoconservatives to take the fall. As the plotters and propagandists of the war, they knew that if Iraq went the way of Vietnam, a search would be conducted for those who had misled America and, yes, lied us into war. Rumsfeld had become the designated scapegoat.

But with their abandonment of Rumsfeld, President Bush was also on notice. The neoconservative agenda mandates escalation: Enlarging the army, more troops in Iraq, widening the war to Syria and Iran, indefinite occupation of the Middle East—as we forcibly alter the mindset of the Islamic world. If Bush does not deliver on that agenda, he, too, will be dismissed as not up to the Churchillian task history has assigned him. And the neoconservatives will abandon him, too, and look elsewhere.

At New Year's 2005, there existed a surplus of war plans for Pax Americana, but President Bush was bumping up against reality: an army tied down, bleeding in Iraq, the soaring costs of war, exploding deficits, a sinking dollar, and an absence of allies willing to fight alongside us, or even assist.

With the Iraqi elections of January 30, and the heartening photos and footage of men and women braving suicide bombers to vote, the Bush policy was again being proclaimed a success. In the middle of a guerrilla war, it was said, democracy had triumphed. But a beautiful wedding is no guarantee of a long and happy marriage. Skeptics noted that, given the returns from Baghdad and the southern provinces, this seemed more a vote for a Shia-dominated Iraq, alongside a Shia-dominated Iran, rather than a harbinger of peace. Within hours after the balloting, as the national lockdown was lifted, Sunni insurgents had returned to the killing fields.

Thus, President Bush confronts the Vietnam dilemma. Does he plunge in deeper in hope of victory in Iraq, risking all, stay the course, or cut his losses and return to a less ambitious foreign policy that secures the country but no longer seeks forcibly to convert a recalcitrant world to democracy? For fifteen years, some of us have warned that if America, in the aftermath of her Cold War victory, refused to adopt a foreign policy rooted in her history and national interests, the world would, to our humiliation, impose such a policy upon us.

Entering his second term, George Bush is there.

Neoconservatism, that cocktail of Big Government liberalism, free-trade globalism, open borders, and endless Wilsonian wars for democracy, had come near to costing George W. Bush the presidency in 2004. Where Nixon and Reagan, running for reelection against liberal Democrats, had rolled up forty-nine-state land-slides, Bush had carried but thirty-one states. Not until the early morning of November 3 did his victory seem secure, with sixteen electoral votes to spare. Had the sixty thousand Ohio voters gone the other way, George Bush would, like his father, have been a one-term president, and the first ever to have been ousted from office in wartime.

Thus it was that by the spring of 2005, President Bush was already embattled and the war for the soul of the GOP had begun. The dividing lines between traditional conservatives and neoconservatives were these:

• Will President Bush defend the borders of his country and halt the endless invasion of illegal aliens from Mexico? Will he jettison an open-borders policy that may be providing a bottomless pool of cheap labor for corporate America, but is undercutting the wages of our working men and women, bankrupting our states, and imperiling the social fabric, cultural unity, and national identity of the United States?

• Will President Bush continue to pursue the free-trade policy of *Wall Street Journal* corporatists that is denuding America of her manufacturing base, outsourcing high-paying jobs to China and India, increasing our dependence on foreign sources for the necessities of our national life, and producing immense trade deficits that are driving down the value of dollar?

• Will the president nominate to the Supreme Court justices who will look to the Constitution—not Warren court precedents—to ring down the curtain on the social, moral, legal, and political revolution that arrogant judges have been imposing on this nation for fifty years, against the will of the people?

• Will the president realize that those who told him the Iraq war would be a cakewalk had another agenda than the national interests of the United States—be it empire, Israel, or Pax Americana? Will he see that America, powerful as she is, has neither the resources nor the ambition to become an imperial nation that dictates to other peoples how they should govern themselves?

The American Republic has never truly been, and must never become, an empire. To do so would be a betrayal of our Founding Fathers and put us on the road to imperial ruin, trod by all the other great Western nations before us. Early in the second term, either the War Party will be put into a cold shower by President Bush, or we are headed for war without end until bankruptcy beckons. With an overstretched army, record trade deficits, a sinking dollar, soaring debt, a budget out of balance, and America isolated in the world, visions of empire must vanish in the cold dawn of reality.

Within the Republican Party there is a fallen banner waiting to be picked up, the banner of true conservatism, rooted in the wisdom of the Founding Fathers and the patriotism of Ronald Reagan. It is the banner of a cause that sees Big Government not as liberator or benefactor, but is ever vigilant against its encroachments, no matter the professed nobility or seeming necessity of the causes in which it advances its claims for greater power. It is a conservatism that rejects globalism for patriotism, and imperialism as un-American. It is a conservatism that has no allegiance or loyalty other than to the United States. It is a conservatism that sees America not as a means to some glorious global end, but as a unique land and people to be loved, cherished, and defended for who and what they are. Who picks up that banner will find a following and will be followed.

ACKNOWLEDGMENTS

This book and its author owe a debt of gratitude to quite a few people. First, to Fredi Friedman, my agent and the editor of four of my previous books, who read some loose chapters in the late spring of 2004, suggested they be titled *Where the Right Went Wrong,* and sent them on to my publisher, Tom Dunne, at St. Martin's. Tom agreed to have a book out by August if a finished work could be completed by the end of June. To Tom and Sean Desmond, my editor at St. Martin's, with whom I worked on *The Death of the West,* my thanks, once again.

Thanks also to old friends Allan Ryskind and Sam Francis for reading and criticizing the manuscript, and for their suggestions, and also to the writers and scholars who reviewed various chapters: Richard D. Fisher Jr., who critiqued the chapter on China; Brian Riedl, budget expert at The Heritage Foundation, who reviewed the Conservative Impersonators chapter, and Allan Tonelson of the U.S. Business and Industry Council, who took a hard and critical look at the Economic Treason chapter. While I agreed with many of their suggestions, I thank them for them all, and give them unconditional absolution for any culpability in the final product.

Finally, my thanks go out to Kara Hopkins and W. James Antle

III of the *American Conservative* magazine, who put in many hours of editing in the final days of preparation, and Veronica Yanos, also of the magazine, for technical assistance in computer translation, of which the author was in dire need.

INDEX